Simply Safety

Robert AG Greenfield

&

Michael JW Morgan

Copyright © 2013 Robert AG Greenfield & Michael JW Morgan

All rights reserved.

ISBN - 10: 1482502046
ISBN-13: 978-1482502046

Dedicated to all those who have lost their lives or have been injured at work and to the families often left to cope.

AUTHORS BIOGRAPHY

Robert Greenfield DipOSH Grad IOSH MBIFM
Director of Safety Health Environmental & Quality for the GSH Group

Robert has over 25 years experience in FM with the last 14 specialising in Safety Health Environmental & Quality (SHEQ) having started his career as a Research and Development Engineer within the Ministry of Defence (Atomic Weapons Research Establishment). Robert has worked in a number of building managing agent companies as well as within the contracting element of the hard FM sector where he has a wealth of experience in the development of Safety, Health, Environmental and Quality (SHEQ) operational strategy of large multi site portfolios.

A major part of Roberts work for the GSH Group involves the strategic management of cross border contracts and this has resulted in Robert gaining experience in the management of safety and health in mainland Europe, India and the USA.

Robert is a regular writer for the British Institute of Facilities Management magazine FM-World and has assisted the Health and Safety Executive (HSE) in the development of the 'Shattered Lives' and 'Asbestos-The Hidden Killer' campaigns and is currently engaged in projects to revitalise the HSE Work at Height micro site and the review of the Workplace Welfare Regulations Approved Code of Practice. .

Robert is the past Deputy Chairman of the British Institute of Facilities Management (BIFM), Past Chairman of the BIFM East Region and the current Chairman of the BIFM Health & Safety Specialist Interest Group.

Robert also sits on the Confederation of British Industry (CBI) Health & Safety Committee, Construction Industry Council (CIC) Health & Safety Committee, Health & Safety Executive (HSE) Asbestos Liaison Group (ALG) and Asbestos Stakeholders Group.

Robert has spoken at many conferences on both Health & Safety, Risk Management and Security topics including the series of joint ATaC (Asbestos Testing & Consulting Group) /BOHS (British Occupational Hygiene Society) seminars across the country where he represented the British Institute of Facilities Management.

Michael J W Morgan CMIOSH, MBIFM, MIIRSM, MIHM, EurOSHM
Chartered Safety and Health Practitioner
Managing Director, Safety Action Services Ltd

Michael has been involved with the Health & Safety Industry for some 25 years. He is an experienced Health & Safety professional with considerable expertise of strategy development, management systems and compliance, coupled with extensive experience at senior levels in Facilities Management and Security.

Michael started his career working for the National Westminster Bank before moving to the Canadian Imperial Bank of Commerce in the City of London in 1974. In the mid 1980ies Michael moved from the banking side of CIBC and became involved in Facilities Management where he eventually became the Security Manager attached to the European Operations Office which covered the United Kingdom, Europe, Africa and the Middle East.

Moving to Ernst & Young in 1988 he worked in the London office for 12 years, specialising in Facilities Management and in particular Health & Safety where he eventually took over the role of the London Health & Safety Manager. In 1999 Michael became the UK Health & Safety Manager, a position he held until he left the firm in December 2000.

In January 2001 Michael started Safety Action Services Limited a Health & Safety Consultancy and Training Company which he has now successfully run for over 11 years

Michael is a Chartered Member of The Institution of Occupational Safety and Health (CMIOSH) and holds as well full Membership of The International Institute of Risk and Safety Management (MIIRSM), The British Institute of Facilities Management (MBIFM) and The Institute of Healthcare Management (MIHM).

Michael is also accredited by the European Network of Safety and Health Professional Organisations (ENSHPO) as a European Occupational Safety and Health Manager (EurOSHM).

Michael sits on and is Deputy Chairman of the British Institute of Facilities Management Health & Safety Special Interest Group (BIFM SIG) (formerly the National Health & Safety Committee) and has been involved with the committee since 1993.

Michael has spoken at many conferences on both Health & Safety and Security topics including the series of joint ATaC (Asbestos Testing & Consulting Group) /BOHS (British Occupational Hygiene Society) seminars across the country where he represented the British Institute of Facilities Management.

In January 2001 Michael started Safety Action Services Limited a Health & Safety Consultancy and Training Company which he has now successfully run 13 years.

SIMPLY SAFETY

INTRODUCTION

This book entitled **'Simply Safety'** covers all of the significant elements of health and safety legislation relevant to the workplace and is written to take employers through a series of stages to ensure compliance with legislation within their workplaces. In other more complex environments such as with specialist manufacturing plants and high risk processes then these legislative requirements and guidance would still apply but would have to be supplemented by specific legislation relevant to that specialist industry and process activity e.g. Oil Refineries, Nuclear industry, offshore platforms etc.

Simply Safety has been designed and written to provide employers with an introduction to a range of legislation that you will come across when carrying out a range of maintenance activities or project works upon a building. We believe that we have come up against the many pitfalls of health and safety over the years and here we attempt to impart some knowledge of how to avoid such problems in the hope that you will succeed in your journey towards compliance and successful health and safety management.

SO WHO IS AN EMPLOYER?

In Simply Safety we always refer to an employer and in our experience an employer will ultimately be an organisation and anyone who is acting as an officer on behalf of the organisation. Therefore this person has a responsibility for management of the health and safety and under health and safety law has a duty to the staff of the organisation together with any visitors including contractors, members of the public and anyone who may be affected by the work of the organisation. In practice the persons responsible for fulfilling health and safety law duties will be anyone within the structure of the organisation e.g. implemented and driven downwards from the Chief Executive Officer, Managing Director, Board Members, Senior Managers, Employers and other managers down to the workforce themselves who let's not forget also have their own duties.

As for who is actually responsible for assisting the employer to comply with their duties within health and safety law then this should be detailed within the organisational arrangements for health and safety and forms a major part of an organisation's Health & Safety Policy. We will explain which organisations require a Health & Safety Policy and how to develop the arrangements within Chapter 2 - Establishing a Health and Safety Culture in Your Organisation.

WHAT ARE THE AIMS OF THIS BOOK?

The main aims of Simply Safety are as follows:

- to enable employers to fulfill their health and safety duties
- to achieve a high level of compliance
- to keep staff, visitors and members of the public safe
- to reduce costs of accidents and downtime
- to improve staff morale
- and to protect the reputation of the organisations brand name

Table of Contents

Authors Biography 4
Introduction 6
    Who is an Employer? 6
    What Are the Aims of This Book Series? 6
    Table of Contents 7
    How This Book Will Help 18
    Key legislation 18

Chapter 1 21
Health and Safety Management 21
Legal framework 21
    Why Health and Safety? 21
    The Courts 24
    Effect of the Health & Safety (Offences) Act 2008 26
    Corporate Manslaughter & Corporate Homicide Act 2007 27
    The High Court 27
    Employment Tribunals 28
Types of law 28
Figure 1.2: Sources and Divisions of Law 31
Enforcement Authorities – Responsibilities and Powers 32
    Health and Safety Executive (HSE) 32
How HSE enforces health and safety 33
    Environmental Health Officer (EHO) 33
    Fire Officer 34
    Employment Medical Advisory Service (EMAS) 34
    The Different Responsibilities and Powers of the Enforcement Authorities
    34
    Powers of Entry and Inspection 35
    Dealing With a Visit by an Enforcement Authority 36
    If faults are found 36
    Interviews by an Inspector 37
    Statutory Notices 37
    Improvement Notices 38
    Prohibition Notices 38
    Appeals 39

Chapter 2 40
Establishing a Health and Safety Culture in Your Organisation 40
    Introduction 40
    What is Health and Safety Culture? 40
    Influencing Safety Culture 40
    Why is Safety Culture important? 41
    Indicators of A Poor Culture? 41
    Indicators of a Positive Culture? 41
    Relationship between Safety Culture & Performance 42
    What does it take to create a positive culture? 43
    Safety Culture Development 43

SIMPLY SAFETY

- EXAMPLE CASE STUDY: 44
- IMPLEMENTING A SAFETY MANAGEMENT SYSTEM..46
- INTRODUCTION 45
- HUMANE 45
- ECONOMIC 45
- LEGAL 45
- HEALTH AND SAFETY ARRANGEMENTS...45
- HEALTH AND SAFETY MANAGEMENT SYSTEM 46
- MAINTAINING THE REGIME 48
- HEALTH AND SAFETY POLICY STATEMENT AND POLICIES 48
- ASSIGNING RESPONSIBILITIES 50
- THE REQUIREMENT FOR COMPETENCE 52
- DEFINITION OF COMPETENCE 52
- RECORD KEEPING AND DOCUMENTATION 53
- COMMUNICATION 53
- COMMUNICATION TO NEW STAFF 54
- COMMUNICATION WITH MANAGEMENT 55
- COMMUNICATION WITH EXTERNAL BODIES 55
- TRAINING 55

Chapter 3 58
Risk Assessment and Management 58
Risk Assessment – Requirements and Definitions 58
There are Some Definitions Which Might be of Help 58

- WHAT IS A HAZARD AND WHAT IS A RISK? 59
- CARRYING OUT A RISK ASSESSMENT 59
- STEP 1 - IS TO IDENTIFY THE HAZARDS..61
- PHYSICAL HAZARDS 61
- PROCESS HAZARDS 62
- MATERIAL HAZARDS 62
- STEP 2 - DECIDE WHO MIGHT BE HARMED AND HOW...62
- STEP 3 - EVALUATE THE RISKS AND DECIDE ON WHAT PRECAUTIONS ARE NEEDED.........63
- STEP 4 - RECORD YOUR FINDINGS AND IMPLEMENT THEM 63
- STEP 5 - REVIEW YOUR RISK ASSESSMENT AND UPDATE IF NECESSARY 65
- SCORING AND RATING RISKS..65
- MANAGING THE RISKS...68
- MANAGING THE RISKS...68
- RISK ASSESSMENTS REQUIRED 69
- THE KEY RISKS 70
- FIRE 70
- DISPLAY SCREEN EQUIPMENT (DSE)..70
- MANUAL HANDLING 71
- ELECTRICITY 71
- FIRST AID 71
- GENERAL WORKPLACE HAZARDS 71
- COSHH..72
- CONTRACTORS 72
- NEW AND EXPECTANT MOTHERS 72
- CHILDREN AND YOUNG PERSONS 73

- Lone Working 73
- Example Risk Assessments 74
- The list of the example Risk Assessments prepared by the HSE are as follows 74
- Shops 74
- Motor Vehicles 75
- Office 75
- Other 75
- Table 3:07 - Risk Assessment Guidance for Some More Common Regulations .. 77

Chapter 4 80
Occupational Health 80
Introduction 80
Work-Related Upper-Limb Disorders (WRULDs) 81
- What are WRULDs? 81
- Preventative Measures 82
- Work Design 82
- Conclusion 82
Noise Control of Noise at Work Regulations 2005 83
- Noise at Work – Health Effects 83
- Do You Have a Noise Problem at Work? 83
- Assessment of Risks (Reg. 5) 85
- Elimination or Control of Exposure (Reg. 6) 85
- Hearing Protection (Reg. 7) 86
- Maintenance and Use of Equipment (Reg. 8) 86
- Health Surveillance (Reg. 9) 86
- Information, Instruction and Training (Reg. 10) 86
- Do I Have to Make Any Checks? 87
Stress 87
Causes of stress 88
- General Management and Culture of the Organisation 88
- Role in the Organisation 88
- Career development 88
- Decision-making/control 88
- Relationships at work 88
- Home/work issues 88
- Job design 88
- Remedies 88
- HSE Management Standards For Work-Related Stress 89
- What are the Management Standards for work-related stress? 89
Smoking 90
Bacterial Illness 90
Occupational Zoonoses 91
Leptospirosis (also known as Weil's disease) 91
Psittacosis (Ornithosis): - 92
Rabies: 92
Anthrax: 93
Newcastle Disease: 93
- Occupational Settings 93
- Occupational Dermatitis 94
- Contact Dermatitis 95

SIMPLY SAFETY

- OTHER OCCUPATIONALLY INDUCED SKIN DISEASES ... 95
- RISK ASSESSMENT ... 95
- HEALTH SURVEILLANCE ... 96
- SOME SUGGESTED STEPS TO COMPLIANCE ARE: ... 96

Manual Handling – Legal Requirements ... 97
- WHAT SHOULD YOU DO ABOUT IT? ... 98

Manual Handling – Assessment ... 98
- T = THE TASK ... 98
- I = THE INDIVIDUAL ... 98
- L = THE LOAD ... 99
- E = THE ENVIRONMENT ... 99

Manual Handling – Reducing The Risk of Injury ... 99
- PROVIDING ADDITIONAL INFORMATION ON THE LOAD ... 99
- ERGONOMICS ... 99
- REVIEWING THE ASSESSMENTS ... 99

Hand-Arm Vibration Syndrome (HAVS) ... 100
- LEGAL REQUIREMENTS ... 100
- MOST AT RISK ... 100
- SYMPTOMS ... 101
- EXPOSURE LIMIT VALUES AND ACTION VALUES (CVWR, REG. 4) ... 101
- RISK ASSESSMENT (CVWR, REG. 5) ... 101

Workstation Requirements ... 102
- LEGAL REQUIREMENTS ... 102
- WORKSTATION EQUIPMENT ... 103
- WAYS OF WORKING ... 104
- EYE AND EYESIGHT TESTS ... 104
- TRAINING AND INSTRUCTION ... 104

Mobile Phones and Driving ... 105
- EMPLOYERS' LIABILITY ... 105

Chapter 5 ... 106
First Aid and Accident Reporting ... 106
Introduction ... 106
Legislation and Publications ... 106
The Employers Legal Duties ... 106
- FIRST AID – WHAT THE LAW REQUIRES ... 109
- ASSESSMENT OF NEED ... 110

Training and qualifications required ... 110
- FIRST AIDERS ... 110
- RENEWING A FIRST AID CERTIFICATE ... 111
- EMERGENCY FIRST AIDERS ... 111
- TRAINED FIRST AIDERS – SUGGESTED ASSESSMENT OF FIRST-AID NEEDS AND NUMBERS REQUIRED ... 113
- COVER FOR LEAVE/ABSENCE OF FIRST AIDERS ... 115

First aid boxes, bags and rooms ... 116
- FIRST AID BOXES ... 116
- OTHER FIRST AID RESOURCES ... 118
- REQUIREMENTS FOR FIRST AID ROOMS ... 118
- SPECIAL REQUIREMENT FOR OFFSHORE WORK ... 119

SPECIAL REQUIREMENTS FOR DIVING...119
RECORD KEEPING OF FIRST AID INCIDENTS..119
ACCIDENT REPORTING WHAT THE LAW SAYS..120
Reporting of Injuries, Diseases and Dangerous Occurrences Regulations 2013 120
    TYPES OF REPORTABLE INJURY 122
    OVER-SEVEN-DAY INJURY REPORTING 122
    DISEASE... 123
    DANGEROUS OCCURRENCE 123
REPORTING AN ACCIDENT.. 123
    ARE YOU AN EMPLOYER OR IN CONTROL OF PREMISES................................ 123
    IF YOU ARE AN EMPLOYER..123
    IF YOU ARE IN CONTROL OF PREMISES.. 123
    IF YOU ARE SELF EMPLOYED..123
    IF YOU ARE A GAS SUPPLIER..123
    IF YOU ARE A GAS ENGINEER...123
    IF YOU ARE WORKING OFFSHORE.. 124
WAYS TO REPORT AN INCIDENT AT WORK..124
    ONLINE... 124
    TELEPHONE.. 124
    REPORTING OUT OF HOURS..125
    ACCIDENT INVESTIGATION AND
    REPORTING... 126
    REPORT ON THE INCIDENT..126
    ADDITIONAL INFORMATION... 126
    CONCLUSIONS.. 127
    ACTIONS TAKEN SINCE THE INCIDENT.. 127
    RECOMMENDATIONS.. 127
    STATEMENTS.. 127
    PHOTOGRAPHS.. 127
    APPENDICES... 127
Keeping Accident/ Incident Investigation Reports...128
TABLE 5.04 Sample Accident / Near Miss Report..129

Chapter 6 130
Fire... 130
Fire Risk Assessment.. 130
    REGULATORY REFORM (FIRE SAFETY) ORDER 2005 (*RR(FS)O 2005*) 130
    AUTHORS NOTE: 130
    WHAT ARE THE KEY DUTIES FOR YOU AS THE EMPLOYER?......................... 131
    THE FIVE STAGES FOR THE PREPARATION OF A FIRE RISK ASSESSMENT ARE AS FOLLOWS:
    132
    DEPARTMENT FOR COMMUNITIES & LOCAL GOVERNMENT 133
    IDENTIFICATION OF POTENTIAL FIRE HAZARDS... 133
    EVALUATE RISKS AND CURRENT CONTROL MEASURES 134
    RECORD YOUR FINDINGS AND ACTIONS... 135
    REVISE YOUR PROCEDURES AS NECESSARY 135
    FIRE LOG BOOK 135
    FIRE WARDENS AND GENERAL STAFF TRAINING 136
    ENFORCEMENT.. 137
    DEFINITIONS OF NOTICES 137

- ALTERATIONS NOTICE 137
- ENFORCEMENT NOTICE 137
- PROHIBITION NOTICE 137
- The Dangerous Substances and Explosive Atmospheres Regulations 2002 137

Chapter 7 138
- Workplace Welfare Provision 138
- Welfare Provision – Overview 138
- Toilets and Washing Facilities 139
- Food and Water 140
- Temperature in the Workplace 141
- Work in Hot or Cold Environments 141
- Smoking 142
- Definitions 142
- Smokefree Vehicles 143
- Private Dwellings 144
- Working from Home 144
- Signage 144
- Signage for SmokeFree Premises 144
- Signage for Smokefree Vehicles 145
- Penalties 145
- Additional Information for the Employer 146
- Smoking Help Lines: 146
- Alcohol and Drugs 146
- The Health and Safety (Safety Signs and Signals) Regulations 1996 146
- Security 147
- Lone Working 147
- In Case of Emergency (ICE) 148
- Ventilation & Lighting 148

Chapter 8 149
- Asbestos Management 149
  - INTRODUCTION 149
  - CONTROL OF ASBESTOS REGULATIONS 2012 150
  - WHAT HAS STAYED THE SAME? 150
  - WHAT HAS CHANGED? 150
  - THE DUTY HOLDER EXPLAINED 151
  - CONTROL OF ASBESTOS REGULATIONS 2012 151
  - HOW TO MANAGE ASBESTOS 152
  - HSE SYSTEM FOR 'MANAGING MY ASBESTOS' 154
  - HOW TO USE THIS FORM 155
  - STEP 1- INTRODUCTION 155
  - STEP 2 - ARE YOU RESPONSIBLE FOR MAINTENANCE OR REPAIR? ... 155
  - STEP 3 - WHEN WAS IT BUILT? 156
  - STEP 4 - WHAT INFORMATION DO YOU HAVE ALREADY? 156
  - STEP 5 - INSPECT YOUR BUILDING 157
  - INSPECTING YOUR BUILDING: 157
  - STEP 6 - DETERMINING PRIORITIES FOR ACTION 157
  - STEP 7 - DECIDE HOW TO DEAL WITH THE DIFFERENT TYPES OF ASBESTOS 158
  - STEP 8 - WRITE DOWN YOUR ASBESTOS MANAGEMENT PLAN 158

- STEP 9 - TESTING FOR ASBESTOS 159
  - TYPES OF SURVEY 159
  - STEP 10 - TELL PEOPLE WHAT YOU'RE DOING 160
  - STEP 11 - GETTING WORK DONE 160
  - IS THE WORK LICENSED? 161
  - LICENSED WORK 161
  - FACILITIES NEEDED 161
  - WHAT YOU SHOULD EXPECT 161
  - LEGAL POINTS TO CONSIDER 161
  - NON-LICENSED WORK 161
- Asbestos Essentials 161
  - STEP 12 - KEEP YOUR RECORDS UP TO DATE 162
  - ASBESTOS RISK ASSESSMENT 162
  - THE BASIC PRINCIPLES FOR THE EMPLOYER (DUTY HOLDER) TO CONSIDER 163
  - TYPES OF SURVEY TO DETERMINE THE PRESENCE OF ASBESTOS 163
  - MANAGEMENT SURVEY 163
  - REFURBISHMENT AND DEMOLITION SURVEYS 164
  - ACCREDITATION/CERTIFICATION OF SURVEYORS 167
  - HOW TO REMOVE ASBESTOS 167
  - ASBESTOS ESSENTIALS FOR UNLICENSED WORK 169
  - WHAT YOU NEED TO DO 169
  - YOUR WORKERS 169
  - WHAT THE PREMISES OWNER (CLIENT) NEEDS TO TELL YOU 169
  - MAIN POINTS: 169
  - DOES THE WORK NEED A LICENCE? 169
  - IS IT NOTIFIABLE NON-LICENSED WORK? 170
  - PLANNING 171
  - MANAGE THE WORK 171
  - DISPOSAL OF ASBESTOS MATERIALS AND WASTE 171
  - ASBESTOS LICENSING UNIT (ALU) 172
  - CHANGES TO THE METHOD OF PAYMENT FOR ASBESTOS LICENCE FEES 172
  - ONLINE REVISED FOD ASB1 APPLICATION FORM 172
  - TRANSITIONAL PERIOD 172

Chapter 9 173
- Building Services 173
- Construction (Design and Management) Regulations 2007 173
- Definitions 173
  - CONSTRUCTION WORK 173
  - NOTIFIABLE PROJECTS 173
  - NON-NOTIFIABLE PROJECTS 174
  - CONTRACTORS AND SELF-EMPLOYED 174
  - DUTY HOLDERS 174
  - THE CLIENT (EMPLOYER) – ROLES AND RESPONSIBILITIES 174
  - CDM CO-ORDINATORS – ROLES AND RESPONSIBILITIES 175
  - DESIGNERS – ROLES AND RESPONSIBILITIES 175
  - PRINCIPAL CONTRACTORS – ROLES AND RESPONSIBILITIES 175
  - CONTRACTORS – ROLES AND RESPONSIBILITIES 176
  - WORKERS – ROLES AND RESPONSIBILITIES 176
  - PARTICULARS TO BE NOTIFIED TO THE HSE 177
  - THE HEALTH AND SAFETY FILE 177

SIMPLY SAFETY

    Brief Description of The Work Carried Out..177
    Work at Height Regulations 2005 (as Amended) 178
    Definitions..178
    Management of Working at Heights 179
    Planning 179
    Other Considerations for the Employer 180
    Weather 180
    Emergency Procedures/Rescue 180
    Training 180
    Place of Work 180
    Equipment 180
    Inspections..181
    Fragile Surfaces 182
    Falling Objects 182
    Confined Spaces 182
    Legislation 183
Electricity at Work Regulations 1989..184
Gas Safety 186
    Legislation 186
    The Gas Safe Register 186
    Employers as Landlords 187
Water 188
Control of Legionella 188
    Introduction 188
    Source 188
    Route of Infection...188
    Legal Requirements 188
    Operation of Cooling Towers...189
    Operation, Maintenance and Inspection of Domestic Water Services 190
    Further Information May Be Found At: 191
Approval of Contractors 191
    Pre-qualification Questions..191
    Site Authorisation / Approval for Work 192
Safe System of Work 192
    Permit to Work 193
    General Permit (to cover high-risk activities) 194
Sick Building Syndrome 194
    Legal Duties 195
    How to Ensure Operation Without Sick Building Syndrome 196
Pressure Systems Safety Regulations 2000...196
Transportable Gas Containers (Gas Cylinders) 197

Chapter 10 199
Provision and Use of Work Equipment Regulations 1998 – Overview......................199
    Legal requirements..199
    What does PUWER do? 199
    To Whom do the Regulations Apply? 200
    Legal requirements of PUWER 1998 – Suitability, Maintenance and Inspection
   200

- SUITABILITY 200
- MAINTENANCE 201
- INSPECTION 201
- INFORMATION, INSTRUCTIONS AND TRAINING 201
- DANGEROUS PARTS OF MACHINERY 202
- GUARDS AND PROTECTION DEVICES 203
- TYPES OF GUARD AND SAFETY DEVICE 203
- PROTECTION AGAINST FAILURE 203
- HIGH OR VERY LOW TEMPERATURE 203
- CONTROLS AND CONTROL SYSTEMS 204
- STOP CONTROLS 204
- POSITION OF CONTROLS 204
- ISOLATION 204
- STABILITY 204
- LIGHTING 204
- MAINTENANCE 204
- MARKINGS / WARNINGS 205

Mobile Work Equipment 205
- EMPLOYEES CARRIED ON MOBILE EQUIPMENT 205
- ROLL-OVER PROTECTION 205
- ROLLOVER PROTECTION FOR FORK LIFT TRUCKS 205
- SELF-PROPELLED WORK EQUIPMENT 205
- REMOTE CONTROLLED WORK EQUIPMENT 206
- DRIVE SHAFTS 206

Lifting Operations and Lifting Equipment Regulations 1998 – Overview 206
- TO WHOM DO THE REGULATIONS APPLY? 207
- LOLER 1998 – DESIGN, INSTALLATION AND MARKING 207
- STRENGTH AND STABILITY 207
- LIFTING EQUIPMENT FOR LIFTING PERSONS 207
- POSITIONING AND INSTALLATION 207
- PATH OF TRAVEL (WHERE FIXED) TO BE PROTECTED BY SUITABLE ENCLOSURE 207
- LIFTING EQUIPMENT MARKING 208
- LOLER 1998 – ORGANISATION OF LIFTING OPERATIONS ... 208
- LOLER 1998 – EQUIPMENT TESTING AND EXAMINING 208
- LOLER 1998 – DOCUMENTATION 209

Dangerous Substances and Explosive Atmospheres Regulations 2002 (DSEAR) 209
- WHAT ARE DANGEROUS SUBSTANCES? 209
- WHAT DOES DSEAR REQUIRE? 210
- WHEN DOES DSEAR APPLY? 210
- WHERE DOES DSEAR APPLY? 211
- WHAT DOES DSEAR REQUIRE? 211
- ASSESSING RISKS 211
- PREVENTING OR CONTROLLING RISKS 211
- CONTROL MEASURES 212
- STORAGE OF FLAMMABLE LIQUIDS IN PROCESS AREAS, WORKROOMS, LABORATORIES AND SIMILAR WORKING AREAS 212
- FLAMMABLE LIQUIDS – RISKS 213
- FLAMMABLE LIQUIDS – PRECAUTIONS AND PROCEDURES 214
- PRECAUTIONS 214
- EMERGENCY PROCEDURES 215

SIMPLY SAFETY

INFORMATION AND TRAINING	215
Scaffolds and Ladders	216
DON'T LET A FALL SHATTER YOUR LIFE	216
Working at Heights	216
SCAFFOLDING	217
LADDERS, STEPLADDERS AND TRESTLES	218
LADDER EXCHANGE	219
Personal Protective Equipment	219
CE MARKING	220
Other Regulations	220
Appendices	227
Appendix 1 - HEALTH AND SAFETY LEGISLATION FOR EMPLOYERS	221
Health and Safety at Work etc. Act 1974	221
EMPLOYER'S DUTIES UNDER HASWA 1974	221
EMPLOYEE'S DUTIES UNDER HASWA 1974	222
THE MANAGEMENT OF HEALTH AND SAFETY AT WORK REGULATIONS (MHSWR) 1999	224
Six Pack Subsidiary Directives	225
PROVISION AND USE OF WORK EQUIPMENT REGULATIONS (PUWER) 1998	225
MANUAL HANDLING OPERATIONS REGULATIONS (MHOR) 1992	225
WORKPLACE (HEALTH, SAFETY AND WELFARE) REGULATIONS 1992	226
PERSONAL PROTECTIVE EQUIPMENT AT WORK REGULATIONS 1992	229
HEALTH AND SAFETY (DISPLAY SCREEN EQUIPMENT) REGULATIONS 1992	229
OTHER LEGISLATION	229
CONTROL OF SUBSTANCES HAZARDOUS TO HEALTH REGULATIONS 2002	230
ELECTRICITY AT WORK REGULATIONS 1989	231
LIFTING OPERATIONS AND LIFTING EQUIPMENT REGULATIONS 1998	231
HEALTH AND SAFETY (FIRST-AID) REGULATIONS 1981	232
HEALTH AND SAFETY (SAFETY SIGNS AND SIGNALS) REGULATIONS 1996	232
REPORTING OF INJURIES, DISEASES AND DANGEROUS OCCURRENCES REGULATIONS (RIDDOR) 1995	233
HEALTH AND SAFETY (CONSULTATION WITH EMPLOYEES) REGULATIONS 1996 AND SAFETY REPRESENTATIVES AND SAFETY COMMITTEES REGULATIONS 1977	234
HEALTH AND SAFETY (YOUNG PERSONS) REGULATIONS 1997	235
CONSTRUCTION (DESIGN AND MANAGEMENT) REGULATIONS 2007	236
CONTROL OF NOISE AT WORK REGULATIONS 2005	238
CONTROL OF VIBRATION AT WORK REGULATIONS 2005	238
EXPOSURE LIMIT AND ACTION LIMIT VALUES (REG 4)	238
VIBRATION RISK ASSESSMENT (REG 5)	239
ELIMINATION OR CONTROL OF EXPOSURE (REG 6)	239
HEALTH SURVEILLANCE (REG 7)	240
INFORMATION, INSTRUCTION AND TRAINING (REG 8)	240
DISABILITY DISCRIMINATION ACT 1995	240
EQUALITY ACT 2010	240
WORK AT HEIGHT REGULATIONS 2005 AND WORK AT HEIGHT (AMENDMENT) REGULATIONS 2007	243
DON'T LET A FALL SHATTER YOUR LIFE'	244
LADDER EXCHANGE	244
CORPORATE MANSLAUGHTER AND CORPORATE HOMICIDE ACT 2007	244

- The Health and Safety Offences Act 2008 246
- Health and Safety Information for Employees (Amendment) Regulations 2009 246
- Chemical (Hazard Information and Packaging for Supply) Regulations 2009 – to be known as CHIP 4 247
- Factories Act 1961 and Offices, Shops and Railway Premises Act 1963 (Repeals and Modifications) Regulations 2009 248
- Health and Safety at Work etc. Act 1974 (Application to Environmentally Hazardous Substances) (Amendment) Regulations 2009 249
- **Appendix 2 - Associations and Organisations - Alphabetical** 250
  - British Institute of Facilities Management (BIFM) 250
  - British Safety Council 250
  - British Standards Institution (BSI) 250
  - Chartered Institute of Building Services Engineers (CIBSE) 250
  - Chartered Institute of Environmental Health 251
  - Construction Best Practice Programme 251
  - Ergonomics Society 251
  - Health and Safety Bulletin 251
  - Health and Safety Executive 251
  - HSE Head Office 251
  - HSE Books 252
  - International Institute of Risk and Safety Management (IIRSM) 252
  - Institute of Engineering and Technology (IET) 252
  - Institute of Occupational Safety and Health (IOSH) 253
  - Lighting Industry Federation 253
  - NHS Stop Smoking Helpline 253
  - Royal Institution of Chartered Surveyors 253
  - Royal Society for the Prevention of Accidents 253
  - Sanitary Medical Disposal Services Association 254
  - Smokefree England 254

Acknowledgements 265

SIMPLY SAFETY

HOW THIS BOOK WILL HELP

Simply Safety will show you how to:

- comply with the relevant health and safety statutes, regulations and directives
- work with enforcement authorities
- set up a health and safety culture and company policy
- manage risk and conduct and review risk assessments
- comply with the law regarding first aid and accidents
- comply with the law regarding working with tools and other equipment
- comply with the law regarding occupational health
- comply with the law regarding building services
- set up and use a range of relevant model policies

KEY LEGISLATION

Some of the Key legislation referenced in this book:

- Building (Amendment) (No3) Regulations 2004 (SI 2004/3210) (B(A)(No3)R 2004)
- Carriage of Dangerous Goods and Use of Transportable Pressure Equipment Regulations 2009 (SI 2009/1348)
- Chemical (Hazard Information and Packaging for Supply) Regulations 2009 (SI 2009/716) (CHIP 4)
- Confined Spaces Regulations 1997 (SI 1997/1713) (CSR 1997)
- Construction (Design and Management) Regulations 2007 (SI 2007/320) (C(DM)R 2007)
- Control of Asbestos Regulations 2006 (SI 2006/2739) (CAR 2006)
- Control of Noise at Work Regulations 2005 (SI 2005/1643) (CNWR 2005)
- Control of Substances Hazardous to Health Regulations 2002 (SI 2002/2677) (COSHH 2002)
- Control of Vibration at Work Regulations 2005 (SI 2005/1093) (CVWR 2005)
- Corporate Manslaughter and Corporate Homicide Act 2007 (CMCHA 2007)
- Dangerous Substances and Explosive Atmospheres Regulations 2002 (SI 2002/2776) (DSEAR 2002)
- Electricity at Work Regulations 1989 (SI 1989/635) (EWR 1989)
- Factories Act 1961
- Factories Act 1961 and Offices, Shops and Railway Premises Act 1963 (Repeals and Modifications) Regulations 2009 (SI 2009/605)
- Fire and Rescue Services (Northern Ireland) Order 2006 (SI 2006/1254) (FRS(NI)O 2006)
- Fire Safety (Scotland) Act 2005 (FS(S)A 2005)
- Fire Safety (Scotland) Regulations 2006 (SI 2006/456) (FS(S)R 2006)
- Gas Appliances (Safety) Regulations 1995 (SI 1995/1629)
- Gas Safety (Installation and Use) Regulations 1998 (SI 1998/2451)
- Gas Safety (Management) Regulations 1996 (SI 1996/551)

- Health Act 2006 (HA 2006)
- Health and Safety (Consultation with Employees) Regulations 1996 (SI 1996/1513) (HS(CE)R 1996)
- Health and Safety (Display Screen Equipment) Regulations 1992 (SI 1992/2792) (HS(DSE)R 1992)
- Health and Safety (First-Aid) Regulations 1981 (SI 1981/917) (HS(FA)R 1981)
- Health and Safety (Miscellaneous Amendment) Regulations 2002 (SI 2002/2174) (HS(MA)R 2002)
- Health and Safety (Safety, Signs and Signals) Regulations 1996 (SI 1996/341) (HS(SSS)R 1996)
- Health and Safety (Young Persons) Regulations 1997 (SI 1997/135) (HS(YP)R 1997)
- Health and Safety at Work etc. Act 1974 (HSWA 1974)
- Health and Safety at Work etc. Act 1974 (Application to Environmentally Hazardous Substances) (Amendment) Regulations 2009 (SI 2009/318)
- Health and Safety Information for Employees Regulations 1989 (SI 1989/682)
- Health and Safety Information for Employees (Amendment) Regulations 2009 (SI 2009/606) (HSIE(A)R 2009)
- Health and Safety Offences Act 2008 (HSOA 2008)
- Legislative and Regulatory Reform Act 2006 (LRRA 2006)
- Lifting Operations and Lifting Equipment Regulations 1998 (SI 1998/2307) (LOLER 1998)
- Management of Health and Safety at Work Regulations 1999 (SI 1999/3242) (MHSWR 1999)
- Manual Handling Operations Regulations 1992 (SI 1992/2793) (MHOR 1992)
- Notification of Cooling Towers and Evaporative Condensers Regulations 1999 (SI 1999/2225) (NCTECR 1999)
- Occupiers Liability Act 1957 (OLA 1957)
- Occupiers Liability Act 1984 (OLA 1984)
- Offices, Shops and Railway Premises Act 1963
- Offshore Installations and Pipeline Works (First-Aid) Regulations 1989 (SI 1989/1671)
- Personal Protective Equipment at Work Regulations 1992 (SI 1992/2966) (PPEWR 1992)
- Pressure Equipment Regulations 1999 (SI 1999/2001) (PER 1999)
- Pressure Systems Safety Regulations 2000 (SI 2000/128) (PSSR 2000)
- Pressure Systems and Transportable Gas Containers Regulations 1989 (SI 1989/2169)
- Provision and Use of Work Equipment Regulations 1998 (SI 1998/2306) (PUWER 1998)
- Quarries Regulations 1999 (SI 1999/2024) (QR 1999)
- Regulatory Reform (Fire Safety) Order 2005 (SI 2005/1541) (RR(FS)O 2005)
- Reporting of Injuries, Diseases and Dangerous Occurrences Regulations 1995 (SI 1995/3163) (RIDDOR 1995)
- Safety Representatives and Safety Committees Regulations 1977 (SI 1977/500) (SRSCR 1997)
- Smoke-free (Penalties and Discounted Amounts) Regulations 2007 (SI 2007/764) (S(PDA)R 2007)

SIMPLY SAFETY

- Work at Height Regulations 2005 (SI 2005/735) (WAHR 2005)
- Work at Height (Amendment) Regulations 2007 (SI 2007/114) (WAH(A)R 2005)
- Workplace (Health, Safety and Welfare) Regulations 1992 (SI 1992/3004) (W(HSW)R 1992

CHAPTER 1
HEALTH AND SAFETY MANAGEMENT

LEGAL FRAMEWORK

WHY HEALTH AND SAFETY?

Good health and safety really makes sense for organisations and as an employer you can actually save costs by implementing simple cost effective procedures designed to control the risks in your workplace. To see an example of organisations who got it wrong and the fines and costs involved then visit the HSE Public Register of Convictions at www.hse.gov.uk/prosecutions and remember the fines imposed here are just the tip of the iceberg as we will go onto examine and remember good effective health and safety is not rocket science and doing the simple things well and involving your staff can pay huge dividends and actually save you costs.

As an employer you may think that your insurance policy will cover you for your losses but in practice uninsured costs can amount to ten times the cost of your insurance premium paid and are made up of legal costs, down time and loss of production in investigating the accident, absence cover, investigation costs including gathering witness statements, in worse cases dealing with the HSE inspector, purchase of new equipment if damaged as a result of the incident to name but a few. The actual costs can be startling. Further information regarding costs of accidents may be found at www.hse.gov.uk/costs

Good health and safety can work in any organisation large or small and save money which otherwise would eat into the profits. As an example this small selection of large companies shown below worked with their employees to reduce absence, improve productivity and saved money. Further case studies may be found at www.hse.gov.uk/business/casestudy.htm

- Pharmaceuticals: AstraZeneca
  http://www.hse.gov.uk/business/casestudy/astrazeneca.htm
  Improving employee wellbeing reduced absence, improved productivity and saved AstraZeneca £200,000 a year on health insurance

- Healthcare: Barts and the London NHS Trust
  http://www.hse.gov.uk/business/casestudy/barts.htm
  By providing a voluntary flu jab, this hospital trust has been able to reduce sickness absence, benefiting all staff, patients and the trust itself

- Construction: Birse Rail
  http://www.hse.gov.uk/business/casestudy/birserail.htm
  By adopting a zero tolerance culture, significant reductions in accidents have improved safety, reduced business interruptions, and strengthened supply chain relations

FOUNDATION OF HEALTH and SAFETY LEGISLATION

The central hub driving Health & Safety legislation in the UK is the Health and Safety at Work

SIMPLY SAFETY

etc. Act 1974, which is sometimes referred to as the 'Umbrella Act', due to the fact that section 16 allows regulations to be introduced and which have had such a fundamental affect upon the workplace e.g. The Six Pack Regulations in 1992.

An employer has a duty to comply with health and safety law as well as having a moral duty and will seek to do this to protect the staff and thus ensure that everybody goes home safely after a day's work and that nobody suffers ill health as a result of their workplace. However if something does go wrong in the workplace and there is a serious accident or indeed if an inspector calls at your workplace, then as an employer you need to think about just how are you going to show that you have complied with the law? It is far better to have a written or an electronic record to prove compliance and thus to prevent any potential for prosecution and the financial, moral and reputational costs associated with such an event.

Under the auspices of UK Health & Safety legislation we all have a responsibility for health and safety and the **Health and Safety at Work etc. Act 1974 (HSWA 1974), s 2(1)**, sums it up as follows:

'It shall be the duty of every employer to ensure, so far as is reasonably practicable, the health, safety and welfare at work of all his employees.'

And from later in the Act (HSWA 1974, s 7):

'Every employee must:

(a)   Take reasonable care for the health and safety of themselves and others who may be affected by their acts or omissions.
(b)   Co-operate with their employer or any other person to enable legal obligations to be met.'

Although there were Acts of Parliament that preceded this legislation, and there has been, of course, a wealth of subsequent regulation, these are still the key words around which any organisation, no matter what sector of industry or commerce it operates in, should base its overall approach to health and safety. However many risk assessments, audits, training courses or other activities related to health and safety you carry out, it is always worth referring back to these phrases to remind yourself of why you are doing them.

Remember:

- A safe workplace is one in which risks to staff have been minimised; absence from work, lost production and down time due to avoidable accidents will be reduced.
- Staff morale is likely to be higher in an organisation where the employer is perceived to be one that takes an active interest in its staff; its approach to health and safety will be one of the ways in which this will be judged.
- Your clients and customers may well use your overall approach to health and safety as one way of judging whether you are someone they wish to do business with; most tenders for services these days ask questions about your health and safety policy.

Health and Safety Management

- A failure to adequately discharge your health and safety duties can have a seriously detrimental effect on your organisation, both financially, in terms of significant fines, and to your company's reputation if it is perceived that you do not take such issues seriously.

- You may be in a position to save money on insurance costs by demonstrating to your insurers that you have considered all health and safety risks and have implemented robust and effective control measures as a result of your robust processes, procedures and risk assessment process.

Negligent health and safety practices may also put organisations at risk of conviction for corporate manslaughter offences as well.

We will cover the requirements of the HSWA 1974 act in more detail in the Appendices later in this book.

SIMPLY SAFETY

The Legal System

THE COURTS

Criminal Courts of England & Wales

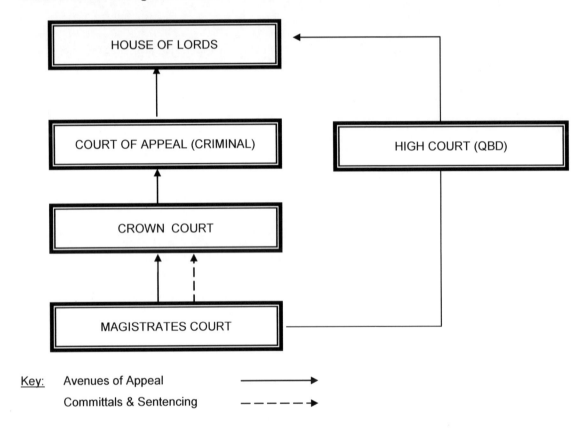

Key: Avenues of Appeal ⟶
       Committals & Sentencing ---▶

Health and Safety Management

Civil Courts of England and Wales

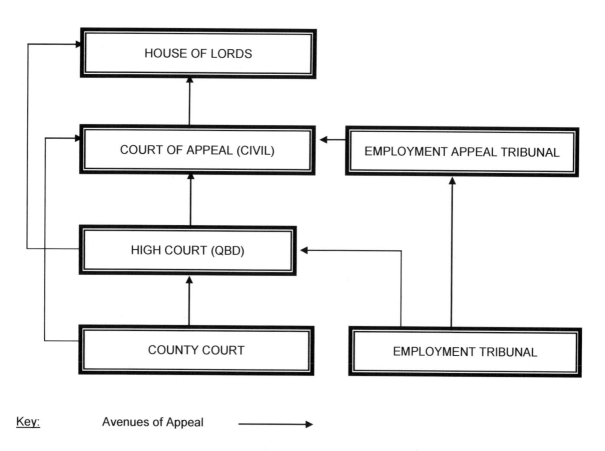

Key: Avenues of Appeal ———▶

Court Structure & Appeal routes

There are two divisions of courts that deal with different aspects of health and safety: **Criminal**, e.g. magistrates' courts and Crown Courts; and **Civil**, e.g. county courts and High Courts (including the Employment Tribunal). Each division has its own hierarchical structure, from lower courts to higher ones, and there is an appeal process from lower courts to higher ones. The House of Lords is the highest court in the UK for both divisions. See Figure 1.1.

The lowest court in the criminal division is the magistrates' court, where most charges are first heard. The magistrates' court can hear all of the offences under Health and Safety at Work etc. Act 1974 (HSWA 1974) and subsidiary legislation; however, when the prosecution believe that the case is too serious to be heard by the magistrates' court they can request to take the case to the Crown Court. In the magistrates' court, upon conviction, employers and/or their organisation can be penalised as follows (together with the addition of costs):

- fines of up to £20,000 for breaches of HSWA 1974, ss 2–6 and up to £5,000 for breaches of any other section or any regulation made under the Act

SIMPLY SAFETY

- fines of up to £20,000 and/or six months imprisonment for failing to comply with an improvement or prohibition notice

The Crown Court is where cases are taken when the matter is considered too serious for the magistrates' court to hear, or where the magistrates' court decides that there is sufficient evidence for the case to be passed on to the Crown Court or when the accused opts for trial by jury. Upon conviction on indictment within the Crown Court, employers and/or their organisation can be penalised as follows (together with the addition of costs):

- an unlimited fine
- and/or up to two years' imprisonment

With regards to failure to comply with Improvement and Prohibition Notices, the fine is unlimited, with a further fine not exceeding £100 per day if the offence is continued.

Appeals on criminal cases from the magistrates' courts are heard in Crown Court, whereas appeals from the Crown Court go to the Court of Appeal (Criminal Division) and from there to the House of Lords.

Penalties for Breaching H&S Legislation

Prosecution is the main means by which the health and safety enforcing authorities (Health & Safety Executive (HSE) and the local authorities Environmental Health Officers (EHO's) deal with those alleged to have committed serious breaches of health and safety law.

Health and safety law provides few sentencing options for the courts, and conviction usually results in a fine for organisations and or directors of those organisations as individuals.

All breaches of health & safety are treated very seriously by the Courts and offenders can expect some pretty heavy financial penalties to be handed out. That said both the authors of this book and the enforcement authorities would rather that organizations make the choice to be proactive and have suitable systems in situ and are compliant with legislation rather than resist the law and place not only their own company at risk but that of their staff and potentially members of the public. The Safety culture of an organization plays an important part in this compliance process and we will cover this subject later in this book.

Remember: If the enforcing authorities consider that they do have to prosecute then the consequences will be serious

For further information on fines handed down by the court system then please visit the HSE website at www.hse.gov.uk

EFFECT OF THE HEALTH & SAFETY (OFFENCES) ACT 2008

Many offences committed on or after 16 January 2009 are subject to higher maximum penalties. For example, for offences relating to breaches of health and safety regulations, magistrates' courts may impose a fine of up to £20,000 as opposed to £5,000 per breach pre January 2009. In addition, imprisonment is a sentencing option in respect of many offences, both in the magistrates' court and the Crown Court. Magistrates are currently limited to imposing custodial sentences up to a maximum of 6 months. However should the case be referred to the Crown

Court then the Judge has the power to impose an unlimited fine and a custodial sentence of up to two years' imprisonment where the accused is an individual rather than a company.

NOTE: The higher penalties are not retrospective and cannot be imposed for offences committed before the 16th January 2009.

Authors Note: From our experience of dealing with accidents we can assure you that the courts do make the most of the penalties available to them when sentencing as not only a way of punishing the organization or individual but also to set an example to other organization's which does focus the mind somewhat and remember its often not just the fines but also the court costs that have to be taken into account as well.

CORPORATE MANSLAUGHTER & CORPORATE HOMICIDE ACT 2007

The legislation has two names because the offence of causing a death without criminal intent is known as manslaughter in England and Wales, and homicide in Scotland (which has a slightly different legal system).

The Act was devised because incidents such as the Potters Bar rail crash had shown a weakness in the legislation such as it was then. In such a complex incident such as this it can be fairly easy to prove that some of the track maintenance workers, are liable in some way because they have breached health & safety, but what of the senior management and executives of the company? It was incredibly difficult to prove that senior managers knew of, and condoned, health & safety breaches for commercial reasons, or in most cases their defence maybe that they simply delegated the task to a subordinate who let them down? Therefore the problem was that of identifying the "controlling mind" within the organization, and thus the Corporate Manslaughter Act was developed to solve this problem.

Section (1) of the act in essence states that: "An organization ... is guilty of an offence if the way in which its activities are managed or organized a) causes a person's death, and b) amounts to a gross breach of a relevant duty of care owed by the organization to the deceased."

Therefore the theory behind the act is the behaviour of the organisation as a whole rather than the behaviour of any particular individual within the organisation. In the act need to identify a specific "controlling mind" has been removed.

Since the Corporate Manslaughter Act is dealing with an organisation there is no point in employing the sanction of imprisonment since you cannot imprison a paper structure. Instead the major penalty that can be imposed is that of an unlimited fine, and guidance produced by the Ministry of Justice suggests that the Courts will not shy away from multi-million pound fines where Judges feel that is an appropriate punishment.

Further information may be found at the following web site:

General principles
http://www.hse.gov.uk/enforce/enforcementguide/court/sentencing-principles.htm

THE HIGH COURT

Under common law, unlimited damages can be awarded by the High Court where it can be shown that, on the balance of probability, the claimant sustained personal injury as a direct

SIMPLY SAFETY

result of the employer's negligence. This applies mainly to claims made by employees against their employer for compensation for injuries arising out of an accident, or for health damage. Cases include claims for work-related upper limb disorders, manual handling injuries and noise-induced hearing loss arising from exposures to harmful agents in the workplace.

Civil claims, especially personal injury claims of less than £50,000, begin in the county court. Claims that come about due to the result of an industrial injury are heard in the High Court, which is presided over by a High Court judge. The judge alone decides the outcome of the claim. Should there be an appeal on a point of law, then the case is referred to the Court of Appeal and from there to the House of Lords when given leave.

The power of the civil court is to award damages/compensation and not to give custodial sentences or fines. The amount of damages/compensation awarded for industrial injury and illness depends upon the extent of the loss suffered as well as other mitigating factors:

- effect on quality of life
- pain and suffering
- loss of earnings
- rate of inflation
- type and permanency of injury or illness

EMPLOYMENT TRIBUNALS

Internal disputes concerning entitlements under the Safety Representatives and Safety Committees Regulations 1977 (SI 1977/500) (SRSCR 1977) that are unresolved are required to be referred to an employment tribunal (HSWA 1974, ss 24(2), 82(1)(c); Industrial Tribunals (Constitution and Rules of Procedure) Regulations 1993 (SI 1993/2687), reg 8(4) and ch 4).

TYPES OF LAW

The two court systems have separate types of law to which they refer. The criminal courts deal with breaches of the law known as criminal liability, whereas the civil courts deal with breaches of common law.

Criminal liability means the responsibilities imposed by statute law and the penalties that can be set by the courts. These penalties can be fines, remedial orders or imprisonment. See Figure 2.2.

Common law is law consisting of decisions of court bound together by precedent into a body of authoritative rules and it is judge made. Breaches of the common law are generally breaches in the tort of negligence. A tort is defined as a private or civil wrong.

Under the rule of common law everyone owes a duty to everyone else to take reasonable care so as not to cause foreseeable harm or injury. This is known as the duty of care.

'An employer, owes a duty of care to all those within his building and to those who may be affected by the work being carried out. The duty of care was defined in 1937 by the House of Lords in a leading case (Wilsons and Clyde Coal Co v English). These duties were identified as all employers having to provide:

- a safe place of work, plant and equipment
- a safe system of work
- competent employees, by means of adequate instruction and supervision

For an employee successfully to sue his/her employer, they must prove to the courts the following three points:

- that the employer owed him/her a duty of care
- that the employer breached that duty
- that the breach caused injury, disease or death to the employee

It should be noted that criminal law and common law are not mutually exclusive under health and safety. Employers can be prosecuted for a breach of the law and, if found guilty, can suffer the appropriate penalty. They can at the same time or later be sued under common law for a breach of the tort of negligence for basically the same offence.

SIMPLY SAFETY

SUMMARY OF TYPES OF LAW

LAW DERIVED FROM TWO MAIN SOURCES, AS FOLLOWS:

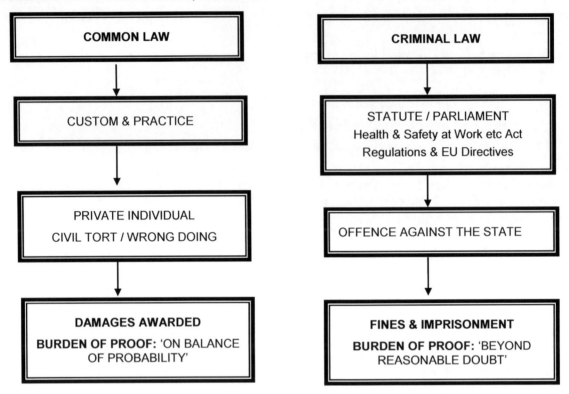

FIGURE 1.2: SOURCES AND DIVISIONS OF LAW

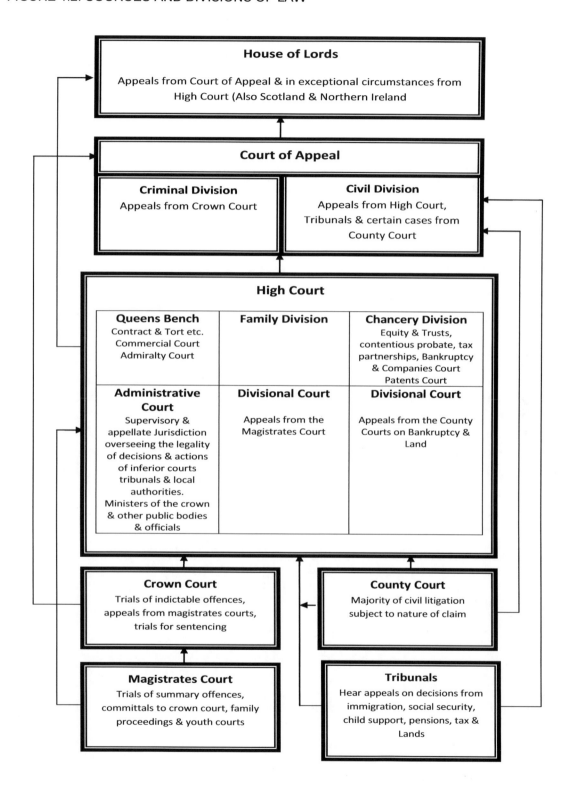

SIMPLY SAFETY

LEGISLATION OVERVIEW

As a member state of the EU the United Kingdom must respond to EU directives by incorporating them into UK law unless they have negotiated an exemption from all or part of that legislation or unless the provisions of the directive concerned can already be shown to be covered by existing statute.

It is likely that an increasing amount of UK health and safety regulation will be derived from EU directives, with the Working Time Regulations 1998 (SI 1998/1833) being a good example from recent years. Because any such directives are subject to a period of consultation and then have to be enacted into UK law, those responsible for health and safety within companies have the opportunity to consider the impact of such legislation both in terms of operation and financially, and plan accordingly. It is important that you take note of the date by which provisions should be implemented and also understand the difference between regulations that may be under discussion (and therefore subject to amendment and revision) and those that have been enacted and have the force of law.

ENFORCEMENT AUTHORITIES – RESPONSIBILITIES AND POWERS

There are various groups that have responsibilities for health and safety within the workplace, and the employer needs to understand who these groups are and for what they are responsible, and probably more importantly their powers. These are as listed below.

HEALTH AND SAFETY EXECUTIVE (HSE)

The HSE consists of a board in essence responsible for setting strategy which is then developed by a senior management team. The board is lead by its chairman and consists of a further nine board appointments which are made by consultation with representative groups, employers, employees and local authorities. The board works within the guidelines laid out by a code of practice as well as an HSE business plan for the next year. The board is then supported by the senior management team, consisting of 12 members who all hold key roles within the HSE.

The main emphasis of the HSE is as follows:

'The prevention of death, injury and ill health in Great Britain's workplaces.'

In practice this means that the HSE will come down hard on people who put others at risk - particularly where there is evidence of deliberate flouting of the law.

Why have Enforcement?

Enforcement ensures that duty holders .e.g. employers

- deal immediately with serious risks;
- comply with the law; and
- are held to account if they fail in their responsibilities.

The HSE in its new form following its merger with the Health and Safety Commission is now better equipped to face the challenges of the ever changing workplace and will retain its independence and commitment to maintaining service delivery through the prioritisation of

Health and Safety Management

resources and continual review its strategy.

In these testing economic times the HSE is keen for our leaders in industry to be aware of their duties as directors to lead health and safety and are actively raising the profile of the free publication, Leading Health & Safety at Work INDG417, which was jointly published by the old Health and Safety Commission and the Institute of Directors. The publication, which is a must for any facilities management directors, details directors' duties to ensure that their organisations have adequate health and safety systems in place to ensure the protection of their staff.

A copy of the document is available at the HSE website at www.hse.gov.uk/pubns/indg417.pdf.

HOW HSE ENFORCES HEALTH AND SAFETY

The HSE Enforcement Policy Statement adopts a wide definition of "enforcement":

- Enforcing authorities may offer duty holders information and advice, both face to face and in writing. They may warn a duty holder that in their opinion, they are failing to comply with the law.
- Where appropriate, they may also serve improvement and prohibition notices, withdraw approvals, vary licence conditions or exemptions, issue formal cautions (England and Wales only), and they may prosecute (or report to the Procurator Fiscal with a view to prosecution in Scotland

In carrying out its enforcement role, HSE follows these internal operational procedures:

- Inspection
- Investigation
- Complaints
- Enforcement decisions
- Notice
- Prosecution
- Major incident
- Penalties
- Work-Related Deaths

For more information please visit the HSE website: -http://www.hse.gov.uk/enforce/enforce.htm

ENVIRONMENTAL HEALTH OFFICER (EHO)

The Local Environmental Health Officer is employed by the relevant County, District or Borough Council and has the same powers as the Health and Safety Inspectors, though their area of operation is different. EHOs are employed to enforce health and safety at work in respect of premises for which they are responsible as well as a wide range of other legislation, including food safety, infectious disease control, housing, pollution and noise control.

SIMPLY SAFETY

FIRE OFFICER

The county council and other unitary authorities employ the Fire Officer. Fire Officers have a range of powers, which are given to them by the new Regulatory Reform (Fire Safety) Order 2005 (SI 2005/1541) (RR(FS)O 2005), which has transposed the powers of the Fire Officer from the old Fire Precautions Act 1971 (FPA 1971). The Fire Officer has the power to enter premises to ensure that the responsible person is complying with their duties under the new RR(FS)O 2005.

EMPLOYMENT MEDICAL ADVISORY SERVICE (EMAS)

The Employment Medical Advisory Service is part of the HSE and provides advice on all aspects of occupational health with the aim of promoting greater awareness of health-related matters in the workplace. The staff at EMAS are all doctors and nurses with specialist qualifications in occupational health.

THE DIFFERENT RESPONSIBILITIES AND POWERS OF THE ENFORCEMENT AUTHORITIES

The HSE and over 380 individual local authorities (LAs) are responsible for the enforcement of health and safety in Great Britain, under the general direction of the Health and Safety Executive Board.

The Health and Safety at Work etc. Act 1974, and related legislation, is enforced either at individual work premises, by HSE, or the relevant LA, according to the main activity carried out there. LAs also enforce other primary legislation relating to pesticides (Food and Environment Protection Act 1985) on a similar basis, as well as storage of explosives and petroleum licensing. The latter aspects are also enforced by Fire Authorities and Trading Standards departments.

The Health and Safety (Enforcing Authority) Regulations 1998 (EA Regulations) allocate the enforcement of health and safety legislation at different premises between LAs and HSE. Some businesses, such as dry cleaning and motor vehicle repair, are enforced either by HSE or LAs depending on the main activity at a particular premise. Responsibility for enforcement at certain premises may be transferred between HSE and Local Authorities by agreement.

LAs are the principle enforcing authority in retailing, wholesale distribution, warehousing, hotel and catering premises, offices, and the consumer/leisure industries. However, HSE may also have some enforcement responsibilities at certain premises. The difference between the HSE inspectors and the EHOs depends upon the area within which one works, as can be seen by the following lists. These lists are not exhaustive and if you are in any doubt as to which authority covers your workplace you should ring the local HSE office and check with them.

The HSE covers the following areas of work:

- factories
- hospitals
- railway systems
- schools

Health and Safety Management

- building sites
- power stations
- fairgrounds

Whereas local authority environmental health officers cover these areas:

- offices
- retail premises
- exhibition premises
- food premises

POWERS OF ENTRY AND INSPECTION

An inspector has many powers to enable him to undertake his duties without interference. Briefly, these powers enable them to undertake the following within premises in their area of jurisdiction:

- enter and search premises without the need for permission at any reasonable time
- gain access to premises if there is a dangerous situation at any time
- call upon the police for assistance in the execution of their duty
- order that locations be left undisturbed until investigations are completed
- take samples of articles or substances in the premises and atmosphere in or within the area of the building
- interview any person
- require the production and inspection of, and to take copies of, any documents
- require the provision of facilities to enable them to carry out their investigations

It should be noted by the employer that failure to co-operate with an inspector carrying out his lawful duty is a criminal offence.

Prior to a visit by an inspector it is important that the employer ensures that legally required information for the business is available or displayed within the premises:

- a current employer's liability certificate
- the signed general statement of policy on safety
- fire certificate, if the premises require one
- an Accident Book
- the poster 'Health and Safety Law – what you should know' is displayed and that the following are entered in the spaces provided:
    - the address of the EMAS office
- that employees have been given the official explanatory leaflet containing the above information if there are no posters available
- that a thermometer has been provided for employees to check the workplace temperature

SIMPLY SAFETY

- that first aid boxes are kept full and that stock is in date
- that the general risk assessment for the workplace and any specific risk assessments are available
- that any required records are available in respect of the following:
    - lifts
    - lifting equipment
    - pressure vessels and compressors
    - electrical equipment (permanent and portable)
    - training for operation of equipment such as fork lift trucks, cranes or mounting of abrasive wheels, where relevant

DEALING WITH A VISIT BY AN ENFORCEMENT AUTHORITY

It is important for the employer to be prepared for a visit by an inspector, which can happen at any time:

- The inspector should be escorted to a suitable room or office.
- The employer needs to meet with the inspector and therefore needs to be informed immediately of the visit (even more so if it is an unexpected visit so that they or a suitable alternative can be sent to meet the inspector).
- The employer is able to provide an explanation of the workings of the company, what it does and who is responsible for what and, in particular, for health and safety.
- Arrangements should be made for the inspector to meet others within the organisation with whom they may wish to talk.
- Arrangements should be made to accompany the inspector around the building, giving them the opportunity of looking at whatever they are interested in.
- Arrangements should be made so that the inspector can talk with members of staff should they wish to do so.
- Copies of maintenance records, risk assessments, audit training records, fire alarm tests and evacuation exercises should be available for the inspector to look at should they so desire.

If faults are found

If at any time during the inspection faults are found, then the employer should ask for advice on putting the matters right. Inspectors from all of the Enforcement Authorities see numerous organisations and their problems and they have useful knowledge that will assist the employer to correct health and safety faults. Generally, inspectors are much happier giving advice that will help put the problem right than they are to begin the lengthy processes involved in the serving of the various notices.

Once the inspector has left the premises it is important that the employer ensures that the situation is discussed and that any corrective actions are delegated to the appropriate persons such as facilities or human resources managers who will take ownership. It is important that management discusses and agrees with those responsible for undertaking the work required to correct the problems spotted, as to what will be done next and by whom. The employer should

Health and Safety Management

expect to receive a subsequent written note from the inspector clarifying matters. The inspector may well ask for more information and will more than likely confirm certain actions that they expect to see at the time of their next visit.

INTERVIEWS BY AN INSPECTOR

Under the Health and Safety at Work etc. Act 1974 (HSWA 1974), s 20(2)(j), an inspector may conduct interviews and take statements. These interviews are normally just a simple part of an inspection visit. However, if during the inspection or interview, the inspector believes that an offence has been or may well be committed they may well decide to use the replies that they receive as evidence for a possible legal action. If this is the case the inspector must take the following steps:

- the inspector must caution the person being interviewed
- the inspector must allow the interviewee to have legal representation present as is their entitlement
- if for some reason there is a break during the questioning (whilst the interviewee is under caution), the interviewing inspector must ensure that when the interview resumes, the interviewee is aware that they still remain under caution
- the inspector must make a record as soon as practicable of the following:
  - the date and place of interview
  - the date of making the record, if different
  - those persons present
  - the fact that a caution has been given
  - the time the interview started and ended
  - the times of any breaks in the interview

Although it seems to vary from area to area, in most cases the inspector will cease questioning as soon as it becomes clear that an offence has been committed and will write to the interviewee advising them of a date time place to attend for a formal interview which will be conducted under the Police and Criminal Evidence Act (PACE) and which will be recorded on tape. As above, all of the same rules apply with regards to the interviewee being under caution.

STATUTORY NOTICES

If during an inspection an inspector discovers something that they believe to be in contravention of the duties set out within the Health and Safety at Work etc. Act 1974 (HSWA 1974) or any of the subsequent pieces of legislation, they can take one of the following options (HSWA 1974, ss 20–22):

- send a letter requiring actions to be taken
- seize, render harmless or destroy any article or substance which is considered to be the cause of imminent danger
- issue an improvement notice which gives a time limit for the work to be carried out which must be at least 21 days (HSWA 1974, ss 24(2), 82(1)(c); Industrial Tribunals (Constitution and Rules of Procedure) Regulations 1993 (SI 1993/2687), reg 8(4) and Sch 4)

SIMPLY SAFETY

- issue a prohibition notice which prohibits the work detailed within the notice
- prosecute any person

Improvement Notices

Improvement notices are served when, in the inspector's opinion, the employer has done the following:

- contravened one or more statutory requirements
- contravened one or more statutory requirements in circumstances that make it likely that the contravention will continue or be repeated

An improvement notice will state that in the opinion of the inspector there is a breach of a specific legal requirement. They will normally issue a schedule that will lay out what actions need to be undertaken to enable the employer to comply with the law. The improvement notice will set a date by which time the inspector will expect all remedial works to be completed. The minimum amount of time that must be given for any rectification works is 21 days after the notice is served, although in practice the time frame is normally longer.

If after the time specified within the improvement notice the employer has not complied with the details outlined within the improvement notice he can be prosecuted.

Prohibition Notices

A prohibition notice is issued by an inspector when he believes that an activity involves a risk of serious personal injury or possible death or that an activity may lead to a risk of serious personal injury or possible death.

When an inspector issues a prohibition notice this is an instruction to the employer to stop the work activity in question immediately. The notice, when issued, must contain the following:

- a statement from the inspector that he is of the opinions given above regarding serious risk of injury or death
- details of the matters that created the risks in question
- a statement that the inspector is of the opinion that an actual breach or an anticipated breach in the regulations has or will occur and he must also give his reasons
- instructions that the activities referred to in the prohibition notice must not be carried out on, by or under the control of the employer unless the matter referred to above has been rectified

In a few cases it is possible that the inspector will allow the prohibition notice to be deferred. This means that the prohibition notice will come into force after a particular work activity comes to an end. The notice will then prohibit a repetition of the work until certain matters are eliminated or controlled.

Health and Safety Management

Should the employer fail to comply with the notice, that is in itself an offence and the organisation may very well be prosecuted.

APPEALS

The employer can lodge an appeal against notices that have been issued.

In the case of an improvement notice this has the effect of suspending the Improvement Notice until the appeal is heard.

In the case of a prohibition notice, which refers to matters believed to be potentially life threatening, the prohibition notice will remain in force while the appeal is heard.

Appeals are heard by employment tribunals, which may do the following:

- uphold the notice
- set aside the notice
- should the notice be confirmed, it is possible that the tribunal may alter some or all of the terms contained therein

CHAPTER 2

ESTABLISHING A HEALTH AND SAFETY CULTURE IN YOUR ORGANISATION

Including promoting a positive health and safety culture and implementing a health and safety system

INTRODUCTION

The health and safety culture of an organisation makes the greatest contribution to its health and safety performance. Unfortunately in some respects this culture is not an easy concept to understand, measure or manage. A good health and safety management system can go some way to setting the scene for developing a good culture, but it goes much deeper than that and is influenced by management from the very top down from the CEO and the board of directors and requires a positive commitment by the company to promote a positive culture with the resulting creation of some important work activities for the management team.

WHAT IS HEALTH AND SAFETY CULTURE?

Defined in pure simple terms: 'it's the way things are done around here'. According to HSG65 "The safety culture of an organisation is the product of individual and group values, attitudes, perceptions, competencies and patterns of behavior that determine the commitment to, and the style and proficiency of, an organisation's health and safety management."

Also (quoting from the Advisory Committee on the Safety of Nuclear Installations) "Organisations with a positive safety culture are characterised by communications founded on mutual trust, by shared perceptions of the importance of safety and by confidence in the efficacy of preventative measures."

Safety culture is not a difficult idea, but it is usually described in terms of concepts such as 'trust', 'values' and 'attitudes'. It can be difficult to describe what these mean, but you can judge whether a company has a good safety culture from what its employees actually do rather than what they say.

INFLUENCING SAFETY CULTURE

Most organisations view health and safety as a direct cost or an overhead to the business with the function being treated as an optional extra or a bolt on function. In reality effective health and safety management will enable the organisation to be more efficient and will provide added value in cost savings achieved through efficiencies and it is in this area where the employer can have an influence upon the Health and Safety arrangements within an organisation.

Some typical areas for the employer where savings may be realised are risk identification prioritisation and mitigation, legal costs associated with accidents and their investigation, down

Establishing a Health and Safety Culture in your Organisation

time for accident investigation, absenteeism, retraining following an accident, insurance claims and other uninsured costs. If the employer can influence the organisation to treat health and safety as an essential function integrated into its overall strategic objectives then this has proven time and time again, through case studies, to save money, protect the brand name and image of the organisation as well as improving staff well-being and morale.

In addition, there is also a vast plethora of legislation to consider, which can have a considerable impact upon the finances of an organisation by way of uninsured costs for fines as well as a black mark against an organisation's reputation through advertisement within the government's Health and Safety Executives' 'name and shame' website and resulting loss of business through a loss in clients' confidence.

Why is Safety Culture important?

Many accidents, incidents and near misses in the workplace occur as a result of unsafe acts or behaviours by staff e.g. failure to follow company procedures, use of inappropriate equipment, poor housekeeping. However unsafe acts or behaviours are normally developed over time and are inherited by staff as a result of systemic failure within the organisation itself and are generally accepted as the root cause of accidents as well as being indicators of a poor safety culture.

Indicators of A Poor Culture?

As an employer you will be able to see typical symptoms around the workplace that indicate a poor culture such as:

- Widespread, routine procedural violations;
- Failures of compliance with health and safety systems;
- Untidy and dirty workplaces
- Poor Leadership e.g. turning a blind eye
- Lack of defined roles and responsibilities
- Use of unsuitable work equipment that is not maintained.
- Poor maintenance of records e.g. statutory
- Staff not wearing or incorrect storage of PPE
- Staff negative attitude to health and safety
- Management decisions that put production or cost before safety.
- Evidence of minor injuries to staff combined with a low accident rate e.g. under reporting

Some of these conditions can be difficult to detect because a poor culture not only contributes to their occurrence, it also means that staff may be inclined to hide or cover-up violations and unsafe practices.

Indicators of a Positive Culture?

The following are indicators to the employer that an organisation has a positive health and safety culture:

- Visible management commitment to safety at all levels in the organisation;

SIMPLY SAFETY

- Good knowledge and understanding of health and safety throughout the organisation;
- Clear definition of the culture that is desired e.g. Values;
- Lack of competing priorities with health and safety (e.g. production, quality, etc);
- Setting of SMART health & safety objectives;
- Visible evidence that investment is made into health and safety, including the
  - Quality of the working environment, equipment provided etc.;
  - Health & Safety seen as a main agenda item at all meetings
  - Proactive training programme
  - Proactive health & safety e.g. opportunities for improvement are dealt with before problems arise;
  - Good communication up, down and across the organisation;
  - A fair and just discipline system;
  - Meaningful consultation of the workforce in all elements of health and safety.

RELATIONSHIP BETWEEN SAFETY CULTURE & PERFORMANCE

If we take the analogy of driving a motor vehicle on a road we can start to explore just how safety culture can influence safety performance by considering the essential components of safe driving, as follows:

- The driver – their experience, attitude etc.
- The design of the car – the safety features (e.g. seat belts, crumple zones, anti-lock brakes, etc.);
- Traffic management - (e.g. the road design & layout, road surface, signage, etc.);

Motor vehicle design these days means that that they are inherently safe for use on the roads and whilst some traffic arrangements on our roads can be confusing at times, they are also inherently safe. However with the best will in the world, even with good systems, it is the attitudes and behaviours of the driver that will ultimately determine the safety performance of driving and, to reach the maximum levels of safety performance, we need all three elements e.g. attitudes, behaviours and systems - to be as good as possible

The actual safety of any organisation may be defined by through the observation of key day-to-day behaviours within an organisation including both management and operational staff and the extent to which these behaviours are encouraged and supported by an effective safety management system. The shared belief and values held within the organisation in the importance of safety, the extent to which an organisation actively strives to ensure health and safety is done properly and always given a high priority is what defines a positive safety culture and will ensure a zero accident environment with zero downtime, zero claims, reduced ill health and sickness and in general the staff will be more productive as they will have a very positive mindset and high morale.

In contrast however if management are not committed to health and safety then there will be evidence of managers walking by poor behaviour and in effect turning a blind eye, safety will not have the focus in meetings that it deserves, safety managers will not be given the support by management and an attitude will likely prevail where accidents and incidents are merely accepted as the norm and as part and parcel of the job. This in effect will have the opposite

Establishing a Health and Safety Culture in your Organisation

effect on most of the points mentioned above and will result in a reactive or fire fighting system which is inefficient and will cost you, as an employer, money off your bottom line.

WHAT DOES IT TAKE TO CREATE A POSITIVE CULTURE?

It is not possible to improve culture directly as it is necessary to work at a number of improving factors that can have a positive influence on culture

Genuine commitment to a strong safety culture means you as the CEO, MD, Directors and Senior Management team of your organisation have the key task to drive Health and Safety down through the organisational structure and to embed this into all areas of the organisation. In reality the following improving factors will all contribute to achieving a positive safety culture:

- Commit time and sufficient resources to workplace safety
- Increase the amount of time managers spend visiting the workplace (not just after an accident);
- Ensure that there is demonstrable safety leadership & visible management commitment to health and safety; this needs to be evident from the priority and resourcing given to safety;
- Ensure that your organisation learns from incidents and accidents and communicates such lessons across the organisation to achieve continual improvements:
- Improve managers non-technical skills (e.g. communication) so that issues are communicated in a respectful way;
- Consult with your workers and really listen to what they say
- Promote good job satisfaction and moral;
- Promote a 'just culture' where blame is only used where someone is reckless;
- Implement a competence assurance program to ensure everyone throughout the organisation has the skills they need to work safely.
- Develop and implement effective and appropriate safety management systems that remove barriers to safe working and foster the correct attitudes and behaviours across your organisation;
- Ensure implementation of return to work and injury management programs for injured staff

SAFETY CULTURE DEVELOPMENT

Safety culture development is complex and slow as old habits die hard and it takes time to motivate and change the attitudes of staff. In addition every organisation will be at a different level of safety culture development across the various elements of their operations, due to the prevalent local conditions and in most cases the attitude of the senior manager towards health and safety. This is important to recognise as safety culture development requires certain key elements to be in place, and working reasonably well, before the next steps can be taken – trying to run before you can walk nearly always ends in frustration and failure. Think of the development as a staircase where you are working to get to the top.

Numerous papers have been written on safety culture and its development and there are countless systems and tools that teams and organisations have developed to measure the culture and attitudes of staff within an organisation some of which are very complex in deed. However in our opinion the development of positive safety culture in your organisation does not

SIMPLY SAFETY

have to be rocket science and if you as an employer concentrate on the development of a simple but effective safety management system which is then implemented properly then this will pay huge dividends to your business in the long run.

EXAMPLE CASE STUDY:

A production facility was experiencing a very substantial number of accidents, the quality of the components in production were in some cases not up to standard and there had been a series of accidents involving fork lift trucks where damage had been caused.

The organisation itself had a full set of policies and procedures, risk assessments, safety management system and really just about every conceivable article of equipment and PPE that would have been the envy of most organisations. So finally the question was asked as to what was going on.

When a simple assessment was carried out by an external health and safety consultant it was evident that the senior management team were merely paying lip service to health and safety and the safety management system had never been implemented effectively, staff had not received proper training and were not aware of their roles and responsibilities with the result that all operational staff considered that health and safety was an activity that someone else would deal with.

A decision was made by the managing director that a step change in health and safety had to be made and he gathered the senior management team and their health and safety manager together and an action plan was drawn and all directors and managers signed up to this in the form of a simple charter.

The organisation took the existing safety management system and in essence simplified this and using the policies and procedures the system was implemented from scratch over a three month period. All staff including directors attended various safety training sessions delivered in house and roles and responsibilities were assigned in a clear and concise manner in such a way that everyone was empowered to take ownership for health and safety and that they were to be held accountable for their actions in a balanced way e.g. no blame culture. Health and safety was driven down through the business by the senior management team but over a relatively short period of time through the effectiveness of safety committee meetings the safety message was then driven up through the business in the opposite direction. Staff from the cleaner up to a senior director now had the confidence to challenge colleagues if they considered that an unsafe act was being carried out.

This was a huge commitment by the organisation but the accident rate reduced to zero within a ten month period, an audit schedule was implemented and within three months the organisation was 100% compliant and incidents resulting in production outage where eliminated. The overall effect on the organisation was that there were significant cost savings and efficiencies gained here and the morale of the staff was high and really demonstrates that safety really does not have to be complicated and fantastic results can be achieved by merely doing the simple basic things properly.

IMPLEMENTING A SAFETY MANAGEMENT SYSTEM

INTRODUCTION

If you as a employer have had a good day at work, spare a thought for the families of workers killed or injured in their workplaces even though there is at times what seems to be a plethora of legislation and regulation to prevent such an occurrence happening.

We have already established the legal reasons as to why an employer must manage health and safety effectively in a proactive way. However, the effects of not maintaining health and safety may be categorised under three headings using the mnemonic of 'HEL', as follows:

Humane
- accident, injury and ill health reduction
- effect on families of injured workers or those killed
- stress and anxiety of injury or ill health

Economic
- loss prevention
- damage to corporate image
- days taken off by staff
- loss of production due to investigation
- uninsured costs (estimated as at least £10 for each £1 insured)

Legal
- civil compensation
- criminal fines
- corporate manslaughter

A more detailed version of the above HEL mnemonic is available as an HSE publication (HSG96).

HEALTH AND SAFETY ARRANGEMENTS

As will be seen in CHAPTER 3 – RISK ASSESSMENT, which covers risk assessment, the *MHSWR 1999, reg 3* requires that the employer identifies precautions to be taken by way of the process of risk assessment. This is taken a stage further in *MHSWR 1999, reg 5*, by describing how to put them into practice by way of a systematic management cycle.

MHSWR 1999, reg 5 requires that the employer must make and implement arrangements for the effective planning, organisation, control, monitoring and review of the preventative and protective measures identified by the risk assessments. Where five or more persons are employed within the organisation then records of these arrangements must be maintained.

The complete Management Regulations and an Approved Code of Practice (ACoP) is contained in the HSE publication L21 detail the HSE's recommended way of conducting Risk Assessment; however this is covered in much more detail in Chapter Three of this book.

SIMPLY SAFETY

HEALTH AND SAFETY MANAGEMENT SYSTEM

The most effective method of achieving a change in health and safety culture is the commitment to and implementation of a formal health and safety management system and there is no doubt that the employer will have some degree of involvement in the process.

There are a number of health and safety management systems seen in organisations, such as ISO 18001 and the HSE's publication *Successful Health and Safety Management*, HSG65, which is also detailed in the British Standard BS 8800:1996, Guide to Occupational Health and Safety Management Systems.

The most common system in use is the HSE system *Successful Health and Safety Management*, HSG65, the mechanics of which may be best remembered by the mnemonic POPIMAR, as follows:

- policy
- organising
- planning
- implementation
- measuring/monitoring
- audit
- review

These key management stages are arranged in a closed loop system of continual improvement as shown below and also in the following diagram:

- identify the issues that need to be addressed,
- set the direction/standards to be achieved,
- plan what needs to be done,
- organise who is going to do it,
- equip them to do so,
- do it,
- check it has been done,
- check that it worked and
- learn from/feedback lessons from this exercise to (continually) improve (the process and outcomes).

Figure 2.4: Key management stages of the HSE *Successful Health and Safety Management* HSG65

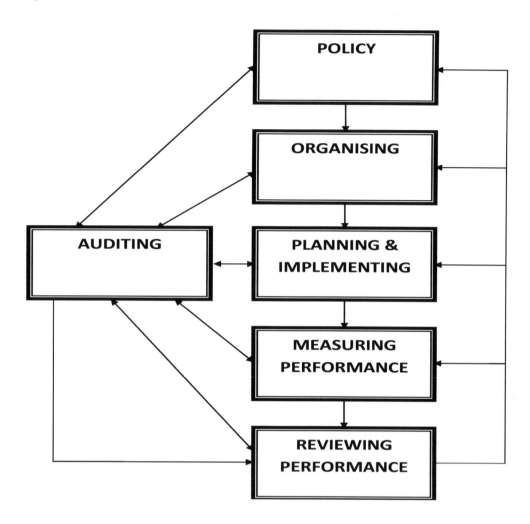

Key stages in this process are described below (many of these will of course be concurrent). The meaning of the terms *Planning, Organisation, Control, Monitoring* and *Review* are defined in full within the HSE document *Successful Health and Safety Management* HSG65, but may be summarised as follows:

- **Health and safety policy** – You need to know from the outset what you are trying to achieve in overall terms, and gain the commitment of the company. Writing (or revising) a health and safety policy, which is a legal requirement, and must be signed by a managing director or similar, is a good way of beginning the process.
- **Planning** – The employer (employer) should set up an effective health and safety management system with which to implement their health and safety policy. This should adopt a systematic approach which identifies priorities and enables objectives to be set. Particular attention should be paid to the policy, the organisation, hazard identification and risk assessment.

SIMPLY SAFETY

- **Organisation** – You will need to have in place the means by which the health and safety policy can be implemented by way of a combination of the following actions:
    - communication of policy to staff
    - organogram with lines of communications
    - roles and responsibilities assigned to staff
    - agreed processes and procedures
    - audit regime to monitor the effectiveness of the policy
    - involvement of staff in risk assessments
    - competence of staff through effective training
- **Control** – Management should take responsibility by leading by example, ensuring that roles and responsibilities have been made adequately clear to staff and ensuring that there are clear and concise lines of communication. Standards and objectives must be set.
- **Monitoring and review** – Monitoring and review of the overall effectiveness of the health and safety management system ensures that routine checks are undertaken and that preventative and protective measures are in place, up to date and effective. There should also be an effective system in place to investigate the root causes of accidents and to establish priorities for any necessary remedial actions.

Maintaining the Regime

Setting up your health and safety culture is not the end of the story; it is only the beginning. Maintaining it is the key as people become complacent and your organisation will change and develop, plus your systems and processes will need to be monitored regularly, otherwise they will, over time, become out of date and inappropriate.

Health and Safety Policy Statement and Policies

Each company employing five or more people must have a written health and policy. This policy should have the following components:

- A general statement of commitment to health and safety; this will indicate that the organisation is aware of its legal responsibilities both to its own staff and others affected by its operations (contractors, visitors etc). It can aim to achieve the minimum level (ie statutory compliance) or can be more ambitious depending on the aspirations and style of the organisation.
- A description of the organisation within the company that is designed to fulfil the objectives and achieve effective two-way communication with staff on issues of health and safety. This should name the roles and individuals responsible for health and safety within the organisation.
- The arrangements within the company for dealing with specific areas of health and safety. For the purposes of this document this section can be reasonably general.
- How the policy will be maintained and reviewed.

The policy will need to be regularly updated and the mechanism and frequency by which this will be achieved should be shown.

Establishing a Health and Safety Culture in your Organisation

The health and safety policy should be of a length and level of detail appropriate to the organisation for which it is prepared. The policy documentation for a small office premises is likely to be less detailed and shorter than that prepared for a nuclear power station or process engineering plant, but the key components will remain the same.

In support of the arrangements section of the health and safety policy statement, procedures should be prepared to cover all key areas of the organisation. Again, the areas to be covered and the level of detail will depend on the size and complexity of the organisation and the risks identified. Core procedures are listed below; however, there may be other areas specific to your organisation that are not listed. In each case the format should be the same: a preamble should identify the aim of the procedure; the main part of the document should describe the procedure; and the final part should outline how the procedure will be implemented, monitored and reviewed.

Suggested list of health and safety procedures:

- accidents and first aid
- asbestos management
- fire procedures including fire risk assessment
- control of substances hazardous to health (COSHH)
- risk assessments
- display screen equipment (DSE)
- manual handling
- personal protective equipment (PPE)
- contractors
- visitors
- vehicles
- smoking
- stress
- lone working
- electricity at work
- young people at work
- security
- noise
- work at height
- workplace welfare

It is important to realise that as well as providing a record of how the company is discharging its health and safety policy, these procedures are pointless unless they can be effectively communicated to staff. This being so, it is a good idea to back up the main procedure, which will be detailed and possibly lengthy, with a shorter, more user-friendly version, which will include the salient points and which, published in booklet form or on a company intranet, is more likely to be read by staff.

SIMPLY SAFETY

Further guidance on Policies and health and safety in general may be found in the new HSE publication titled 'Health & Safety made simple – The basics for your business', which can be downloaded from the HSE website at:

http://www.hse.gov.uk/simple-health-safety/simplehealthsafety.pdf

ASSIGNING RESPONSIBILITIES

The *Health and Safety at Work etc. Act 1974* makes it clear that it is the employer that is responsible for providing a safe workplace, and failure to do so may result in legal penalties imposed by statutory authorities. The employer, in the person of the chief executive or responsible director, may delegate health and safety duties to one or more employees, or even to external resources (such as health and safety consultancies) but they cannot delegate responsibility. Nor is this an insurable risk; any fines imposed due to failures of health and safety must be met by the business.

Equally, it is important to realise that if the failure is due to bad advice or negligence by someone within the company who has been delegated health and safety responsibilities, then they may be penalised or face prosecution. So, it is important if you are charged with some of these responsibilities that these are taken seriously.

Indeed, a key part of an effective health and safety culture is ensuring that all the various areas of the policies are the direct responsibility of a particular person or post holder. It will be unlikely, even in a small organisation, that the company's health and safety manager is responsible for the maintenance of all policies and processes; in larger organisations it will simply be impossible.

For example, it may be the job of the maintenance manager to control contractors within the workplace and run the permit to work system and control access to plant rooms. It may be the job of the security manager to ensure that visitors are informed of the company's health and safety policy when they enter the building. It is important that you allocate yourself, or are aware of where the various responsibilities lie for maintaining policies, whoever has developed the policies in the first place.

It is essential that all staff is well versed in their roles and responsibilities and take ownership and accountability for their actions, because any ambiguity can lead to misunderstandings which is when safety can and often breaks down and in time leads to unnecessary accidents.

A list of key areas of responsibility is shown in the table below. Using this as a guideline you may add other company specific responsibilities to the list. You may wish to break down some of the headings into smaller subdivisions, where different personnel have departmental responsibilities or where different people handle different aspects of an area.

Key responsibilities within Your Organisation are shown in Table 2.01 on the next page.

Establishing a Health and Safety Culture in your Organisation

Table 2:01 - Key Responsibilities within Your Organisation

AREA	KEY RESPONSIBILITIES	PERSON RESPONSIBLE
Fire Precautions	Organising practice evacuations	
	Training of fire marshals and staff	
	Fire risk assessment	
	Portable fire equipment maintenance	
	Fire alarm maintenance	
	Fire marshal lists	
	Upkeep of fire log	
	Checks on escape routes/fire doors	
Maintenance	Organising fixed wiring tests	
	Portable appliance testing	
	Gas safety checks	
	Lift safety tests	
	Operating permit to work system	
	Eyebolt testing	
H&S Policy Statement	Communicating and updating	
Training	Induction	
	First aiders	
	Manual handling	
	DSE evaluations	
Risk Assessments	Carrying out, maintaining and updating	
First aid	Maintaining supplies	
Accidents	Maintaining accident book, investigating incidents, preparing reports	

SIMPLY SAFETY

THE REQUIREMENT FOR COMPETENCE

One of the main duties placed on a employer by the *Health and Safety at Work etc. Act 1974* is to ensure the health, safety and welfare of those affected by their undertaking. One of the important aspects of this duty is indicated in the HSE guidance HSG65 Successful Health and Safety Management as 'competence'.

From a health and safety management point of view there are two elements of competence, which should be considered by the employer, as follows:

- Competence of the workforce in carrying out their tasks.
- Competence of the person charged with the provision of advice on health and safety matters.

DEFINITION OF COMPETENCE

The *Oxford English Dictionary* defines 'competent' as being adequately qualified or capable and also as being effective. This practical definition is borne out by the meaning given to it in the *Management of Health and Safety at Work Regulations 1999 (SI 1999/3242), reg 7* when referring to the competence of health and safety assistance. In *reg 7(5)*, a person is deemed to be competent if they have an adequate combination of training and experience or knowledge.

The definition of competence also includes the qualities that the person needs in order to adequately fulfil the tasks required of them as part of the function in which they are competent. This is a very practical definition and provides three aspects to competence:

- Knowledge of the subject.
- Experience to apply that knowledge correctly.
- Personal qualities to undertake their functions effectively.

Although the Management Regulations are referring to the competence of the health and safety advisor, the definition is a reasonably good one for determining the meaning of competence in any workplace context.

Competence is therefore a combination of appropriate practical and theoretical knowledge and the ability to apply that knowledge in a work situation. The degree of competence for performing or supervising a particular task must be proportional to the complexity of the task and the associated risks. For example, a person assembling and erecting a tower or scaffold would need to have a higher level of competence than a person using it.

Generally a competent person should be capable of:

- Undertaking the specified activity safely, at their level of responsibility.
- Understanding the potential risks related to the activity that they are to carry out.
- Detecting and reporting any defects or omissions.
- Recognising any implications for the health and safety of themselves and others.
- Capable of specifying appropriate remedial actions that may be required.
- Refusing to do a particular task if the potential risk is assessed as too great.

Establishing a Health and Safety Culture in your Organisation

Record Keeping and Documentation

An essential part of a successful health and safety culture is the maintenance of records and documentation; both those required for statutory compliance and those that you need yourself to make your job easier. Ideally all the documents should be in one place, readily accessible. Often this will not be practical but, at the very least, your health and safety file should include a table indicating the location of all the records.

The table below indicates the key documents that may be required in your organisation. There are some documents that are common to all companies, others will depend on the size of the organisation and the type of premises you occupy; for example if you have lifts in your building or if you have gas boiler plant.

Table 2:02 - Suggested Key Records for Your Organisation

RECORD/DOCUMENT	COMMENT
Health and Safety Policy Statement	Display on notice boards
Employer's Liability Insurance Certificate	Display on notice boards
Health and Safety Poster (What you should know)	Display on notice boards
Fire Risk Assessment	Copy available to all staff and for review and Inspection
Fire Precautions	Issued to all staff
Fire Marshals list	Display on notice boards, intranet etc
Portable Fire Equipment	Copy of maintenance test sheet
First Aiders List	Display on notice boards, intranet etc
Accident Book B 1510	Location published to all staff
General Risk Assessment	Including actions taken, measures in place
Training Records	Including fire marshals, first aiders, manual handling general fire training etc
COSHH assessments	Including contractors' assessments
Minutes of Safety Committee and Other Meetings	Including safety inspections
Maintenance Records	Including electrical, lift, water treatment etc

SIMPLY SAFETY

COMMUNICATION

The best health and safety system in the world will have no value unless it is effectively communicated. As well as formal training courses communication of health and safety issues to staff on a regular basis is the most effective means of communication there is and will be essential in the development of a health and safety culture.

How you should communicate will depend on what is appropriate to your company and what works best:

- notice boards
- induction packs
- company intranet
- health and safety newsletter
- minutes of meetings
- leaflets for particular campaigns

The key in all cases, especially when trying to communicate to staff in general, is to make the information simple and palatable. There is no point, however tempting, in giving the full detailed background to every policy that is implemented if that means it doesn't get read and is therefore ignored.

The communication process has a number of different elements and you may well be a key conduit. Communication will have to include the following.

Communication to Staff in General

This may have several purposes:

- reinforce initial training
- advise staff of particular issues
- communicate change in company policies in response to changes in the workplace
- advise on the implication of new regulations or statutes
- publicise results of incident investigations

Remember too that this is a two-way process; nothing will damage your health and safety culture more than if issues raised by staff are, or appear to be, ignored. Even if the issue raised is spurious or does not require action this must be communicated.

Communication to New Staff

This is a process that may be carried out in conjunction with your HR or personnel department:

- advising of company health and safety policy
- explaining fire procedures

Establishing a Health and Safety Culture in your Organisation

- how incidents should be reported
- specific training for particular roles

Communication with Management

This can be a neglected part of the overall communication process. It is essential that management at all levels, whether nominally involved in the maintenance of health and safety processes or not, is kept informed of all issues. Not only is senior management formally responsible for health and safety within your organisation, but also at the end of the day it is senior managers who will have to demonstrate a commitment to health and safety issues and who will have to authorise the resources to enable you to do your job. Management should be informed of the following:

- all incidents/accidents and the actions taken in response
- the health and safety implications of any changes to the business
- the implications of any changes to health and safety legislation on the business
- the implications of the results of any audits or inspections to the business

Communication with External Bodies

There are a number of areas where health and safety managers must maintain a dialogue with external bodies. These will include:

- statutory and reporting bodies; Fire Brigade, Environmental Health, HSE etc
- other companies who may be affected by your business
- your contractors

TRAINING

The amount of training you need to provide and the means of delivery will again depend on your organisation. A list of key training areas is provided in the table shown on the next page but you will need to evaluate other areas where training is required and this can be derived from your general risk assessment. For instance, you may have business processes in your company that require specific specialist training.

Remember that all staff require some health and safety training, whatever their duties. The requirement for this training is enshrined both in the *Health and Safety at Work etc. Act 1974 (HSWA 1974)* and the *Management of Health and Safety at Work Regulations 1999 (SI 1999/3242) (MHSWR 1999)*. There are general training issues such as training in fire and emergency procedures and accident prevention. Then there are more job specific areas, which may not apply to everyone, such as manual handling and use of PPE.

Also, do not forget one essential person, namely yourself. If you have been given specific health and safety responsibilities then you must be competent to carry them out, otherwise you may put others at risk, however well-intentioned you are, simply through lack of knowledge. Suitable health and safety qualifications are provided by organisations such as BIFM training, IOSH, British Safety Council and NEBOSH.

SIMPLY SAFETY

The first stage in any training programme is the evaluation of training needs. This must consider both the task to be carried out and the abilities and competence of the person carrying it out. This evaluation will vary in complexity from task to task and person to person. For example, the evaluation of training needs in respect of all staff for the purposes of fire awareness may be relatively simple, while that for a maintenance handyman will be less so, and will require careful thought and discussion both with the individual concerned and the line manager.

Best practice is for an organisation to prepare a matrix of all jobs in existence within the business and then matching each job to a list of essential training and desirable training. This will then allow a training needs analysis (TNA) to be completed which will identify any gaps in the essential training thus producing a the basis of a training programme.

Table 2:03 - Key Training Requirements

TRAINING	FOR WHOM	DELIVERY METHOD
Induction Training	All staff, regular contractors	Written guidelines, talk by health and safety manager, supplemented by role specific training
Health and Safety General	Competent person, health and safety manager, line managers	Certified external course by approved body
Fire Awareness	All staff	Written fire procedures, practice evacuation exercises
Fire Marshal Training	Fire marshals, security staff, employers	External course by certified trainer
First Aid	Appointed persons, first aiders, security staff, employers	External course by certified trainer
Manual Handling	Delivery and portering staff, post room staff, maintenance staff	Depending on job content, in-house review of key guidelines or external course by approved trainer
Electrical Awareness	Maintenance staff, health and safety manager	External course by certified trainer if job content warrants
Display Screen Equipment	All staff using computers as a regular part of their job	Written guidance notes supplemented by specialist support as required
Specialist Training	Dependent on processes involved which may be specific to particular organisation	Dependent on task

Establishing a Health and Safety Culture in your Organisation

Note that all training must be recorded and must be reviewed regularly to ensure it is current. For example, the date of any first aid training must be recorded and the need for refresher courses must be flagged.

Do not forget that, apart from staff, your regular contractors must receive appropriate training for your workplace, for example on fire precautions and evacuation procedures, and the same is true for temps, contract employees and visitors.

CHAPTER 3
RISK ASSESSMENT AND MANAGEMENT

RISK ASSESSMENT – REQUIREMENTS AND DEFINITIONS

Risk assessment is the key to providing a safe workplace and as such is one of the most important tasks of any Employer. Unless you have assessed the risks present in your workplace, you will have no idea of what systems and procedures to put in place, and as a result your measures may be woefully inadequate, or may simply address generic risks, some of which, are not applicable to your workplace.

Health and safety law is now quite explicit on the need for risk assessments and where an organisation employs five or more employees then the risk assessment must be recorded. The *Management of Health and Safety at Work Regulations 1999 (SI 1999/3242) (MHSWR 1999), Reg 3* states that every employer shall make a suitable and sufficient assessment of the following specific risks:

- the risks to the health and safety of his employees to which they are exposed whilst they are at work *(SI 1999/3242, Reg 3(1)(a))*
- the risks to the health and safety of persons not in his employment arising out of or in connection with the conduct by him of his undertaking *(SI 1999/3242, reg 3(1)(b))*

Where five or more staff are employed, the employer is bound to carry out a general risk assessment and record the findings *(SI 1999/3242, Reg 3(6))*.

There are also specific areas – such as asbestos, fire, display screen equipment, manual handling, young persons and new and expectant mothers – where specific risk assessments are required. For a longer list please refer to Table 3:07 - Risk Assessment Guidance for Some More Common Regulations later in this chapter

There are Some Definitions Which Might be of Help
- **Hazard:**
  Something with the potential to cause harm in other words a situation at the workplace capable of causing harm (i.e. capable of causing personal injury, occupationally related disease or death).
- **Risk:**
  the chance of a hazard actually causing injury or disease. It is measured in terms of consequences and likelihood
- **Risk Management:**
  the overall process of risk identification, risk analysis, control of risks and risk evaluation

Risk Assessment and Management

- **Risk Control:**
  that part of risk management which involves the implementation of policies, standards, procedures and physical changes to eliminate or minimise adverse risks

WHAT IS A HAZARD AND WHAT IS A RISK?

The first thing that needs to be understood is what, in health and safety the terms, 'hazard' and 'risk' actually mean. Many times in life the terms risk and hazards are mixed up and mean the same thing; however, in health and safety each has its own meaning. A simple explanation is as follows:

- A **Hazard**
  is something that has the potential to cause harm.
- A **Risk**
  is the likelihood of that harm occurring.

There are several definitions of risk and this issue can quickly become more complicated than it need be. At its most basic, risk in this context is the probability of a workplace hazard causing harm combined with the severity of the harm that may be caused.

It is worth looking at one example to show how these three elements interact. If as part of your business operations you use chemicals, then that is a hazard. If the chemicals have the capacity to cause serious injury and if they are stored in an area accessible to general staff then that represents a serious risk. If, on the other hand, the chemicals are generally benign unless drunk in large quantities, and if they are kept in a secure controlled area and are accessible only to highly trained staff then the risk is minimal. Thus hazard does not automatically equal risk.

Your role in carrying out risk assessment is to consider all these elements:

- What are the hazards?
- Who is likely to be affected?
- What is the potential for harm from these hazards?

Once you have considered all these issues you will then be in a position to put in place the measures to address these risks and, importantly, you can allocate your possibly limited resources on addressing the priority risks with the greatest potential for harm. Your aim in each case should be first and foremost to eliminate the risk or, if this is not possible, to put such control measures in place that the potential for harm is reduced to an absolute minimum.

CARRYING OUT A RISK ASSESSMENT

Please also see the sample risk assessment proforma at Table 3:01.

There are five key stages in carrying out a risk assessment and different areas to examine. Whether you are taking over an existing system or implementing a health and safety system from scratch it is as well to start with a clean sheet of paper. This will enable you to consider the workplace with a fresh pair of eyes without preconceptions. You will also not be influenced by previous assessments that may now be out of date.

Another issue to consider is that unless the premises are small it is best not to carry out the risk assessment in one go or on your own. Two pairs of eyes are better than one, and even if your colleague is untrained they may pick up things that you miss. If you try to tackle the whole

SIMPLY SAFETY

workplace in one go then you may well miss areas or assume that one set of circumstances prevails throughout the premises.

Dialogue with your colleagues is also essential. You may not be aware of all the processes and tasks that go on in your workplace or what the implications are; you will need to discuss these issues with departmental managers, supervisors and the like. It is also likely that you will need to discuss issues with your regular contractors, such as your maintenance company or your window-cleaning contractor etc.

The Health and Safety Executive has provided useful guidance on conducting risk assessments. They break it down into five simple steps:

- identify the hazards
- assess the personnel affected
- evaluate the risks and current control measures
- record your findings
- review the assessments regularly or when anything in the process changes
-

Use a basic template as you walk round to summarise your findings, an example is shown in TABLE 3:04

Table 3.01 - Basic Risk Assessment Template

HAZARD	POTENTIAL HARM	WHO MIGHT BE HARMED	EXISTING CONTROL MEASURES	RESIDUAL RISK *	RECOMMEND ACTIONS FURTHER CONTROL MEASURES	RESIDUAL RISK *	WHO IS RESPONSIBLE	DUE DATE	COMPLETED DATE

This will enable you to capture the basic data that you will use to progress your assessment. Now let us go through the steps one by one.

Risk Assessment and Management

STEP 1 - IS TO IDENTIFY THE HAZARDS

The first thing that you as an employer needs to do is to work out how your employees and others in your work area could be harmed whilst at work. Because you tend to work in the same building every day it is easy to overlook some hazards, so there are some simple tips hints that should enable you to identify the hazards that matter:

- Walk around your workplace and look at what could reasonably be expected to cause harm, remember to look with a critical eye and don't discount anything at this stage.
- Talk to your employees or their representatives and ask them what they think. It is more than possible that they may have noticed things that are not immediately obvious to you.
- Look at the manufacturers' instructions for your equipment and at the Material Safety Data Sheets for any chemicals or substances that you may have in the workplace as they can be very helpful in spelling out the hazards and putting them in their true perspective.
- Check with your trade association or professional body, as many produce very helpful guidance for free.
- Go through your accident and ill-health records as these may very well-help identify some of the less obvious hazards.
- Don't forget to think about the long-term hazards that could affect people's health at work (e.g. do you have noisy equipment that could mean high levels of noise or are your staff etc exposed to harmful substances) as well as any safety hazards.
- Pay a visit the HSE website (www.hse.gov.uk). The HSE publishes a great deal of practical guidance on where hazards occur and how to control them as well as sample risk assessments for various types of business.

The hazards will depend very much upon the nature of your workplace. In the initial survey you should err on the side of caution and record as much as possible; where necessary trivia can be discounted later. Areas you might consider in the physical workplace include the following:

- entrances and exits to the building, including loading bays
- common areas and staircases
- general office areas
- plant rooms
- storage areas
- kitchens and toilets
- roofs

There are several types of hazard:

Physical Hazards

Physical Hazards can be a variety of things such as premises, equipment or People. When you are looking at premises and equipment these might be steep fire escape stairs, frayed carpets, trailing leads and so on. Do not only consider these issues at the time you are looking at them but consider how an area might become hazardous at another time, for example an external fire escape at night could present more of a hazard if lighting is inadequate, or a marble floor in reception could become more hazardous during wet weather. Also consider the overall environment; is a particular area very noisy for example? Or does a particular room get very hot? Alternatively think about the different seasons, does an external area become more hazardous when covered with snow or ice.

SIMPLY SAFETY

Process Hazards

These would involve identifying the work activities carried out, such as manual handling, window cleaning or general maintenance activities and considering the specific hazards that these bring. Talk to the people actually carrying out these tasks as well as observing them, consider the training they have been given, the equipment that they are using and any protective equipment they have to use.

Material Hazards

Consider the materials and substances used in the various areas of the workplace, such as cleaning chemicals, fuel for vehicles, oils and lubricants in maintenance tasks. Consider whether the Material Safety Data Sheets and Manufacturers' Instructions are available and how accessible they are to those that need them.

An important point to make is that at an early stage you should be aware of your own limitations in evaluating hazards in some areas. For example as you walk around plant rooms you may simply not know what all the plant does and how it functions at different times; enlist the help of your maintenance engineer or other qualified person to answer your questions. This is especially true when trying to understand the hazards associated with tasks or processes.

Typically the types of people that need to be considered are as follows:

STEP 2 - DECIDE WHO MIGHT BE HARMED AND HOW

Having completed the walk round your workplace / premises you now need to be clear as to who might be harmed for each of the hazards that you have identified. This will help you identify the best way of managing the risks. Don't worry, this doesn't mean you have to list everyone by name, but rather identify the groups of people (e.g. office workers, people working in the storeroom, those in the engineering workshop, cleaners or even passers-by etc.).

In each case, identify how they might be harmed, i.e. to what type of injury or ill health might they be susceptible. For example, shelf stackers may suffer back injury from repeated lifting of boxes.

Remember that there are some workers that will have certain particular requirements who may be at particular risk, e.g.

- new and or expectant mothers,
- new employees
- young workers,
- people with disabilities.

As an employer you will need to give extra thought to those who may be affected for some hazards e.g.

- cleaners, visitors, contractors, maintenance workers etc, who may not be in the workplace all the time;
- members of the public, if they could be hurt by your activities;

The other area where you as an employer may be exposed and need to consider is where you share your workplace, you will need to think about how your work affects others that are present,

Risk Assessment and Management

as well as how their work affects your staff. Involve these people in your discussions and remember to ask your staff if they can think of anyone you may have missed.

STEP 3 - EVALUATE THE RISKS AND DECIDE ON WHAT PRECAUTIONS ARE NEEDED

Now that you have spotted the Hazards and have decided who might be harmed and how they might be harmed, you now have to decide what you are going to do about them. The law requires you to do everything 'reasonably practicable' to protect people from harm. This involves weighing a risk against the trouble, time and money needed to control it. You can work this out for yourself, but the easiest way is to compare what you are doing with good practice.

Thus the first thing you need to do is to look at what you're already doing. Think about what controls you already have in place and how the work is organised. Now compare this with good practice in your industry and see if there's anything else you should be doing to bring yourself up to standard. In asking yourself this, consider the Hierarchy of Control Measures Table 3:06 Managing the Risks): -

In using these ask yourself:

- Can I get rid of the hazard altogether?
- If not, how can I control the risks so that harm is unlikely?

When controlling risks, apply the principles below, if possible in the following order:

- try a less risky option (e.g. switch to using a less hazardous chemical);
- prevent access to the hazard (e.g. by guarding);
- organise work to reduce exposure to the hazard (e.g. put barriers between pedestrians and traffic);
- issue personal protective equipment (e.g. clothing, footwear, goggles etc); and
- provide welfare facilities (e.g. first aid and washing facilities for removal of contamination).

Improving health and safety need not cost a lot. For instance, placing a mirror on a dangerous blind corner to help prevent vehicle accidents is a low-cost precaution considering the risks. Failure to take simple precautions can cost you a lot more if an accident does happen.

It is vital that you involve your staff and other workers so that you can be sure that what you are proposing to do will work in practice and won't introduce any new or additional hazards.

The HSE's website (www.hse.gov.uk), is a good source of "good practice" advice or again contact your trade association or professional body

STEP 4 - RECORD YOUR FINDINGS AND IMPLEMENT THEM

The next step in this process is to put the results of your risk assessment into practice as this will make a difference when looking after people and your business.

It is important to ensure that you write down the results of your risk assessment (use the template risk assessment shown earlier), and share the results with your staff and other people

SIMPLY SAFETY

working in your building / area etc. This will help to provide you with the encouragement to make the necessary changes. Note that if you have fewer than five employees (including yourself) you do not have to write anything down, however we strongly recommend that you do as it is useful when you come to review the risk assessment at a later date, for example if something changes, but also to provide proof that you have done a risk assessment and have considered the hazards and risks..

When writing down your results don't try to be complicated, keep it simple, for example: -

- 'Tripping over rubbish; - bins provided, staff instructed to use bins, weekly housekeeping checks to be undertaken', or
- 'Fume from welding: - local exhaust ventilation used and regularly checked'.

The Health & Safety Executive (HSE) do not expect a risk assessment to be perfect, but it must be suitable and sufficient. To do this you will need to be able to show that:

- a proper check was made;
- you asked and found out who might be affected;
- you dealt with all the significant hazards, taking into account the number of people who could be involved;
- the precautions are reasonable, and the remaining risk is low; and
- you involved your staff or their representatives in the process.

If, like many businesses, you find that there are quite a lot of improvements that you could make, big and small, don't try to do everything at once. Look carefully at the list of improvements that are required and prioritise them, prepare a plan of action to deal with the most important things first. Ensure that you monitor your plan and that the improvements are planned over a reasonable period of time. Health and Safety Inspectors generally acknowledge the efforts of businesses that are clearly trying to make improvements.

A good plan of action often includes a mixture of different things such as:

- a few cheap or easy improvements that can be done quickly, perhaps as a temporary solution until more reliable controls are in place;
- long-term solutions to those risks most likely to cause accidents or ill health;
- long-term solutions to those risks with the worst potential consequences;
- arrangements for training employees on the main risks that remain and how they are to be controlled;
- conduct regular checks to make sure that the control measures you have put in place stay in place; and
- that there are clear responsibilities detailed i.e. who will lead on what action, and by when.

Remember, prioritise and tackle the most important things first. As you complete each action, tick it off your plan.

Risk Assessment and Management

STEP 5 - REVIEW YOUR RISK ASSESSMENT AND UPDATE IF NECESSARY

It is a well known fact that few workplaces stay the same. Sooner or later, you will bring in new equipment, new substances and procedures that in turn can lead to new hazards. It makes sense, therefore, to review what you are doing on an ongoing basis. Every year or so it is important to formally review where you are and to make sure you are still improving, or at least not sliding back. This is why we often refer to risk assessments as Living Documents in that they are always being worked upon and where possible improved.

Make a date in you diary once a year or so to look at your risk assessment again, review them. Have there been any changes in the process, the machinery, the chemicals / substances, the workers that need to be addressed? Are there improvements you still need to make? Have your workers spotted a problem, don't be afraid to ask them?

Have you learnt anything from accidents or near misses in your workplace or perhaps in a business that is local to you? Whatever you do you must make sure that your risk assessment stays up to date.

When you are running a business it's all too easy to forget about reviewing your risk assessment – until something has gone wrong and by then it's too late. As we said earlier why not set a review date for your risk assessments now? Write it down and note it in your diary as an annual event, at least you can prepare for the review in advance and ensure that you have set aside the time.

It is important however that during the year, if there is a significant change, don't wait for the annual review. Check your risk assessment and, where necessary, amend it and ensure that you let your people know of any changes. If possible, it is best to think about the risk assessment when you're planning your change – that way you leave yourself more flexibility.

SCORING AND RATING RISKS

Do not be put off by this process; it is not complicated (and is not by any means essential) but it is a useful way of formally assessing the risks within your organisation and will allow you to prioritise your actions. The way the system works is by assigning a score to each element of the risk assessment matrix. As you recall the risk is a product of the likelihood that the hazard will cause harm combined with the severity of the harm that may be caused. Take into account the control and risk reduction measures that have already been put in place.

Develop definitions that make sense to you but do not overdo it. The following example works well:

SIMPLY SAFETY

Table 3:02 - Probability of Hazard Occurring

Almost certain	5
Likely	4
Possible	3
Unlikely	2
Rare	1

Table 3:03 - Potential Impact of Hazard

Catastrophic / Death	5
Major	4
Moderate	3
Minor	2
Negligible	1

You can of course add other definitions if you feel you need greater flexibility, but for most organisations this should be enough. By marking your risks using these scores and then multiplying the figures together you get a rough guide to the most serious risks that you need to tackle, although of course this is still a subjective process; merely assigning numbers in this way does not make it scientific. So a hazard that would very probably lead to an incident (that is, a score of three) and which had potentially serious consequences (score three again) would attract a rating of nine, putting it at the top of your list.

The simple proforma with two examples in Table 3:04 will describe this process better.

Risk Assessment and Management

Table 3:04: Risk Assessment Proforma

HAZARD	PROBABILITY	SCORE	SEVERITY	SCORE	RISK SCORE
Nosing's on rear fire stairs are badly worn in places; potential trip hazard	Possible if staff do not take care	3	Could cause serious injury if fall occurs	4	12
Lorries have to reverse into busy loading bay	Loading bay is manned and mirrors have been provided	1	Possible trapping injury	4	4

You will see that, although useful, this type of scoring can only ever be a guide and should not be followed rigidly. Always pay more attention to the probability than to the severity. In other words if a hazard has been so managed that the likelihood of it leading to an incident is almost non-existent, the severity of its actually taking place is almost academic. It is essential, therefore, to assess the residual risk, not the risk if measures had not already been taken.

Below there is a simple matrix that you can use to see how serious the problem is.

Table 3:05 – Risk Matrix

LIKELIHOOD	SEVERITY / CONSEQUENCE				
	None (1)	Minor (2)	Moderate (3)	Major (4)	Catastrophic (5)
Rare (1)	1	2	3	4	5
Unlikely (2)	2	4	6	8	10
Possible (3)	3	6	9	12	15
Likely (4)	4	8	12	16	20
Almost Certain (5)	5	10	15	20	25

See also the Risk Assessment Proforma at Table 3:04.

SIMPLY SAFETY

MANAGING THE RISKS

Carrying out the assessment and recording the results is only the first step in the process. Of course, the crucial step comes now: dealing with the issues that you have identified. For each of the risks you have identified you need to consider and record a number of things:

- Location of the risk.
- Who is affected?
- How they may be affected.
- What controls have been put in place?
- What additional measures should be put in place?
- Who should carry out the work involved?
- Target date for completion.

You can either compile a single table that lists all these issues or, possibly more effectively, put together a proforma for each risk with an overall summary sheet. The proforma can then be issued to those who are responsible for implementing the changes.

Please also see the sample Risk Assessment Proforma at Table 3:04.

MANAGING THE RISKS

Once you have identified the risks, there are likely to be a number of different types of measures that are required to reduce the risk to the lowest possible.

The hierarchy of control is generally as follows:

- Eliminate the hazard.
- Reduce the hazard.
- Prevent contact with the hazard.
- Introduce a safe system of work.
- Personal protective equipment.

The ultimate and most satisfactory method is to remove the cause of the risk altogether. The following hierarchy of control measures will help you to identify what additional control measures will need to be taken to reduce the risk to an acceptable level. It is important to remember that some corrective measures are better than others and some are very ineffective as controls. The table below shows control measures in descending order of effectiveness.

Risk Assessment and Management

TABLE 3:06 – HIERARCHY OF CONTROL MEASURES

\	HIERARCHY OF CONTROL MEASURES
Elimination	e.g. stop using altogether or by the use of alternatives, design improvements, change of process
Substitution	e.g. replacing a hazardous chemical / process with one with less risk
Use of Barriers	e.g. isolation/segregation; guarding
Use of Procedures	e.g. safe systems of work, limiting exposure time
Use of Warnings	e.g. signs and labels, audible alarms
Use of PPE *	To be used only as a last resort

* PPE = Personal Protective Equipment

With each identified risk you should start off with this aim in mind rather than trying to work around the status quo. Of course, in many cases this course of action will not be available to you and you must consider alternatives:

- Information and Communication: - Advise staff through procedures, signage, notices etc of the risk and of the measures needed to combat it.
- Training: - Provide effective training to affected staff involved in the process concerned.
- Substitution: - If the risk involves a hazardous substance look for less toxic or dangerous alternatives.
- Adapt: - Change the workplace so that the risk is reduced; change the type of flooring you have in a slippery area for example, or ban general staff from using a busy goods inwards area as a means of access.
- Contract out: - If the process is dangerous look at using a specialist contractor instead of your own staff.

RISK ASSESSMENTS REQUIRED

Some of the area where risk assessments are compulsory:
- COSHH
- Carcinogens
- Contractors – engagement and management of
- Display Screen Equipment (PCs)
- Dangerous Occurrence (i.e. - sharps management)

SIMPLY SAFETY

- Electricity
- Fire
- Lifting Operations and Lifting Equipment
- Lone Working
- Manual Handling and Lifting
- New and Expectant Mothers
- Provision of Work Equipment
- Radiation / Laser use
- Stress
- Working at Heights
- Violence and Aggression
- Young Persons and Children

THE KEY RISKS

Every workplace will have its own risks. However there are certain areas that are likely to be more naturally hazardous than others. Also as well as the issues that are identified by your own risk assessment remember that there are key areas where your need to carry out an assessment is prescribed by law. You must, for example, carry out a specific fire risk assessment for your premises and this process is described in Chapter Six on Fire under the section entitled - The Five Stages for the Preparation of a Fire Risk Assessment.

To assist you as the employer, a set of bullet point notes and in some cases a hierarchy of control measures, have been highlighted for the key risks that you as the employer is likely to encounter.

A list of some key risks is provided below.

Fire

- carry out specific risk assessment
- prepare evacuation procedures
- reduce and control amount of combustible materials
- install adequate portable fire appliances
- maintain fire alarm system
- train staff and fire marshals
- protect means of escape

Display Screen Equipment (DSE)

- carry out individual workstation assessments
- implement necessary corrective actions
- train staff
- provide guidance documents
- follow up problems by referral to Occupational Health
- maintain records of actions

Risk Assessment and Management

Manual handling

- reduce need for lifting operations where possible
- split heavy loads or use mechanical aids
- train staff concerned and provide general advice
- consider the following (**T.I.L.E.**) in your assessment:
    - **Task** – process involved, is it repetitive?
    - **Individual** – are they fit enough? Do they have a medical condition that might affect their ability to lift or are they pregnant?
    - **Load** – heavy, hot/cold, rough?
    - **Environment** – is it dark, hot / cold, is there restricted space?

Electricity

- advise staff of the risks
- provide training for maintenance staff
- ensure only competent staff work on electrical systems
- inspect and test all appliances (Portable Appliance Testing PA Testing) frequency depending on risk, e.g. location and usage)
- reduce reliance on adaptors and trailing leads
- ensure five-yearly fixed system testing is completed and any faults rectified

First aid

- undertake assessment of risk considering the following:
    - accident history of site
    - processes undertaken on site
    - remoteness of site from hospital/ambulance station
- provide adequate trained first aiders
- provide well-stocked first aid boxes

General workplace hazards

- keep all floor coverings in good repair
- make all storage accessible (provide ladders and step ladders if necessary)
- keep all corridors clear of obstructions
- keep all plant roofs and risers locked
- maintain hygiene standards
- ensure weekly inspection of workplaces
- ensure general risk assessment is undertaken on annual basis or if significant changes are made to workplace or processes

SIMPLY SAFETY

COSHH

- ensure that a hierarchy of control measures is deployed as follows (but in all cases sufficient instruction, information, training and supervision must be provided):
    - elimination of product – use safer alternative
    - reduction in use
    - isolation by enclosure
    - control by management process
    - personal protective equipment – as last resort only
- obtain relevant manufacturers' safety data sheets
- maintain an inventory of hazardous substances on site
- undertake a COSHH assessment for each hazardous substance present on site (see 2.211A for example)
- keep substances under controlled conditions in accordance with manufacturers' recommendations
- post appropriate notices
- ensure your contractors provide relevant information

Contractors

Contractors bring a special series of risks into the workplace, especially when major works are taking place alongside normal work activities. However, essentially the same process can be used. You as the employer must discuss with the contractor in detail their work process'. They should produce Risk Assessments as well as their method statements for you, which will help you evaluate the risks involved in their work for you. All but the most routine work by contractors should be carried out under your permit to work scheme (see *The Section on Permits To Work*), which will offer you the chance to impose your controls on their work.

Prior to any contractor being allowed to carry out work on site the employer should complete some basic checks on the contractor to ensure that they are competent to undertake the work. The following is a list of items to check:
- contractors' health and safety and environmental policies and procedures
- details of insurance
- samples of completed risk assessments and method statements
- training and competency of operatives and management team for undertaking the intended work
- details of accident records and any prosecutions or improvement notices
- references that may be taken up

New and Expectant Mothers

- ensure that staff handbook/procedures includes details of duty for females to inform company when they are pregnant
- ensure that a room is set aside for feeding of infants or for expectant mothers to take rest break, if required, e.g. First Aid room is ideal if not in use

Risk Assessment and Management

- ensure that an Expectant Mothers Risk Assessment is completed at intervals and to include the following:
    - consider working hours or shift patterns
    - workstation suitability
    - tasks involved, e.g. avoid bending and lifting heavy weights
    - consider any substances being used by expectant mother or being used nearby (refer to manufacturers' safety data sheet and COSHH assessment)
    - consider ease of evacuation in an emergency

Children and Young Persons

Whether you as the employer is able to employ such persons will no doubt depend upon the work you undertake and your organisation's insurance cover. In addition, there is also the decision to be taken as to whether the child/young person is suitable for employment and this must be determined by taking a risk assessment approach.

First, the Employer should be aware of the definition of a child and young person, which are as follows:

- Child is defined as being under the minimum school leaving age
- Young Person is any person who has yet to attain the age of 18 years of age

Any Risk Assessment is to include:

- consideration of the lack of maturity, experience and perception of hazards
- their physical size, strength and ability
- the potential duration and exposure to physical work, conditions and any chemical hazards
- the amount of supervision that may be required and could actually be provided
- consideration of the nature of training that may be required

Lone Working

This subject can be a problem for the Employer but with adequate and robust procedures then the risks may be managed efficiently. A lone working checklist/questionnaire is also a useful system to ensure all eventualities are covered.

The main risks associated with lone working may be found in the following scenarios:

- out of hours call outs
- working at remote un-manned sites
- remote plant rooms and roof areas
- driving between location

SIMPLY SAFETY

Lone working risk assessment to consider:

- competency of operative for tasks involved in activity
- remoteness of plant room/site
- ease of access
- task involved, eg high risk/low risk
- vulnerability to/risk from violence aggression
- control measures that may be implemented

Control measures that may be deployed:

- 'man down' system
- mobile phone
- two-way radio
- vehicle tracking
- agreed communication between control room or security guard, eg hourly contact by agreed means

EXAMPLE RISK ASSESSMENTS

The Health & Safety Executive, in trying to simplify health & safety for businesses and the Employer, have produced a number of sample risk assessments which show how some small and medium-sized businesses have approached risk assessments. These risk assessments are produced as examples and the Employer should not just cut and paste it and put their company name to it as this would not satisfy the law - and would not adequately protect their staff or others in the workplace. As every business is different you the Employer needs to think about the hazards and controls that exist within their business as well as what else may be required according to your company's needs.

The list of the example Risk Assessments prepared by the HSE are as follows

Shops

- Betting Office
- Butchers
- Charity Shop
- Cleaning a Large Retail Premises
- Cleaning a Shopping Centre Concourse
- Convenience Store / Newsagent
- Drycleaners
- Estate Agency
- Food Preparation and Service
- Hairdressing salon
- Off Licence
- Travel Agent

Risk Assessment and Management

Motor Vehicles
- Car Parking Attendants
- Motor Vehicle Bodyshop
- Motor Vehicle Repair Shop
- Motor Vehicle Showroom
- Private Hire
- Road Haulage

Office
- General Office Cleaning

Other
- Administration Work in a Manufacturing Company
- Call Centre
- Chilled Warehousing
- Cold Storage and Warehousing
- Contract Bricklayers
- Factory Maintenance Work
- Maintenance of Flats
- Night Club
- Plastering Company
- Poultry farm
- Pub
- Village Hall
- Warehouse
- Woodworking

The examples listed above show the kind of approach the HSE expects an Employer in a small business or workplace to take. As stated earlier they are not generic risk assessments that an Employer can just put their company name on and adopt wholesale without any thought. Doing that would not satisfy the law and it would not protect people effectively.

Even where the hazards are the same, you as the Employer may find that the control measures you adopt may have to be different from those in the examples to meet the particular conditions in your workplace.

As the Employer you need to remember that a risk assessment will only be effective if you and your staff act upon it as every business is different; you need to think through the hazards and controls required in your business for yourself and it is also important that you as the Employer follow through with any actions required and reviews them on a regular basis.

The HSE state that if in the opinion of the Employer the example assessments do not exactly represent their industry, the Employer needs to choose the one closest to their requirements and

SIMPLY SAFETY

adapt it for their own workplace and should use their chosen Risk Assessment as a guide to think about:

- some of the hazards in their business
- the steps they need to take to control the risks.

To access the example risk assessments go to the HSE web site at the following link: - http://www.hse.gov.uk/risk/casestudies/index.htm And Please ***DON'T JUST COPY THEM.*** Use them as a basis to start your own.

However if none of the above are suitable and if you as the Employer work in a low risk office-based environment you can complete your risk assessment quickly and easily by using the HSE's new web-based tool. In this section the Employer can select the risks and actions that are relevant for their workplace and then save and print their completed risk assessment. To access this resource the Employer should go to the HSE web site at: - http://www.hse.gov.uk/risk/office.htm and click on the "Begin office risk *assessment"*

Risk Assessment and Management

TABLE 3:07 - RISK ASSESSMENT GUIDANCE FOR SOME MORE COMMON REGULATIONS

REGULATION	PURPOSE OF RISK ASSESSMENT	WHO HAS TO ASSESS THE RISK?	WHOSE RISK SHOULD BE ASSESSED?	WHAT RISKS SHOULD BE ASSESSED?	WHEN TO ASSESS
Management of Health & Safety at Work	To identify measures which need to be taken to comply with the requirements and prohibitions imposed by or under the relevant statutory provisions.	1) Employers. 2) Self-employed people.	1) Employees (at work). 2) Self-employed people (at work). 3) People not in employment who may face risks arising out of, or in connection with, the conduct by the employer or self-employed person of his undertaking.	Risks to health and safety of people listed in previous table.	Prior to commencement of work
Manual Handling	To consider the questions set out in column 2 of Schedule 1 relating to the factors listed in that schedule.	1) Employers. 2) Self-employed people.	Manual handling operations to be undertaken by employees or self-employed people.	Manual handling operations which involve a risk of injury.	Make assessment of all such manual handling operations to be undertaken which involve risk of injury where it is not reasonably practicable avoid the need for employees or self-employed to undertake those manual handling operations.
Personal Protective Equipment	To determine whether the personal protective equipment is	1) Employers 2) Self-employed people.	PPE which an employer or self-employed person is required to ensure is	Risks to health and safety which have not been avoided by other means. Assessment	Assessment to be made before choosing personal protective

SIMPLY SAFETY

	suitable.		provided.	includes: 1) definition of characteristics which the PPE must have in order to be effective against the risks (taking into account any risks which the equipment itself may create) 2) comparison of the characteristics of the PPE available with the required characteristic.	equipment which has to be provided.

REGULATION	PURPOSE OF ASSESSMENT	WHO HAS TO ASSESS THE RISK?	WHOSE RISK SHOULD BE ASSESSED?	WHAT RISKS SHOULD BE ASSESSED?	WHEN TO ASSESS
Display Screen Equipment	To assess workstations for health and safety risks to which users/operators are exposed.	Employers	Workstations which: 1) are used by employees who habitually use DSE as a significant part of their normal work; or 2) have been provided to operators (self-employed people who habitually use DSE as a significant part of their normal work).	Risks to health and safety to which users and operators are exposed in consequence of using the workstations.	As soon as possible after starting work
Noise	1) To identify which employees and self-employed people are exposed	Employers and self-employed people to ensure a competent person makes the assessment.	Employees and self-employed. Any other person at work who may be affected by the employer's work.	Exposure to noise.	Assessment to be made when any employee or self-employed person is

Risk Assessment and Management

	2) To provide the employer (*sic*) or self-employed person with information, with regard to the noise, as will aid compliance with Regulations 7,8,9 and 11.				likely to be exposed to the first action level or above or to the peak action level or above.
Control Of Substances Hazardous to Health	To identify risk to enable a decision to be made on the measures to take to prevent or adequately control exposures.	1) Employers 2) Self-employed people.	Employees and the self-employed liable to be exposed to substances hazardous to health by any work. Other people who may be affected by the employer's work.	Risks to health resulting from work involving exposure to substances hazardous to health. Assessment should include the steps that need to be taken in order to comply with other requirements of the Regulations.	Assessment to be made before work begins

REGULATION	PURPOSE OF ASSESSMENT	WHO HAS TO ASSESS THE RISK?	WHOSE RISK SHOULD BE ASSESSED?	WHAT RISKS SHOULD BE ASSESSED?	WHEN TO ASSESS
Asbestos	1) To identify type of asbestos 2) To determine the nature and degree of exposure 3) To set out steps to reduce exposure to lowest level reasonably practicable.	1) Employers 2) Self-employed people.	1) Employees 2) Self-employed 3) Other people who may be affected by the work activity.	Exposure of people to asbestos.	Assessment to be made before work begins.
Lead	To determine the nature and degree of exposure to lead.	1) Employers 2) Self-employed people.	1) Employees. 2) Other people at work on the premises where lead is being used..	Exposure of people to lead.	Assessment to be made before work begins.

SIMPLY SAFETY

CHAPTER 4

OCCUPATIONAL HEALTH

INTRODUCTION

It is a requirement that organisations must address occupational health, as well as safety in the workplace under the *Management of Health and Safety at Work Regulations 1999* and it is one of the many duties of the Employer to ensure that this happens. Of the 26.4 million working days lost overall (on average 15 days per case of work-related illness or workplace injury). the Health & Safety Executive estimates that 22.1 million were due to work-related ill health and 4.4 million due to workplace injury. It is estimated that Workplace injuries and ill health (excluding cancer) cost society an estimated £14 billion in 2009/10

The effective management of occupational health and the avoidance of occupational ill health will save organisations money by ensuring that they are not having to pay for staff being off sick and are retaining their skills and experience rather than paying out for temporary staff or placing undue strain on work colleagues who are having to cover during absence not to mention the potential for negligence claims for injury and ill health.

Generally occupational health is involved with:

- aiding employees in their return or rehabilitation to work after illness or injury
- assisting the disabled to access work and examining their requirements especially with fire evacuation
- managing all work-related illness
- monitoring employees health and the effects of work on health as well as health on work

Organisations will in most cases need to obtain specialist advice to enable them to effectively assess and manage the occupational health risks within their business. Such advice may come from competent persons within the larger organisation but such support may have to come from external Occupational Health Service Provider who may have to be sourced by the Employer with the exact services provided depend upon the risks, the numbers of personnel involved, and the nature of the organisations business.

NOTE: Medical information is deemed to be confidential to the individual and his or her medical advisor, and therefore employers do not have an automatic right to know an employee's medical diagnosis or treatment regime.

However there is much that you as the Employer can undertake for your own people / staff without involving a specialist Occupational Health Service Provider. The following pages should be used as a guide.

Occupational Health

WORK-RELATED UPPER-LIMB DISORDERS (WRULDS)

Musculoskeletal problems affecting the upper limbs are common in the general population. Symptoms include aches and pains, difficulty in movement and swelling. Links between some work activities and these disorders have long been recognised.

WHAT ARE WRULDS?

As the Employer you need to recognise that Work-Related Upper-Limb Disorders can occur throughout industry and are not specific to one particular sector. You need to realise that musculoskeletal conditions can arise spontaneously and without any link to work; however, they should also remember that WRULD's can be caused or made worse by work, although other activities may be involved in some cases. In the past many of the occupational diseases and conditions were acquired through working with physical products and materials in industry. However, in more recent times the increasing shift of staff from manual to office-based work activities has arisen out of the move of industry from manufacturing to the service industry. As a result, many of the occupational diseases and conditions are changing, either in terms of cause or in the relative incidence of the conditions.

The Employer needs to be aware that some musculoskeletal conditions are reportable under the *Reporting of Injuries, Diseases and Dangerous Occurrences Regulations 1995 (SI 1995/3163) (RIDDOR),* which are also covered in Chapter 5 First Aid and Accident Reporting

- cramp of the hand or forearm due to repetitive movements
- carpal tunnel syndrome
- hand-arm vibration syndrome
- beat conditions (of head, knee or elbow)
- traumatic inflammation of the tendons of the hand or forearm or of the associated tendon sheaths

The Employer, to be able to combat the onset of WRULDs so far as is reasonably practicable, needs to recognise some of the possible causes of WRULD's. These can be grouped into three general causes:

- Force – the application of undesirable manual force
- Frequency and duration of movement, including unsuitable rates of working or repetition of a single element
- Awkward posture of the hand, wrist, arm or shoulder

Employers should be aware that problems may be caused by only one of the causes mentioned above. However it is found that more often problems are caused by a combination or interaction between two or all three of the causes. WRULD's can occur therefore in jobs that require the following:

- repetitive finger, hand or arm movements
- twisting movements
- squeezing, hammering or pounding
- pushing, pulling, lifting or reaching movements

SIMPLY SAFETY

The Employer should remember that both office and manual jobs can cause WRULD's. The following are all potential causes:

- assembly line work
- meat and poultry preparation
- keyboard users
- hand tool and powered tool users

PREVENTATIVE MEASURES

In all cases the Employer must ensure that suitable and sufficient risk assessments are undertaken (See chapter 3 Risk Assessment and Management). These risk assessments should concentrate on identifying whether specific risk factors are present and the degree to which they may affect the likelihood of injury. Many people find that a checklist helps them decide and a sample risk assessment forms can be found at Table 3:04: Risk Assessment Proforma.

Sample Risk Assessments can also be found free in some HSE documents from HSE Books and the HSE web site.

Following on from the risk assessment the Employer must then undertake such remedial actions as may be required. These could be based on ergonomics. Ergonomics is concerned with the 'fit' between the user, equipment and their environments. It takes account of the user's capabilities and limitations in seeking to ensure that tasks, functions, information and the environment suit each user. These ergonomic principles refer to either work design or organisational arrangements such as the following:

WORK DESIGN

- Reduce force levels – reduce the force required, spread the force, get a better mechanical advantage, consider the effects of any hand protection already provided, maintenance of tools, training.
- Reduce highly repetitive movements – to include job enlargement, mechanisation, automation, reduction of machine pace.
- Postural changes – redesign or modify the operation or product, alter the tools or controls, move the part or move the operator.

The Employer will also need to look at the organisational set-up and arrangements. This will certainly involve some form of training and instruction. It is important that considerations are given to new employees who could be at greater risk of WRULDs considerations. Another possible solution is job rotation (periods of working on other tasks, not involving similar repetitive movements).

CONCLUSION

The Employer is more likely to succeed with the preventative measures if they:

- involve workers and their safety representatives early and at every stage
- provide information and training to all those involved
- design the job to fit the worker

Occupational Health

CONTROL OF NOISE AT WORK REGULATIONS 2005

The main aim of the Noise Regulations is to ensure that workers' hearing is protected from excessive noise at their place of work, which could cause them to lose their hearing and/or to suffer from tinnitus (permanent ringing in the ears).

As the Employer, you must assess and identify measures to eliminate or reduce risks from exposure to noise so that you can protect the hearing of your employees.

Where the risks are low, the actions you take may be simple and inexpensive, but where the risks are high, you should manage them using a prioritised noise-control action plan.

Where required, ensure that:

- hearing protection is provided and used;
- any other controls are properly used; and
- you provide information, training and health surveillance.

NOISE AT WORK – HEALTH EFFECTS

Noise at work can cause hearing loss that can be temporary or permanent. People often experience temporary deafness after leaving a noisy place e.g. a noisy plant room. Although hearing recovers within a few hours, this should not be ignored. It is a sign that if you continue to be exposed to the noise your hearing could be permanently damaged. Permanent hearing damage can be caused immediately by sudden, extremely loud, explosive noises, e.g. from guns or cartridge-operated machines.

But hearing loss is usually gradual because of prolonged exposure to noise. It may only be when damage caused by noise over the years combines with hearing loss due to ageing that people realise how deaf they have become. This may mean their family complains about the television being too loud, they cannot keep up with conversations in a group, or they have trouble using the telephone. Eventually everything becomes muffled and people find it difficult to catch sounds like 't', 'd' and 's', so they confuse similar words.

Hearing loss is not the only problem. People may develop tinnitus (ringing, whistling, buzzing or humming in the ears), a distressing condition which can lead to disturbed sleep.

Remember:

Young people can be damaged as easily as the old.

Noise can also be a safety hazard at work, interfering with communication and making any warnings given harder to hear.

DO YOU HAVE A NOISE PROBLEM AT WORK?

This will depend on how loud the noise is and how long people are exposed to it. As a simple guide you will probably need to do something about the noise if any of the following apply:

SIMPLY SAFETY

- Is the noise intrusive - like a busy street, a vacuum cleaner or a crowded restaurant - for most of the working day?
- Do your employees have to raise their voices to carry out a normal conversation when about 2 m apart for at least part of the day?
- Do your employees use noisy powered tools or machinery for more than half an hour each day?
- Do you work in a noisy industry, e.g. construction, demolition or road repair; woodworking; plastics processing; engineering; textile manufacture; general fabrication; forging, pressing or stamping; paper or board making; canning or bottling; foundries?
- Are there noises due to impacts (such as hammering, drop forging, pneumatic impact tools etc), explosive sources such as cartridge operated tools or detonators, or guns?

The Control of Noise at Work Regulations 2005 (SI 2005/1643) (CNWR 2005) replaces the **Noise at Work Regulations 1989 (SI 1989/1790).**

CNWR 2005 provides a framework for you the Employer to prevent or reduce risks to health and safety from exposure to noise at work by providing exposure limit values and action values (reg. 4), as follows:

Lower Exposure Action Values are:

- a daily or weekly personal noise exposure of 80 db (A-weighted); and
- a peak sound pressure of 135 db (C-weighted)

Upper Exposure Action Values are:

- a daily or weekly personal noise exposure of 85 db (A- weighted); and
- a peak sound pressure of 137 db (C-weighted)

Exposure Limit Values are:

- a daily or weekly personal noise exposure of 87 db (A-weighted); and
- a peak sound pressure of 140 db (C-weighted)

The HSE have also issued guidance on the regulations and these are:

- Controlling Noise at Work. The Control of Noise at Work Regulations 2005. Guidance on Regulations. L108, ISBN 0 7176 6164 4. Freely available from the HSE web Site at - - http://www.hse.gov.uk/pubns/priced/l108.pdf
- Noise at Work. Guidance for employers on the Control of Noise at Work Regulations 2005. Leaflet INDG362 (rev1). This is available in packs of 10, ISBN 0 7176 6165 2. Freely available from the HSE web Site at - http://www.hse.gov.uk/pubns/indg362.pdf
- Protect your hearing or lose it. Pocket card INDG363 (rev1) available in packs of 25, ISBN 0 7176 6166 0. Freely available from the HSE web Site at - http://www.hse.gov.uk/pubns/indg363.pdf

The Employer can also find within the HSE website a Noise microsite as well as a 'Noise Calculator', which is a good simple means to help you work out your daily and weekly noise exposures, and is available either within the above mentioned HSE Guidance document (L108) or on-line at www.hse.gov.uk/noise/calculator.htm

Occupational Health

Table 4:01 - Framework

PROVISION	EMPLOYER'S DUTIES
Reduce risk	Eliminate at source or reduce to a minimum
Assess and where necessary measure exposure	Where are, or are likely to be, exposed to noise at or above the Lower Exposure Action Value of 80dB(A)
Assessment period	8 hours or one week
Provide information and training to workers and reps	80 dB(A) and 112 Pa
Workers' right to hearing checks/audiometric testing	85 dB(A) by or under the responsibility of a doctor. To be available at 80 dB(A) and 112 Pa where risk indicated
Health surveillance	Provisions to ensure appropriate health surveillance where risk indicated
Make hearing protection available	80 dB(A) and 112 Pa
Hearing protection to be worn	85 dB(A) and 140 Pa selected to eliminate risk or reduce to a minimum
Limit on exposure	87 dB(A) and 200 Pa at the ear
Programme of control measures	85 dB(A) and 140 Pa
Delimit areas, put up signs and control access	85 dB(A) and 140 Pa where technically feasible and the risk of exposure so justifies
Workers reps to receive information	At or above 80dB(A)

The duty laid upon you as the Employer is a general duty to reduce risk at source and if this is not technically feasible to then provide hearing protection. The undertaking of a risk assessment of noise exposure best does this.

ASSESSMENT OF RISKS (REG. 5)

Noise risk assessments need to be made by a competent person who is properly trained and, has the necessary equipment and ,are to be carried out for employees who are liable to be exposed to noise levels at or above the lower Exposure Action Value of 80 dB(A). The noise risk assessment is undertaken to identify measures required to eliminate or reduce risks, control exposures and protect employees. Finally, a record of what measures are to be taken to reduce exposure is maintained in the form of an action plan.

ELIMINATION OR CONTROL OF EXPOSURE (REG. 6)

Once the findings of the assessment are known then the following actions need to be undertaken:

SIMPLY SAFETY

- Reduce exposure to noise by elimination at source or to as low as is reasonably practicable by means other than ear protectors, e.g. change the process, enclose the source of noise, increase the distance of the employee from the noise.
- If employees are likely to be exposed to noise at or above the upper Exposure Action Value then you as the Employer must implement a programme of organisational and technical measure to reduce exposure to levels as low as is reasonably practicable.

You as the Employer must ensure that employees are not exposed to noise above the Exposure Limit Value.

HEARING PROTECTION (REG. 7)

- The Employer is to provide hearing protection to employees who are exposed to noise at or above the lower Exposure Action Value, upon request.
- If an employee is exposed to noise at or above the upper Exposure Action Value and the Employer is unable to reduce the noise level by other means to below the upper Exposure Action Value, then personal hearing protection is to be provided
- Hearing Protection Zones are to be established by the Employer where employees are likely to be exposed to noise at or above the upper Exposure Action Value.

MAINTENANCE AND USE OF EQUIPMENT (REG. 8)

- The Employer shall ensure, so far as is practicable, that anything provided by him for the benefit and protection of an employee under these regulations is fully and properly used and maintained in good working order.
- In addition, any employee provided with such hearing protection equipment shall use the equipment properly and report any defects to his Employer.

HEALTH SURVEILLANCE (REG. 9)

- It is sometimes beneficial if you as the Employer obtains a baseline reading for the condition of a new starters hearing especially if they have previously worked in a noisy environment or have worked in a call centre using headsets, as this may prevent claims for hearing loss at a later stage.
- The Employer is to provide health surveillance to employees where the noise risk assessment identifies that they are at risk to their health from exposure to noise.
- Personal records of health surveillance must be maintained and made available to both the employee to which they pertain and also the enforcing authority if required.
- If an employee is found to have identifiable hearing damage then you as the Employer must have the employee examined by a doctor whereupon if, in the opinion of the doctor, the damage is likely to be as a result of exposure to noise then you as the Employer shall:
    - Provide information of the findings to the employee.
    - Undertake a review of the noise risk assessment.
    - Review the measures taken to comply with Regs 6, 7, and 8.
    - Consider moving the employee to alternative work that does not involve exposure to noise.
    - Continue health surveillance with the employee affected and in addition review the hearing of other employees exposed in a similar way.

INFORMATION, INSTRUCTION AND TRAINING (REG. 10)

It is your duty as the Employer to ensure that appropriate information, instruction and training is provided on the following subjects:

- Risks to hearing.
- Control measures to be used.
- The Exposure Action Values and Exposure Limit Values.
- Results of the significant findings of the noise risk assessment.
- Provision of personal hearing protection and its correct use.
- How to report defects.
- The importance of and how to detect and report signs of potential hearing damage.
- The arrangements for health surveillance.
- Safe systems of work.

DO I HAVE TO MAKE ANY CHECKS?

As an Employer you need to make sure that employees use hearing protection when required to. You may want to:

- include the need to wear hearing protection in your safety policy. Put someone in authority in overall charge of issuing them and making sure replacements are readily available;
- carry out spot checks to see that the rules are being followed and that hearing protection is being used properly. If employees carry on not using it properly you should follow your normal company disciplinary procedures;
- ensure all managers and supervisors set a good example and wear hearing protection at all times when in hearing protection zones;
- ensure only people who need to be there enter hearing protection zones and do not stay longer than they need to.

STRESS

There is a subtle difference between stress and the kind of pressure which we all face in our daily lives and in fact it is needed for motivational purposes and to ensure that we perform to our best ability. However it is when we experience too much pressure without the opportunity to recover that we start to experience stress. Stress in the workplace can present a big problem for the Employer but by recognising this fact, taking proper advice and working with your staff, it can successfully be prevented and also allow you to comply with the law.

What is stress? Stress is the reaction people have to excessive demands or pressures, whether it be in their home life or at work. In the workplace it arises when people try to cope with the tasks, responsibilities or other types of pressure connected with their jobs but find difficulty, strain or worry in doing so. Stress triggers complex changes in the body's processes, causing physiological changes and affecting the way people think, feel and behave.

There is no specific legislation on controlling or preventing stress at work. However, you as the Employer should note that under the *Health and Safety at Work etc. Act 1974 (HSWA 1974)* there is a general duty to ensure, so far as is reasonably practicable, that your workplaces are safe and healthy. Under the *Management of Health and Safety at Work Regulations 1999 (SI 1999/3242) (MHSWR 1999)* again you as the employer are required to assess the nature and extent of risks to health in your workplace, and then to base you control measures on the results

SIMPLY SAFETY

of the risk assessment. Employers have a legal duty to take reasonable care to ensure that health is not put at risk through excessive and sustained levels of stress arising from work activities, i.e. to treat stress like any other health hazard.

CAUSES OF STRESS

There are a number of possible causes of stress within the workplace and it is quite often a result of a mixture of these causes. The following are generally accepted as the main causes.

GENERAL MANAGEMENT AND CULTURE OF THE ORGANISATION

- lack of clear corporate objectives and values
- poor communication
- lack of management support and development for staff
- lack of management and staff consultation

ROLE IN THE ORGANISATION

- employee's role within the organisation unclear
- conflicting objectives and priorities
- high level of responsibility for people

CAREER DEVELOPMENT

- career uncertainty
- career stagnation
- job insecurity or redundancy

DECISION-MAKING/CONTROL

- low participation in decision-making
- lack of control over work

RELATIONSHIPS AT WORK

- poor relationships with superiors
- interpersonal conflict, including bullying, violence, sexual or racial harassment

HOME/WORK ISSUES

- conflicting demands of work and home
- dual career problems

JOB DESIGN

- ill-defined work
- work overload or under-load
- shift working
- unsocial work hours

REMEDIES

The remedies are not always in the hands of you the Employer; however you can play their part by ensuring that the following remedies are put in place within your area:

Occupational Health

- Provide good management, which includes having regard for people's attitudes.
- Ensure that there are appropriately open and understanding attitudes to stress. It should be realised that work-related stress is a problem for the organisation and not the individual employee.
- Ensure that jobs are able to be undertaken, matching the job with the person undertaking it.
- Look at the management style and ensure that it is consistent, concerned, communicative and caring.
- Manage periods of change so as to reduce any uncertainty.
- Provide help, support and training.

HSE MANAGEMENT STANDARDS FOR WORK-RELATED STRESS

What are the Management Standards for work-related stress?

The Health and Safety Executive takes stress very seriously and has developed a set of Management Standards for work related stress.

The Management Standards define the characteristics, or culture, of an organisation where the risks from work-related stress are being effectively managed and controlled.

The Management Standards cover six key areas of work design that, if not properly managed, are associated with poor health and well-being, lower productivity and increased sickness absence. In other words, the six Management Standards cover the primary sources of stress at work.

These are:

- **Demands** – this includes issues such as workload, work patterns and the work environment.
- **Control** – how much say the person has in the way they do their work.
- **Support** – this includes the encouragement, sponsorship and resources provided by the organisation, line management and colleagues.
- **Relationships** – this includes promoting positive working to avoid conflict and dealing with unacceptable behaviour.
- **Role** – whether people understand their role within the organisation and whether the organisation ensures that they do not have conflicting roles.
- **Change** – how organisational change (large or small) is managed and communicated in the organisation.

The Management Standards represent a set of conditions that, if present, reflect a high level of health well-being and organisational performance.

They:

- demonstrate good practice through a step-by-step risk assessment approach;
- allow assessment of the current situation using surveys and other techniques;
- promote active discussion and working in partnership with employees to help decide on practical improvements that can be made;
- help simplify risk assessment for work-related stress by:
  - identifying the main risk factors for work related stress
  - helping employers focus on the underlying causes and their prevention and

SIMPLY SAFETY

- providing a yardstick by which organisations can gauge their performance in tackling the key causes of stress

Further reference should be made to the HSE's Stress web site at - www.hse.gov.uk/stress/

SMOKING

On 1 July 2007 England became 'smokefree'. The new law was introduced to protect employees and the public from the harmful effects of second-hand smoke. As from 1 July 2007 it became against the law to smoke in virtually all enclosed public places, workplaces and public and work vehicles. There are very few exemptions from the law. Indoor smoking rooms in virtually all public places and workplaces are no longer allowed.

- Employers of smokefree premises and vehicles have legal responsibilities to prevent people from smoking at work.
- The law requires no-smoking signs to be displayed in all smokefree premises and vehicles.
- The law applies to anything that can be smoked. This includes cigarettes, pipes (including water pipes such as shisha and hookah pipes, Narghile pipes, or Qalyan pipes), cigars and herbal cigarettes.
- Failure to comply with the new law is a criminal offence. Penalties and fines for smokefree offences are set out below:
    - **Smoking in smokefree premises or work vehicles**: a fixed penalty notice of £50 imposed on the person smoking or a maximum fine of £200 if prosecuted and convicted by a court.
    - **Failure to display no-smoking signs**: a fixed penalty notice of £200 imposed on whoever manages or occupies the smokefree premises or vehicle or a maximum fine of £1,000 if prosecuted and convicted by a court.
    - **Failing to prevent smoking in a smokefree place**: a maximum fine of £2,500 imposed on whoever manages or controls the smokefree premises or vehicle if prosecuted and convicted by a court.
- Local councils are responsible for enforcing the new law. They offer information and support to help businesses and employers to meet their legal obligations under this law.

You as the Employer can find further information on the Smoke Free England website at www.smokefreeengland.co.uk.

BACTERIAL ILLNESS

Where there is a potential for occupational exposure, you as the Employer must be aware that micro-organisms which are hazardous to human health are included in the Control of Substances Hazardous to Health Regulations 2002 (SI 2002/2677) (COSHH 2002). Ill health may arise by exposure to agents, some of which are covered in brief below. It is vital that risk assessments are undertaken for all activities that deal with animals and areas where these and other diseases can be contracted. It is also vital that suitable information, training, instruction and supervision are given to all workers involved in work activities covering this type of work.

Occupational Health

OCCUPATIONAL ZOONOSES

Occupational Zoonoses are microorganisms, which are hazardous to human health and transmitted from animals to humans. Several of the more common types are also reportable under the *Reporting of Injuries, Diseases and Dangerous Occurrences Regulations 1995 (SI 1995/3163) (RIDDOR 1995)*

The Employer needs to understand that the risk to an individual depends on the following:

- current incidence in the UK
- infectivity of the organism
- the route of transmission
- the vulnerability of the individual
- the severity of the disease
- controls currently in place

The assessment of risk by you the Employer should be followed by confirmation, if necessary, of means of prevention and control. Health surveillance would be required only where there is a reasonable likelihood that an identifiable disease may arise from occupational exposure and for which there are valid detection techniques.

Appropriate information should be given to employees regarding the health risks from microorganisms, the symptoms, which may indicate infection, and the precautions which should be taken. Some occupational zoonoses of relevance in the Local Authority–enforced sector include the following - *(SI 1995/3163, Sch 3)*::

Leptospirosis (also known as Weil's disease) –

Leptospirosis is a disease caused by infection with bacteria of the genus *Leptospira* that affects humans as well as other mammals, birds, amphibians, and reptiles.

Though recognised among the world's most common diseases transmitted to people from animals, Leptospirosis is nonetheless a relatively rare bacterial infection in humans. The infection is commonly transmitted to humans by allowing water that has been contaminated by animal urine to come in contact with unhealed breaks in the skin, the eyes, or with the mucous membranes. Outside of tropical areas, Leptospirosis cases have a relatively distinct seasonality with most of them occurring between August–September/February–March.

Humans become infected through contact with water, food, or soil containing urine from infected animals. This may happen by swallowing contaminated food or water, or through skin contact. The disease is not known to be spread from person to person and cases of bacterial dissemination in convalescence are extremely rare in humans.

Leptospirosis is common among water-sport enthusiasts in specific areas as prolonged immersion in water is known to promote the entry of the bacteria. Surfers and white-water paddlers are at especially high risk in areas that have been shown to contain the bacteria, and can contract the disease by swallowing contaminated water, splashing contaminated water into their eyes or nose, or exposing open wounds to infected water. Rowers are also sometimes

SIMPLY SAFETY

known to contract the disease and in October 2010 British Rower Andy Holmes MBE died after contracting Leptospirosis / Weil's Disease.

As an Employer you should be aware that there are certain high risk occupations that include but *are not limited to*:-

- Veterinary medicine
- Livestock handling, slaughter and meat production
- Farming involving immersion in water
- Leading and instructing adventure sports such as caving, rafting, kayaking, trekking, etc.)
- Manual work in the wastewater industry
- Pest control involving any carrier species (not just rats)
- Work in underground confined spaces (tunnels, mines, etc. with a wild mammal presence)

Personal Protection

Any such work should be subject to a full Risk Assessment and Method Statement undertaken by the Employer. It should note that for general activities, protection of broken skin using waterproof dressings or clothing is the most important factor, but where there is a risk of aerosol spray (for example when pressure-washing or performing veterinary or meat preparation tasks) then eye and face protection is advised to prevent liquid droplets from entering the mouth or eyes. Goggles and a simple paper dust mask will be adequate in most cases. Clothing will be non-infectious once dried and washed, so full coveralls are not essential unless there are associated hazards that demand them. Workers should be given facilities to wash their hands, including soap or antibacterial gel, so they can remove any contaminant from their skin after an accidental exposure.

For situations where workers may accidentally immerse themselves (by falling into water) there is no reasonable way for the Employer to prevent them inhaling and ingesting some water, so the Employer needs to identify and provide protective measures to prevent the fall in the first place – i.e. barriers, covers or fall protection harnesses. It is important to remember that water which is likely to contain Leptospira is equally likely to contain many other harmful bacteria, viruses or chemicals.

Psittacosis (Ornithosis): -

Psittacosis is an infection caused by the bacterium *Chlamydophila psittaci*. This is acquired by contact with infected birds. The disease varies from a flu-like illness to an atypical pneumonia with the possible involvement of other major organs. The number of cases is known to be increasing in England and Wales, with most of those caused by bird contact associated with pet birds. Occupations at risk include all those who deal with 'pet' birds such as cockatiels, parakeets, parrots, and macaws, and poultry.

Rabies:

Rabies is an acute viral infection that is nearly always fatal. Transmission is usually through saliva via the bite of an infected animal, with dogs being the main transmitter of rabies to humans. The World Health Organization has estimated the annual number of human rabies deaths to be between 40,000 and as high as 70,000. Most of these deaths take place in developing countries, particularly in South and South East Asia. A UK woman died in May 2012 as a result of rabies from a dog bite whilst on holiday in Asia, but incidents in the UK are rare.

Anthrax:

Anthrax is a bacterial infection caused by *Bacillus anthracis*, spores of which can survive in the environment for years or decades. It is primarily a disease of herbivorous mammals, though other animals and some birds, particularly carrion birds, can also contract it. It is caused by the handling of infected wool, hides, hair and skins that release spores into the atmosphere, which may then be inhaled. Spores thus enter the body through broken skin or the alveoli. The infection can cause blisters, which then spread. This can lead to the victim becoming very ill, which can be fatal.

Newcastle Disease:

A non life-threatening conjunctivitis; fever and flu-like symptoms caused by virus spread via aerosols from infected birds. Although rare in the UK, there is a slight potential for exposure to pet shop workers.

OCCUPATIONAL SETTINGS

A wide variety of occupations and premises exist where contact with animals or their products may occur. (Please note that the following lists are illustrative, not exhaustive).

Professions

- Abattoir workers
- Bat workers
- Dog handlers/dog wardens
- Farmers and farm workers (working farms and open farms)
- Fish farmers and wild-catch fishers
- Forestry workers
- Horse handlers/grooms
- Meat inspectors
- Poultry farmers and workers
- Shepherds
- Sewage workers
- Veterinarians and other veterinary staff
- Wildlife workers
- Wildlife photographers
- Workers in hides, wool or bonemeal

Premises

- Abattoirs and cutting premises
- Aquaria and fish farms
- Aviaries and wildfowl sanctuaries
- Animal sanctuaries, kennels and catteries
- Farms - dairy, fish, livestock, poultry etc.

SIMPLY SAFETY

- Leisure and water sports facilities
- Open farms and other similar premises open to the public
- Pet shops and similar retail outlets
- Research and diagnostic laboratories
- Quarantine premises
- Zoos and wildlife parks

Table 4:02 - Sample Biological Agents' Checklist

BIOLOGICAL AGENTS CHECKLIST	YES	NO
Are you, your workers or others affected by your work activities exposed to any risk from biological agents?		
Have you assessed the risks arising from such exposure?		
Have you established policies and procedures to prevent/control any risk?		
Have you provided appropriate information and/or instruction to relevant people identified as potentially at risk?		

OCCUPATIONAL DERMATITIS

Occupational Dermatitis is common. It is estimated that somewhere in the region of four million working days are lost in the UK each year because of skin disease, the total cost to British industry running into millions of pounds. No occupation can be considered entirely free from the hazard of skin diseases but it must be remembered that not all skin diseases are of occupational origin.

Dermatitis can often be related to workplace factors. It is characterised by redness, itching, scaling, rashes, hives or blistering of the skin.

The two common forms of dermatitis usually seen in the workplace are allergic dermatitis and irritant contact dermatitis. When the skin comes into contact with certain substances at work, this can cause occupational dermatitis to occur. Things which might cause occupational dermatitis include cleaning products, organic solvents, metalworking fluids, cement, adhesives, other chemicals, and even certain plants.

The skin provides natural protection as long as the surface layer remains intact and undamaged by any wounds, solvents or irritants. Partial gaps in the barrier layer are made by sweat glands and hair follicles, which are consequently more vulnerable to penetration. The nature of the substance, the degree, duration and frequency of exposure to the substance and individual susceptibility determine how much skin damage will result from any particular substance. It is therefore important that you, the employer takes stock of what substances are used within the workplace and ensures that not only are the risk assessments undertaken but that suitable and

Occupational Health

sufficient information, training, instruction and supervision si provided for employees. Employees should also be consulted as to any substances to which they may be allergic.

CONTACT DERMATITIS

Symptoms show as eczema and itching. Substances causing occupational dermatitis are divided into two groups known as irritants and sensitisers:

- Irritants: These can be divided into 'weak' and 'strong' irritants. Weak irritants require frequent multiple exposures, often over prolonged periods. Chronic irritants as these are known include a wide range of substances including weak acids and alkalis, soaps, detergents, organic solvents and water-based metalworking fluids (soluble oils). Irritants act directly on the skin through chemical reactions.

- Sensitisers: These are substances capable of causing the allergic type of contact dermatitis in a two-stage process, first inducing contact sensitisation by penetration of barrier layer and then provoking an immunological delayed allergy over about seven days. With sensitisers, skin reactions may not be caused on initial contact, but after repeated exposure, some people will have an allergic reaction.

As the employer you have an important role in controlling workplace exposures to agents which cause occupational dermatitis and in providing appropriate health surveillance and encouraging employees to report symptoms at an early stage.

OTHER OCCUPATIONALLY INDUCED SKIN DISEASES

- Contact urticaria ('hives' or nettle rash) gives a shorter-lasting rash than contact dermatitis. It may be caused, for example, by rubber latex in protective gloves.

- Inflammation of the hair roots known as oil acne (from mineral oil, usually in cutting oils).

- Ulcerative conditions, for example cement burns from wet cement.

- Skin cancers caused by excessive exposure to UV radiation or from exposure to carcinogenic substances (e.g. mineral oils that have not been solvent refined or severely hydro treated).

- Photo dermatitis: this is where the skin develops a hypersensitivity to UV radiation, which can be triggered by certain chemical agents such as citrus oils used for degreasing purposes).

- Physical agents: things such as heat, light, humidity (e.g. chapping of hands of agricultural workers).

RISK ASSESSMENT

As the Employer you need to identify any agents that are known to have risks of skin damage by using the following:

SIMPLY SAFETY

- suppliers' labels and literature and the Material Safety Data Sheets (MSDS) also known as the Hazard Data Sheets
- company / industry guidance or information regarding known potentially sensitive occupations

You then need to assess whether any exposure of the skin to that substance poses a significant risk, and then decide what control measures are required.

HEALTH SURVEILLANCE

This is required where there is exposure to a substance known to be associated with skin disease and where, under the particular conditions of the work, there is a reasonable likelihood that the disease may occur. Where health surveillance is legally required, cases of occupational skin disease should be actively sought in the workplace, together with the keeping of appropriate health records. In cases of doubt as to whether surveillance is necessary, the Employer will need to obtain advice from an occupational physician or medical practitioner.

Table 4:03 - Sample Occupational Health Checklist

OCCUPATIONAL HEALTH CHECKLIST	YES	NO
Have you identified all occupational health hazards in your workplace?		
Have you carried out risk assessments covering all work procedures where there may be a health risk, identifying who might be harmed and how big the risks are?		
Have you used the risk assessments to help decide what action you need to take?		
Do you monitor and review the measures in place to control health risks?		
Do you inform, instruct and train employees in relation to work-related health risks?		

SOME SUGGESTED STEPS TO COMPLIANCE ARE:

- Identify all known primary skin irritants and sensitisers which the employer's risk assessment shows to be used in the workplace.
- Implement effective control measures to reduce the risk of exposure. Consider substitution of these potential skin irritants / sensitisers with agents that have lower skin reactivity. Provide adequate hygiene facilities, soaps and barrier creams, and appropriate PPE (e.g. gloves and coveralls).

Occupational Health

- Encourage early reporting of symptoms by your staff and protect the individual from further exposure while the cause of the symptoms is fully investigated. Other individuals in the same work group may have similar skin problems. You should review all of your risk assessment and risk management strategies / control measures etc. You will need to investigate any employees' concerns and consult with your safety representatives and employees.
- Establish contact with your employee at an early stage to ensure that they have access to the appropriate advice and support from their GP, and where available your Occupational Health Service. It may be necessary for a referral to be made to a dermatologist and the individuals Doctor or your Occupational Health Service can advise.
- It is important that you set up regular health surveillance for all employees that have been exposed or are likely to be exposed to an agent which may cause occupational dermatitis. You will need to consult with an occupational health professional, to agree the extent and frequency of surveillance. A health record should be maintained for each individual and it should be noted that records should be maintained for 40 years.

- As the Employer you must ensure that exposure is controlled to prevent triggering further skin problems if an individual has developed occupational dermatitis. If a doctor confirms that an employee is suffering from occupational dermatitis, this must be reported as an occupational disease to the HSE under RIDDOR 1995.
- As the Employer you will have to explain to your staff, the likely workplace causes of occupational dermatitis and how to recognise the symptoms. You will need to provide information and training to your staff on skin hygiene and skin care at work, the correct use and maintenance of PPE, and the reporting procedures.
- You need to promote good personal hygiene and good housekeeping in the workplace and encourage employees who are potentially at risk of occupational dermatitis to examine their skin regularly.

MANUAL HANDLING – LEGAL REQUIREMENTS

A recent survey found that 38% of all over-three-day injuries reported each year to HSE and local authorities are caused by manual handling e.g. the transporting or supporting of loads by hand or by bodily force and can occur whenever people are at work in offices, factories, hospitals, construction sites etc. In addition the most recent survey of self-reported work-related illness estimated that 1.1 million people in Great Britain suffered from musculoskeletal disorders (MSDs) caused or made worse by their current or past work. According to the latest averaged Labour Force Survey (LFS) estimates there are around 60 000 reportable non-fatal handling injuries a year. This gives a handling injury rate of 210 (95% confidence interval (CI) 190 to 240) per 100 000 workers. The LFS estimates that 940 000 days were lost due to handling injuries. This is a huge cost to industry and in particular employers working within their organisations.

The *Manual Handling Operations Regulations 1992,* as amended in 2002 *(SI 1992/2793) (MHOR 1992)*, apply to manual handling operations, defined as 'any transporting or supporting of a load (including the lifting, putting down, pushing, pulling, carrying or moving thereof) by hand or by bodily force (*SI 1992/2793, Reg 2*).

SIMPLY SAFETY

WHAT SHOULD YOU DO ABOUT IT?

Consider the risks from manual handling to the health and safety of your employees - the rest of this booklet will help you to do this. If there are risks, the Regulations apply.

Consult and involve your workforce. Your employees and their representatives know first-hand what the risks in the workplace are. So they can probably offer practical solutions to controlling them.

You as the Employer are subject to a clear hierarchy of measures to meet your duties under these regulations. As the Employer you must ensure the following, that you:

- avoid the need for hazardous manual handling, so far as is reasonably practicable
- assess the risk of injury from any hazardous manual handling that cannot be avoided and
- reduce the risk of injury from hazardous

MANUAL HANDLING – ASSESSMENT

It is essential that your staff are involved in the completion of the assessment as they often know the problems that will be faced and ways of dealing with them. To help in making this task easier in itself the assessment can be divided into four major components, which need to be considered and can be remembered by use of the mnemonic **T I L E** (**T**ask, **I**ndividual, **L**oad, **E**nvironment).

T = THE TASK

As the Employer you need to consider the following questions:

- Is the load held or manipulated at a distance from the trunk?
- Does the task involve:
  - twisting the trunk?
  - stooping?
  - reaching upwards?
  - combining risk factors?
  - excessive lifting or lowering distances?
  - excessive carrying distances?
  - excessive pushing or pulling of the load?
  - positioning the load precisely?
  - a risk of sudden movement of the load?
  - frequent or prolonged physical effort?
  - insufficient rest or recovery periods?
  - a rate of work imposed by a process?
  - the importance of posture?
  - handling while seated?
  - team handling?

I = THE INDIVIDUAL

This is perhaps one of the most important parts of the assessment that the Employer has to undertake. You need to refer each question, in some way, to each member of the workforce involved in the task to establish the following elements:

- if the task requires unusual strength, height etc
- if the job puts at risk those who might be pregnant or have a disability or a health problem
- if the task requires special information or training in its safe performance

L = THE LOAD

As the Employer you need to consider various aspects of the load, is it:

- heavy
- bulky or unwieldy
- difficult to grasp
- unstable, or if its contents are likely to shift
- sharp, hot or otherwise potentially damaging

E = THE ENVIRONMENT

When considering the working environment the following points have to be taken into account:

- space constraints preventing good practice
- uneven, slippery or unstable floors
- variations in levels of floors or work surfaces
- extremes of temperature or humidity
- ventilation problems or gusts of wind
- poor lighting conditions

MANUAL HANDLING – REDUCING THE RISK OF INJURY

PROVIDING ADDITIONAL INFORMATION ON THE LOAD

Where it is not reasonably practicable to avoid employees undertaking MHO at work which involve a risk of their being injured, the employer must also provide general indications and, where it is reasonably practicable to do so, precise information on the weight of each load *and the heaviest side of any load whose centre of gravity is not positioned centrally.*

ERGONOMICS

Take an ergonomic approach, fitting the operations to the individual rather than the other way around. Particular consideration should be given to the provision of mechanical assistance where this is reasonably practicable (for example, a sack truck, a hand-powered hydraulic hoist). As the Employer you should involve your workforce in the process and, again, industry-specific guidance could be a useful source of information.

REVIEWING THE ASSESSMENTS

It is the duty of the Employer to review the risk assessments that have been undertaken if in the following circumstances:

SIMPLY SAFETY

- new information becomes apparent
- there is a change in the MHO
- a reportable injury occurs

Further information can be found in:

- HSE website www.hse.gov.uk
- HSE publications such as:
    - Are you making the best use of lifting and handling aids (INDG 398) - http://www.hse.gov.uk/pubns/indg398.pdf
    - Getting to grips with manual handling INDG 143 - http://www.hse.gov.uk/pubns/indg143.pdf)

HAND-ARM VIBRATION SYNDROME (HAVS)

Hand arm vibration syndrome describes a range of medical conditions caused by prolonged use of hand-held power tools, which can have an adverse effect on the hands and arm of the users. Without effective control measures, operatives using such equipment can suffer damage known as hand-arm vibration syndrome, also known as vibration white finger (VWF). The employer has duties to reduce and control the risks of HAVS.

This is a disorder that affects blood vessels, muscles, joints and nerves of the hand, wrist and arm. If the condition is ignored it can become extremely painful and can lead to disability.

In addition medical conditions may be caused by exposure to work processes and activities, which involve vibration being transmitted through the hands.

LEGAL REQUIREMENTS

The *Control of Vibration at Work Regulations 2005 (CVWR)* set out legal duties upon you the Employer to protect your employees from the effects of vibration by assessing the risk of damage to staff and to ensure that there are adequate control measures in place. There are also requirements for manufacturers and suppliers of equipment to ensure that equipment is supplied with the lowest practicably obtainable values for vibration.

MOST AT RISK

The risk is dependent upon the actual amount or dose of vibration received by an individual and will depend on the magnitude of vibration emitted by the hand tool or process and the length of time that it is used each day.

The operatives that are at most risk are those who use the following tools although this is not an exhaustive list:

- hammer drills
- jig saws
- needle guns
- sanders and angle grinders
- vibratory compactors
- vibrating pokers
- concrete breakers

- chipping hammers

SYMPTOMS

As the Employer you need to be aware of the tools that your operatives are using and to provide them with information on the correct use of the tools and the symptoms to look out for. These symptoms will include the following:

- tingling and numbness of the fingers
- in cold and wet weather conditions the fingers go white, then blue, then red and are very painful
- the affected operative cannot feel things with their fingers
- they have difficulty in picking up small items
- they lose strength in their hands
- they feel pain, tingling or numbness in their hands, wrists and arms

As the Employer you should be aware that medical conditions such as Carpal Tunnel Syndrome caused by exposure to hand held vibrating tools is a prescribed disease and is therefore reportable to the HSE under the *Reporting of Injuries Diseases and Dangerous Occurrences Regulations 1995 (RIDDOR)*

EXPOSURE LIMIT VALUES AND ACTION VALUES (CVWR, REG. 4)

Exposure limit values are daily exposure levels that as the Employer you must ensure are not exceeded (except in certain circumstances).

Exposure Action Values are daily exposures which if reached or exceeded place immediate duties upon the employer to reduce the risk.

Table 4:04 - Exposure Action Values

The values are:

VIBRATION TYPE	DAILY EXPOSURE LIMIT VALUE	DAILY EXPOSURE ACTION VALUE
Hand Arm	5 m/s2A(8)	2.5 m/s2A(8)

RISK ASSESSMENT (CVWR, REG. 5)

As the Employer you need to look at the tasks to be undertaken which may put your workers at risk and undertake a risk assessment. You will need to look at taking the following measures:

SIMPLY SAFETY

- whether the task can be undertaken without the use of vibrating power tools
- if the work cannot be undertaken without using vibrating power tools then low vibration tools should be specified / used
- ensure that all tools are correctly maintained and are regularly tested under the portable appliance testing regime
- ensure that all power tools are stored correctly when not in use as this prevents the handles becoming cold
- ensure that all cutting tools are kept sharp
- ensure that the employees using such tools are monitored by a site supervisor as to how long they are using these types of tools
- provide suitable and sufficient information, training and instruction to those at risk, ensuring that they understand the risks involved and the protection measures
- wherever possible, ensure that those using these tools wear gloves while using the equipment

Hand-arm vibration exposure calculator

The HSE has produced a calculator as part of the package to support the Control of Vibration at Work Regulations 2005 and to assist the employer in calculating exposures for hand-arm vibration. The calculator along with further information may be found on the HSE website at:

http://www.hse.gov.uk/vibration/hav/vibrationcalc.htm

WORKSTATION REQUIREMENTS

LEGAL REQUIREMENTS

The *Health and Safety (Display Screen Equipment) Regulations 1992 (SI 1992/2792) (HS(DSE)R 1992)* require that the Employer protects the health of workers using Display Screen Equipment (DSE) by reducing the risks from working with DSE, including standard office visual display units (VDUs). The definitions used in the regulations (*SI 1992/2792, Reg. 1(2)*) include the following:

- **User**: This term means an employee who habitually uses DSE as a significant part of his/her normal work.
- **Operator**: This term means a self-employed person who habitually uses DSE as a significant part of his/her normal work.
- **Workstation**: This term includes any assembly of DSE, accessories, furniture and immediate work environment.

The regulations require that you as the Employer undertake an assessment or an analysis of the workstations used by users and operators (*SI 1992/2792, Reg.* 2). The assessment should be suitable and sufficient, systematic, appropriate to the degree of risk, comprehensive and consultative (*SI 1992/2792, reg 2*

It is recommended that except in very simple cases the assessment is recorded and kept available for future reference. The law requires that the assessment should also be reviewed in the light of any changes in the workstations or users / operators etc (*SI 1992/2792, Reg 2(2)*). Any risks identified must be reduced to the lowest extent reasonably practicable as quickly as possible (*SI 1992/2792, reg 2(3)*).

WORKSTATION EQUIPMENT

The display screen must be well defined, with the following:

- clear characters
- stable, flicker-free image
- adjustable brightness and/or contrast
- easy swivel/tilt
- free from glare and reflections

The keyboard must comply with the following:

- be separate from the screen
- be tiltable
- have space in front to support arms and hands
- have a matt, non-reflective surface
- have a suitable layout and key characteristics
- have adequately contrasted and legible symbols

The work desk should have the following:

- a large, low reflectant surface
- a document holder available (if required)
- adequate space for comfortable position

The work chair should be as follows:

- stable
- have a five star base
- allow the worker easy freedom of movement
- have adjustable seat height, backrest height and backrest tilt
- have a footrest available (if required)

The environment needs to include the following:

- space available dimensioned and designed to allow change of posture
- lighting that is as follows:
    - is satisfactory
    - has secondary adjustable lighting as appropriate
    - avoids glare by layout of workplace and/or design of lighting
    - includes control of daylight by suitable window coverings
- ways of avoiding distracting noise
- temperature that is suitable and does not cause discomfort
- all electro-magnetic radiation (except visible light) reduced to negligible levels

SIMPLY SAFETY

- an adequate level of humidity maintained

For human/computer interface, software must be as follows:

- be easy to use
- be adapted to the user's level of knowledge
- not be able to check the user performance without their knowledge
- provide a system to provide feedback to the user
- allow for information to be displayed in a format/pace adapted to the operator

WAYS OF WORKING

In any job, it is essential that work organisation issues be addressed to ensure that psychological components are satisfactory and that stress and work pressures are not problematic. When designing jobs the Employer needs to reduce the risks of DSE-related health problems. Individual needs will vary depending on the work done but the following measures should be considered:

- Reduce work pressure by reducing the workload.
- Take into consideration the risks of prolonged periods of DSE work when setting deadlines.
- Allow users to have a choice as to when to take their breaks. The length of break required is not set down in law although it is recommended that a break is approximately 10 minutes in every hour. Shorter, more frequent breaks should be encouraged rather than longer, infrequent breaks. Users should be encouraged to take micro-pauses of 10–15 seconds every 10 minutes.
- Incorporate non-DSE tasks into users' work routines, e.g. filing, telephoning.
- Increase control over pace and content of work.

EYE AND EYESIGHT TESTS

Users are to be provided with appropriate eye and eyesight tests upon request. The cost of these tests, and any prescribed corrective appliances (for DSE use only), must be met by you the Employer. There are many ways in which this can be administered by you which can be through direct contact with an Ophthalmic Optician or a group of Ophthalmic Opticians or through a Voucher System.

TRAINING AND INSTRUCTION

It is your duty as the Employer to ensure that sufficient information, training and instruction are provided for all users. This should include details of hazards and risks identified by the assessments, and procedures and arrangements that have been put in place to deal with these and other aspects of the DSE regulations.

Guides on display screen equipment and RSI are available from the HSE.

Occupational Health

MOBILE PHONES AND DRIVING

Driving well is a complicated task, involving both psycho-motor and cognitive skills. Hand-held mobile phones are likely to interfere with both, whereas using a hands-free mobile phone is likely to interfere with concentration and perceptual faculties.

Rule 127 of the Highway Code states:

> 'You must exercise proper control of your vehicle at all times. Never use a hand-held mobile phone or microphone when driving. Using hands-free equipment is also likely to distract your attention from the road. It is far safer not to use any telephone while you are driving – find a safe place to stop first.'

The use of a hand-held mobile phone while driving is an offence, and if anyone is caught doing so, they will receive a £60 fixed penalty or a maximum fine on conviction in court of £1,000. (Lorry, bus and coach drivers face a fine of £2,500.) The offence also attracts three penalty points.

The use of a hands-free phone may also impair a person's driving and lead to the imposition of the fixed penalty, or even a prosecution on the grounds that they did not exercise 'proper control' over their vehicle or that they were driving without due care and attention. These penalties could lead to the loss of their licence which may jeopardise their ability to do their job, so it is not worth the risk and it recommended that you as the employer adopt a policy of Non-Use of any mobile phones whilst in control of a vehicle.

EMPLOYERS' LIABILITY

Under the *Road Vehicles (Construction and Use) Regulations 2003 (SI 2003/182)*, an offence of 'causing or permitting' another person to drive while using a hand-held phone or other similar device was created. Employers may, therefore, be prosecuted if they require their employees to use their phones when driving.

The Department for Transport (DfT) has stated that employers cannot expect their employees to make or receive mobile phone calls while driving. This must be reflected in the company's health and safety policy and risk management policy. Information from the DfT indicates that employers will not be liable simply for supplying a telephone or for telephoning an employee who was driving. However, employers must send a clear message to employees that they are forbidden to use their hand-held mobile phones while driving and their employer will not require them to make or receive calls when driving.

As the Employer, you should inform your staff that, when driving, hand-held mobile phones should be switched off, or, if switched on, the calls should be left to go through to voicemail. Once it is safe to stop, the member of staff can then check for messages and return calls. As the Employer you should ensure that company policy specifies that using a hand-held phone or similar device while driving is a criminal offence and will be treated as a disciplinary matter.

Against this legal background, it is recommended that the you as the Employer formulates a policy on the use of mobile phones, to ensure the safety and well-being of its company car drivers while on the move, as well as to clarify the ground rules for mobile phone usage generally.

SIMPLY SAFETY

CHAPTER 5
FIRST AID AND ACCIDENT REPORTING

INTRODUCTION

Every employer has a duty to provide First Aid assistance to their employees and to those who work for them in whatever capacity. This will very much depend on the type of work being undertaken, where the work is being done, the type of worker and their experience as well as the location of the work. This chapter will provide you with the information that you need to determine the equipment and facilities that you as an employer will have to provide as well as the type of training you need to provide to ensure that you have competent First Aid provision. This chapter will also guide you as to the type of training that is needed and how often it should be provided.

The second part of the chapter looks into the requirement for an employer to report to the Enforcement Authorities certain types of incidents and accidents as well as details on how to prepare an accident report etc.

LEGISLATION AND PUBLICATIONS

The legislation referred to within this section is as follows

- The Health and Safety (First-Aid) Regulations 1981 (HS(FA)R 1981)
- The Health and Safety (First Aid) Regulations 1981. Approved Code of Practice (ACoP) and guidance
- The Offshore Installations and Pipeline Works (First-Aid) Regulations (SI 1989/1671)
- The Diving at Work Regulations 1997 (SI 1997/2776)
- The Reporting of Injuries, Diseases and dangerous Occurrences Regulations 1995

The Health and Safety (First Aid) Regulations 1981 ACoP publication can be accessed and down loaded from the following web page: - http://www.hse.gov.uk/pubns/books/l74.htm

The Offshore Installations and Pipeline Works (First-Aid) Regulations ACoP can be accessed and down loaded from the following web page: - http://www.hse.gov.uk/pubns/priced/l123.pdf

The Reporting of Injuries, Diseases and dangerous Occurrences Regulations 1995 and Guidance can be accessed and down loaded from the following web page: - http://www.hse.gov.uk/pubns/priced/l73.p

FIRST AID TRAINING PROVIDERS

"The Health and Safety (First Aid) Regulations 1981 have been amended to remove the requirement for HSE to approve first aid training and qualifications. These changes took effect as from 1st October 2013.

First Aid and Accident Reporting

The change is part of the HSE's work to reduce the burden on businesses and put common sense back in to health and safety, whilst maintaining standards. The new approach applies to businesses of all sizes and from all sectors and means that businesses have more flexibility in how they manage their provision of first aid in the workplace. However the potential drawback is that Businesses will now have to assess the Trainers, and the courses, that they utilise to ensure that they do comply with the requirements of the regulations and specifically their own needs.

To assist the employer the HSE guidance documents clarify what the law requires and provide practical help to businesses in assessing and understanding their first aid needs. Where a first aider is required, the guidance documents make it clear that the employer is free to select a training provider who is best suited to those needs.

The First Step – The Needs Assessment

As the employer you will need to make an assessment of your first-aid needs to establish what provision for first aid is required. This will obviously depend upon your workplace, taking into account, a number of things including but not limited to the size and location of your work, the nature of your work activity as well as the number of employees you have.

Having undertaken your First-Aid Needs Assessment you may find that it indicates that a first-aider is unnecessary, however the minimum requirement for any business is to appoint a person to take charge of the first-aid arrangements. The roles of this appointed person include

1. looking after the first-aid equipment and facilities
2. calling the emergency services when required.

The appointed person can also provide emergency cover, within their role and competence, where a first-aider is absent due to unforeseen circumstances.

In most cases the findings of your First-Aid Needs Assessment may identify that you require trained first aiders are required. There are no hard and fast rules on exact numbers, and you will need to take into account all the relevant circumstances of your particular workplace and it is recommended that you use the guidance chart found in TABLE 5.01 - CHECKLIST FOR ASSESSMENT OF FIRST-AID NEEDS

Criteria Expected of First Aid Training Providers

The HSE has produced guidance on selecting a first aid training provider that sets out the criteria that a competent training provider should be able to demonstrate.

These criteria include:

- the qualifications expected of trainers and assessors;
- monitoring and quality assurance systems a training company has in place;
- teaching and standards of first-aid practice;
- syllabus content; and
- the information included on a certificate.

SIMPLY SAFETY

The Options in the Selection of a First Aid Training Provider

First Aid Training is available from a wide range of providers including:

- those who choose to offer regulated qualifications (first aid qualifications regulated by the qualification regulators - Ofqual, SQA and the Welsh Government),
- those who operate under voluntary approval schemes for example, a trade or industry body having quality assurance schemes accredited by a third party (e.g. UKAS),
- those who operate independently of any such scheme for example, where a training provider chooses to demonstrate their competence to an employer by providing evidence that they meet the criteria set by HSE, or
- from one of the Voluntary Aid Societies (St John Ambulance, British Red Cross and St Andrew's First Aid).

Where additional or specialist training may be required due to the work activity, for example in the outdoor education industry, as the employers you will be able to choose the most appropriate specialist provider to meet your identified training needs – and therefore potentially avoid duplication in training.

All training providers will need to be able – and should be prepared to demonstrate - how they satisfy the criteria set by HSE. Clarity in this area will be beneficial to both employers and first aid training providers, however, the Health and Safety at Work Etc Act clearly places a duty on the employer to select a competent training provider.

Regulated Qualifications

Regulated Qualifications are nationally recognised and can be obtained from a training centre for an 'awarding organisation' (AO).

These AO's are recognised by qualification regulators (Ofqual, SQA or the Welsh Government):
-
- Ofqual is the regulator of qualifications, examinations and assessments in England.
- SQA (the Scottish Qualifications Authority) and
- the Welsh Government carry out similar functions in Scotland and Wales.

A number of AOs deliver training for the purposes of first aid at work.

These AO's have dedicated policies and quality assurance processes and must approve and monitor their training centres to ensure training meets a certain standard. Regulators stipulate that AO's and their training centres must work in compliance with the Assessment Principles for First Aid Qualifications (which can be found on the Skills for Health website (http://www.skillsforhealth.org.uk/) and other key criteria, including the competence of trainers and assessors and the content of quality assurance systems.

A list of Ofqual/SQA/Welsh Government recognised AOs who can deliver training for the purposes of first aid at workcan be found on this site (http://www.hse.gov.uk/firstaid/efaw.htm)

First Aid and Accident Reporting

Further HSE guidance on selecting a first aid training provider is also available for free download from the HSE site at the following address - http://www.hse.gov.uk/pubns/geis3.pdf .

The above changes do not alter the duties and responsibilities already placed on employers. Businesses still have a legal duty to make arrangements to ensure their employees receive immediate attention if they are injured or taken ill at work.

THE EMPLOYERS LEGAL DUTIES

The Regulations require employers to provide adequate and appropriate equipment, facilities and personnel to ensure that their employees receive immediate attention if they are injured or taken ill at work. It should be noted that these Regulations apply to all workplaces including those with less than five employees and to the self-employed. Detailed information can be found in the ACoP detailed above in the Legislation section.

FIRST AID – WHAT THE LAW REQUIRES

First aid is a vital part of any workplace whatever the size and wherever it is located.

To fully understand what is required under the law it is imperative that the terms quoted within the regulations are fully understood by all concerned.

The term **First Aid** is defined as follows (*SI 1981/917, Reg 2(1)*):

- 'treatment for the purpose of preserving life and minimising the consequences of injury or illness, until help from a doctor or nurse is obtained.'
- 'treatment of minor injuries, which would otherwise receive no treatment or which do not need treatment by a doctor or nurse.'

The term **First Aider** is defined as follows (*SI 1981/917, Reg 3*):

- 'a person who holds a current training certificate issued by an organisation whose training and qualifications were, at the time of the issue of the certificate, approved by the Health and Safety Executive for the purpose of the HS(FA)R 1981.'

The Regulations place a duty on the employer to do the following (*SI 1981/917, Reg 3*):

- provide adequate first aid equipment and facilities appropriate to the type of work or operations undertaken
- appoint a sufficient number of suitable and trained people to render first aid to employees injured or who become ill at work
- make provision to cover annual leave, planned, unplanned and exceptional absences of first aiders or appointed persons
- inform employees of the first aid arrangements, including the location of equipment and personnel

The Employer who is in the position of having to decide upon what level they should base their first aid requirements will first need to undertake a risk assessment (as required under the *Management of Health and Safety at Work Regulations 1999 (SI 1999/3242)*) to enable them to better understand their needs.

SIMPLY SAFETY

ASSESSMENT OF NEED

How much first aid needs to be provided by you as the the /employer very much depends upon the circumstances within each workplace. It is recommended that the employer records the results of their assessment of first aid requirements, which should include looking at the following:

- The nature of the work being carried out – if the risk assessment indicates a comparatively low risk to health and safety, a first aid kit and an appointed person may suffice. With increasing levels of risk the greater the need for qualified first aiders, first aid rooms etc. See the recommendation chart below.
- The size of the organisation – dependent upon the number of employees etc, the need for certain first aid provisions increases or decreases.
- The past history and consequences of accidents – a study of the company's accident books and records will help determine the type of material that needs to be provided as well as the type of cover that is required.
- Local medical amenities – for example where are the nearest hospitals, medical facilities (doctors etc), ambulance depot etc?
- The nature and distribution of the workforce – for example, are there employees that are at a greater risk (young workers, trainees etc)? Does the work involve shift working and where are the locations of specific work groups?
- The needs of peripatetic workers those travelling as well as remote and lone workers.
- Certain groups may need to carry a personal first aid kit as well as a means for emergency communication etc

The results arrived at from the assessment will help the Employer to decide where his/her company lies in relation to the type and number of first aiders they require. As can be seen from Table 5:01 AND 5:02 there are two types of first aiders: an emergency first aider; and a first aider. The difference between the two is covered below

TRAINING AND QUALIFICATIONS REQUIRED

The Employer needs to find people who are willing to undertake the duties of either an Emergency First Aider or a First Aider. They should ideally be office based, or based where the employees are working, and be able to cope in an emergency. The reason for this is that cover must be provided within the workplace at all times that employees and others are present and they must be able to leave their work immediately to enable them to respond to an emergency.

FIRST AIDERS

First Aiders are required to attend a competence-based training course in first aid provided by an organisation that has been specifically licensed to provide first aid training. The training courses involve at least 18 hours of training and are run over a minimum of three days but can also be run at evening classes at a local college.

The course generally covers the following:
- resuscitation
- management of an unconscious casualty
- bleeding control

First Aid and Accident Reporting

- various medical conditions
- causes and management of shock, asphyxia, burns, fractures and poisons
- current first aid legislation
- specific problems or situations if requested

Upon successful completion of the course the candidate receives a First Aid Certificate, which lasts for three years. As the Employer you should note that the Health & Safety Executive (HSE) strongly recommends that First Aiders undertake annual refresher training, over half a day, during any three-year FAW/EFAW certification period. Although this is not mandatory, this will help qualified first-aiders maintain their basic skills and keep up to date with any changes to first-aid procedures. The training organisations that provide the qualification training are able to can run the recommended annual refresher courses.

RENEWING A FIRST AID CERTIFICATE

The certificate needs to be renewed by successful attendance at a refresher training course, currently every three years, and can be renewed up to three months prior to the certificate's expiry date. Re-qualification after the expiry of the certificate will necessitate the candidate attending another full three-day course.

EMERGENCY FIRST AIDERS

Emergency First Aiders are required to attend competence-based training in first aid, which lasts for generally one day. Emergency First Aiders are NOT first aiders and should not be called upon to take on the duties of a first aider unless they have received suitable and sufficient training.

The appointed persons training course covers emergency first aid in the following topics:

- management of heart attack
- resuscitation
- dealing with an unconscious casualty
- choking
- wounds
- fits
- burns
- basic legislation

The HSE guidance is aimed at giving you, the Employer more flexibility in determining their first aid needs or requirements. The guidance provides for a three day First Aider at Work Training Course and for the provision of a one-day course in Emergency First Aid at Work (EFAW) for smaller businesses.

All FAW qualified First Aiders have to attend a two-day re-qualification course every three years if they are to retain their certificate, otherwise they will have to retake the full three day course if their current certificate expires prior to their re-qualification (even by one day). The HSE do strongly recommend that annual refresher training is undertaken for all qualified first aiders. The HSE state that although it is not mandatory for annual refresher courses to be provided, it will help First Aiders maintain their basic skills and keep up to date with any changes to first aid procedures. They go on to say that if guidance is followed the Employer should be best placed to meet their legal responsibilities

SIMPLY SAFETY

The above regulations came into force in 2009 and The Employer did not have to retrain all their first aiders as soon as the implementation date was reached (31 October 2009). First aiders with a valid first aid at work (FAW) certificate would only enter the new arrangements when their certificate expired. This meant that it would take up to three years post-implementation before all first aiders in the workplace were captured within the new training structure and this would have been by 31st October 2012. Thus all First Aiders are now subject to the new regulations detailed above.

First Aid and Accident Reporting

TRAINED FIRST AIDERS – SUGGESTED ASSESSMENT OF FIRST-AID NEEDS AND NUMBERS REQUIRED

TABLE 5.01 - CHECKLIST FOR ASSESSMENT OF FIRST-AID NEEDS

Hazards (use the findings of your risk assessment and take account of any parts of your workplace that have different work activities/hazards which may require different levels of first-aid provision)	
Point to consider	**Impact on first-aid provision**
Does your workplace have low-level hazards, like you might find in offices and shops?	The minimum provision is: • an appointed person to take charge of first-aid arrangements; • a suitably stocked first-aid box.
Does your workplace have higher level hazards, such as chemicals or dangerous machinery? Do your work activities involve special hazards, such as hydrofluoric acid or confined spaces?	You should consider: • providing first-aiders; • additional training for first-aiders to deal with injuries caused by special hazards; • additional first-aid equipment; • precise siting of first-aid equipment; • providing a first-aid room; • informing the emergency services.
Employees	
Point to consider	**Impact on first-aid provision**
How many people are employed on site?	Where there are small numbers of employees, the minimum provision is: • an appointed person to take charge of first-aid arrangements; • a suitably stocked first-aid box. Where there are large numbers of employees you should consider providing: • first-aiders; • additional first-aid equipment; • a first-aid room.
Are there inexperienced workers on site, or employees with disabilities or particular health problems?	You should consider: • additional training for first-aiders; • additional first-aid equipment; • local siting of first-aid equipment.

SIMPLY SAFETY

	Your first-aid provision should cover work experience trainees.
Accidents and Ill Health	
Point to consider	**Impact on first-aid provision**
What Injuries and illnesses have occurred in your workplace and where did they happen?	Make sure your first-aid provision caters for the type of injuries and illness that might occur in your workplace Monitor accidents and ill health and review your first-aid provision as appropriate.

Working arrangements	
Point to consider	**Impact on first-aid provision**
Do you have employees who travel a lot, work remotely or work alone?	You should consider: • issuing personal first-aid kits; • issuing personal communicators/mobile phones to employees.
Do any of your employees work shifts or work out of hours	You should ensure there is adequate first-aid provision at all times people are at work.
Are the premises spread out, eg are there several buildings on the site or multi-floor buildings?	You should consider provision in each building or on each floor.
Is your workplace remote from emergency medical services?	You should: • inform the emergency services of your location; • consider special arrangements with the emergency services.
Do any of your employees work at sites occupied by other employers?	You should make arrangements with other site occupiers to ensure adequate first-aid provision. A written agreement between employers is strongly recommended.
Do you have enough provision to cover for your first- aiders or appointed persons when they are absent?	You should consider: • what cover is needed for annual leave and other planned absences; • what cover is needed for unplanned and exceptional absences.
Non-employees	
Point to consider	**Impact on first-aid provision**
Do members of the public visit your	Under the Regulations, you have no legal

First Aid and Accident Reporting

premises?	duty to provide first aid for non-employees, but HSE strongly recommends that you include them in your first-aid provision.

TABLE 5.02 - - LIST OF NUMBERS OF FIRST AIDERS REQUIRED AS SET DOWN IN THE REGULATIONS

1 From your risk assessment, what degree of hazard is associated with your work activities?	2 How many employees do you have?	3 What first-aid personnel do you need?
Low hazard e.g. offices, shops, libraries	Less than 25	At least one appointed person
	25-50	At least one first-aider trained in EFAW
	More than 50	At least one first-aider trained in FAW for every 100 employed (or part thereof)
Higher hazard e.g. light engineering and assembly work food processing, warehousing, extensive work with dangerous machinery or sharp instruments, construction, chemical manufacture	Less than 5	At least one appointed person
	5-50	At least one first-aider trained in EFAW or FAW depending on the type of injuries that might occur
	More than 50	At least one first-aider trained in FAW for every 50 employed (or part thereof)

COVER FOR LEAVE/ABSENCE OF FIRST AIDERS

The legislation requires that First Aid personnel must always be available when people are at work. It is therefore important that you as the Employer ensures that there are sufficient trained

SIMPLY SAFETY

personnel, who are First Aiders or Emergency First Aiders, to cover for holidays, training courses or sicknesses that may reduce the numbers of first aid personnel available on your site/s compared to the recommended number shown in Table 5:02

FIRST AID BOXES, BAGS AND ROOMS

FIRST AID BOXES

As a minimum one first aid box with sufficient contents must be made available for each workplace; however, in larger premises there will be a requirement for a larger number of first aid boxes.

All first aid boxes etc should be easily identified and should contain a white cross on a green background.

They should meet these criteria:

- suitably stocked with a minimum of contents
- easily accessible
- near to hand-washing facilities if possible

They should not contain any tablets or medicines.

Where there is no special risk within the workplace the suggested contents of a first aid box is as set out in Table 5:03 – suggested Minimum Contents for a First Aid Box

TABLE 5.03 -: SUGGESTED MINIMUM CONTENTS FOR A FIRST AID BOX

Item	Number
A leaflet giving general guidance on first aid (e.g. HSE leaflet *Basic advice on first aid at work*)	1
Individually wrapped sterile adhesive dressings (assorted sizes) (blue for catering personnel)	20
Sterile eye pads, with attachment	2
Individually wrapped triangular bandages (preferably sterile)	4
Safety pins	6
Medium-sized, individually wrapped sterile unmedicated wound dressings (approx. 12cm x 12cm)	6
Large, sterile, individually wrapped unmedicated wound dressings (approx. 18cm x 18cm)	2
Individually wrapped moist cleansing wipes	2
Disposable gloves	1 pair

First Aid and Accident Reporting

It should be noted that there is no mandatory list of contents and other contents are permissible. Additional materials that might be identified as necessary could include scissors, adhesive tape, disposable aprons and so on. Where there is a special first aid requirement or circumstance the first aid box should reflect this need.

It is important to ensure that the stocks within the first aid boxes are maintained. First aid boxes should be subject to a regular check to ensure that stock levels are maintained and as such it may be necessary to hold larger stocks of first aid supplies elsewhere to enable shortages to be made up quickly.

First aid stocks should be regularly inspected to ensure that they are still within date. Any out of date items should be disposed of safely.

OTHER FIRST AID RESOURCES

Where mains tap water is not readily available for eye irrigation, at least one litre of sterile water or saline solution (9%) in sealed, disposable containers should be provided.

Travelling first aid kits should be provided to those who travel as part of their function, that is peripatetic workers (these should include those who drive as a major part of their job). The contents of these differ slightly from the contents of the first aid boxes detailed above. A suggested list of contents is as follows:

- a leaflet giving general guidance on first aid (eg HSE leaflet – *Basic advice on first aid at work*)
- six individually wrapped sterile adhesive dressings
- two individually wrapped triangular bandages (preferably sterile)
- two safety pins
- one large, sterile, individually wrapped unmedicated wound dressing (approx. 18cm x 18cm)
- individually wrapped moist cleansing wipes
- disposable gloves

REQUIREMENT FOR FIRST AID ROOMS

First aid rooms are normally required only where the risk assessment shows that the organisation is operating within high-risk industries. This would mean that the types of industries such as large construction sites, slaughterhouses, chemical manufacturers etc, are likely to require a first aid room. Where this is the case then the first aid rooms need to have the following:

- a bed/couch with waterproof covering
- clean pillows and blankets
- heating, lighting and ventilation
- a storage area for first aid supplies
- a desk and a chair
- a telephone
- a sink with hot and cold running water, soap and towels
- a source of drinking water and cups

SIMPLY SAFETY

- a foot-operated pedal bin with suitable bin liners etc for the safe disposal of clinical waste (normally yellow bags suitably marked)
- a record book to record incidents, treatment etc

The room must also comply with the following, it must:

- be kept clean and tidy
- be available for use whenever there are people at work
- have enough space for the positioning of a couch to enable people to work in the room
- have easily washable surfaces

If the first-aid room(s) cannot be reserved exclusively for giving first aid, as the Employer you need to make sure that the first-aid facilities can be made available quickly if necessary. For example, you should consider the implications of whether:

(a) the activities usually carried out in the room can be stopped immediately in an emergency;

(b) the furnishings and equipment can be moved easily and quickly to a position that will not interfere with giving first aid;

(c) the storage arrangements for first-aid furnishings and equipment allow them to be made available quickly when necessary.

SPECIAL REQUIREMENTS FOR OFFSHORE WORK

Industry specific legislation exists for the offshore industry to take account of the remoteness and difficulties of access to medical and health care expertise. The *Offshore Installations and Pipeline Works (First-Aid) Regulations (SI 1989/1671)* came into force in 1989. The regulations require the person in control (such as an installation operator or the Employer) to provide suitable first aid and medical facilities, as well as sufficiently trained and competent first aiders and offshore medics. The Employer/person in control) should assess the level of first aid and health care provision needed on individual installations or barges. This will include how many trained offshore medics and first Aiders are needed, the amount and type of equipment and the types of drugs supplied. A minimum equipment list: *First aid and medical equipment on offshore installations*, has been produced by the United Kingdom Offshore Operators' Association (UKOOA).

The Employer/person in control has to ensure that adequate basic health care and first aid is provided for everyone on the installation or barge, including visitors and contractors. This extends to people working on certain associated vessels (e.g. during installation commissioning or decommissioning). The person in control also has to make arrangements for a Registered Medical Practitioner to supervise the offshore medic and give advice if necessary. This practitioner is usually based onshore. The offshore medic would normally have responsibility for the sickbay. The size, siting / location, layout and facilities of the sickbay should be sufficient to provide accommodation and medical support for an ill or injured person for up to 48 hours – for further information refer to the UKOOA publication: - "Industry Guidelines for First Aid and Medical Equipment on Offshore Installations: -
http://www.oilandgasuk.co.uk/cmsfiles/modules/publications/pdfs/HS013.pdf

First Aid and Accident Reporting

SPECIAL REQUIREMENTS FOR DIVING

Diving at work covers a wide range of activities from deep saturation diving in support of the offshore oil and gas industry to recreational instruction by a professional instructor. The 'Diving Industry' can be considered as a number of sectors where people need to go underwater to work. With the exception of the recreational sector, diving is primarily a method of getting to a work site that happens to be underwater.

Under the *Diving at Work Regulations 1997 (SI 1997/2776)*, a diving contractor (the Employer) is required to provide first aid and medical equipment during a diving project. In the event of a diving medical incident, the diving supervisor remains in control of any action to be taken.

As part of diver training and assessment, commercial divers in Great Britain are taught diving physiology (which includes the function of the nervous and musculoskeletal systems), and diving medicine (which includes decompression illness and ear problems).

At the same time as the diver undertakes training and assessment, as the Employer you must ensure that the diver also gains an HSE first aid at work qualification. This provides training in the immediate initial treatment to reduce the effects of the common injuries or illnesses suffered at work, for example bleeding, fractures, shock, burns and respiratory arrest.

This qualification is valid for three years. It may be renewed at a first-aid training organisation recognised by the HSE. As the Employer you need to ensure that the refresher training is commenced before the current certificate expires. If the retraining is undertaken up to three months before the expiry date, the new certificate will be valid from the original expiry date. If the certificate expires a full First Aid at Work course will have to be taken again.

RECORD KEEPING OF FIRST AID INCIDENTS

It is good practice to record all incidents attended by first aid personnel and it is therefore important that a record book is kept. This book is not the statutory Accident Book BI 510 but a separate one within which the following information can be entered:

- the date, time and place where the incident occurred
- a description of the injury or the illness
- details of the injured person – name, job title, area of work etc
- details of the first aid treatment given
- details of the disposal of the injured person, ie to hospital, home, back to work
- in the event of onward transmission of the injured party to hospital or home, details of the mode of transport, who accompanied the person and the time of departure
- the name and signature of the first aider or person who dealt with the injured party

SIMPLY SAFETY

ACCIDENT REPORTING – WHAT THE LAW REQUIRES

Note that as from 1st October 2013 new requirements came into force with respect to the RIDDOR reporting requirements and the new regulations became legislation.

REPORTING OF INJURIES, DISEASES AND DANGEROUS OCCURRENCES REGULATIONS 2013

The provisions of RIDDOR 1995 have now been superseded and as from 1 October 2013 the changes that were introduced to the Reporting of Injuries, Diseases and Dangerous Occurrences Regulations (RIDDOR) are intended to simplify the mandatory reporting of workplace injuries for businesses / employers, while ensuring that the data collected gives an accurate and useful picture of workplace incidents.

The Reporting of Injuries, Diseases and Dangerous Ocurrences Regulations 2013 (RIDDOR) is a single piece of legislation that requires employers to look at certain situations that occur within the workplace and report them through a centralised point to the Health and Safety Executive (HSE) or Local Authority, dependent upon their industry sector.

From this information, health and safety experts can produce a clear picture of how we're managing health and safety within the UK, and whether there are any areas that the HSE needs to target – for instance if there is an increase in particular accidents or incidents within a certain sector.

For a large number of companies a reportable accident, dangerous occurrence or case of disease (a RIDDOR incident) is generally a rare event. However employers should be aware that they do occur and that the employer may well have duties under these regulations. The regulations state that it is the duty of the responsible person' to report RIDDOR incidents and that' regulation 2 (1)(2) clearly sets out the definition of "The Responsible Person" and in the main this is classed as the employer *(SI 2013/1471, reg 3(1)(2))*.

To allow employers and businesses time to familiarise themselves with the changes, the HSE have developed the following information to support duty holders with the requirements.

WHAT HAS CHANGED?

The changes follow a recommendation by Professor Ragnar Löfstedt in his report 'Reclaiming health and safety for all: An independent review of health and safety legislation'. The process for implementing the changes was implemented as from October 2013, having obtained Parliamentary approval.

The main changes are to simplify the reporting requirements in the following areas:

- The classification of 'major injuries' to workers is being replaced with a shorter list of 'specified injuries'.

First Aid and Accident Reporting

- The existing schedule detailing 47 types of industrial disease is being replaced with eight categories of reportable work-related illness.
- Fewer types of 'dangerous occurrence' will require reporting.

There are no significant changes to the reporting requirements for:

- Fatal accidents.
- Accidents to non-workers (members of the public).
- Accidents which result in the incapacitation of a worker for more than seven days.

GUIDANCE

The following guidance will apply as from 1st October 2013: -

TYPES OF REPORTABLE INJURY

Deaths

All deaths to workers and non-workers, with the exception of suicides, must be reported if they arise from a work-related accident, including an act of physical violence to a worker.

Specified Injuries to Workers

The list of 'specified injuries' in RIDDOR 2013 replaces the previous list of 'major injuries' in RIDDOR 1995. Specified injuries include (regulation 4):

- a fracture, other than to fingers, thumbs and toes;
- amputation of an arm, hand, finger, thumb, leg, foot or toe;
- permanent loss of sight or reduction of sight;
- crush injuries leading to internal organ damage;
- serious burns (covering more than 10% of the body, or damaging the eyes, respiratory system or other vital organs);
- scalpings (separation of skin from the head) which require hospital treatment;
- unconsciousness caused by head injury or asphyxia;
- any other injury arising from working in an enclosed space, which leads to hypothermia, heat-induced illness or requires resuscitation or admittance to hospital for more than 24 hours.

Over-Seven-Day Injuries to Workers

This is where an employee, or self-employed person, is away from work or unable to perform their normal work duties for more than seven consecutive days (not counting the day of the accident).

SIMPLY SAFETY

Injuries to Non-Workers

You must report injuries to members of the public or people who are not at work if they are injured through a work-related accident, and are taken from the scene of the accident to hospital for treatment to that injury. Examinations and diagnostic tests do not constitute 'treatment' in such circumstances. There is no need to report incidents where people are taken to hospital purely as a precaution when no injury is apparent.

If the accident occurred at a hospital, the report only needs to be made if the injury is a 'specified injury' (see above).

Reportable Occupational Diseases

Employers and self-employed people must report diagnoses of certain occupational diseases, where these are likely to have been caused or made worse by their work:

These diseases include (regulations 8 and 9):

- carpal tunnel syndrome;
- severe cramp of the hand or forearm;
- occupational dermatitis;
- hand-arm vibration syndrome;
- occupational asthma;
- tendonitis or tenosynovitis of the hand or forearm;
- any occupational cancer;
- any disease attributed to an occupational exposure to a biological agent

Reportable Dangerous Occurrences

Dangerous occurrences are certain, specified near-miss events. Not all such events require reporting. There are 27 categories of dangerous occurrences that are relevant to most workplaces. For example: -

- the collapse, overturning or failure of load-bearing parts of lifts and lifting equipment;
- plant or equipment coming into contact with overhead power lines;
- the accidental release of any substance which could cause injury to any person. Certain additional categories of dangerous occurrences apply to mines, quarries, offshore workplaces and certain transport systems (railways etc). For a full, detailed list, refer to the online guidance at: www.hse.gov.uk/riddor.

Reportable Gas Incidents

If you are a distributor, filler, importer or supplier of flammable gas and you learn, either directly or indirectly, that someone has died, lost consciousness, or been taken to hospital for treatment to an injury arising in connection with the gas you distributed, filled, imported or supplied, this can be reported online.

First Aid and Accident Reporting

If you are a gas engineer registered with the Gas Safe Register you must provide details of any gas appliances or fittings that you consider to be dangerous to the extent that people could die, lose consciousness or require hospital treatment. This may be due to the design, construction, installation, modification or servicing, and could result in:

- an accidental leakage of gas;
- inadequate combustion of gas; or
- inadequate removal of products of the combustion of gas.

It is important to note that the amendments to the Reporting of Injuries, Diseases and Dangerous Occurrences Regulations (RIDDOR) 1995 that make up the Reporting of Injuries, Diseases and Dangerous Occurrences Regulations (RIDDOR) 2013 do not affect how an incident at work is reported and the criteria that determine whether an incident should be investigated.

REPORTING AN INCIDENT

ARE YOU AN EMPLOYER OR IN CONTROL OF PREMISES

If you are an employer

If you are an employer, you must report any work-related deaths, injuries, cases of disease, or near misses involving your employees wherever they are working.

If you are in control of premises,

If you are in control of premises, you must report any work-related deaths and injuries to members of the public and self-employed people on your premises, and dangerous occurrences (some near miss incidents) that occur on your premises.

If you are Self-employed

If you are working in someone else's work premises and suffer either a major injury or an over-seven-day injury, then the ***person in control of the premises*** will be responsible for reporting, so, where possible, you should make sure they know about it.

If there is a reportable accident while you are working on your own premises or in domestic premises, or if a doctor tells you that you have a work-related disease or condition, then ***you*** need to report it.

If you are a Gas supplier

If you are a distributor, filler, importer or supplier of flammable gas and you learn, either directly or indirectly that someone has died or suffered a major injury in connection with the gas you distributed, filled, imported or supplied, then this must be reported immediately.

If you are a Gas Engineer

If you are a gas engineer registered with the Gas Safe Register, you must provide details of any gas appliances or fittings that you consider to be dangerous, to such an extent that people could die or suffer a major injury, because the design, construction, installation, modification or servicing could result in:

- an accidental leakage of gas
- inadequate combustion of gas or

SIMPLY SAFETY

- inadequate removal of products of the combustion of gas

NOTE. The Gas Safe Register replaced CORGI gas registration in Great Britain on 1st April 2009.

If you are Working offshore

Operations Notice 30, which was revised and reissued in April 2012 provides extensive guidance on the reporting procedure for offshore workers.

WAYS TO REPORT AN INCIDENT AT WORK

ONLINE

The employer should complete the appropriate online report form listed below. The form will then be submitted directly to the RIDDOR database. The employer will receive a copy for their records.

- F2508 Report of an injury
- F2508 Report of a Dangerous Occurrence
- F2508A Report of a Case of Disease
- OIR9B Report of an Injury Offshore
- OIR9B Report of a Dangerous Occurrence Offshore
- F2508G1 Report of a Flammable Gas Incident
- F2508G2 Report of a Dangerous Gas Fitting

TELEPHONE

All incidents can be reported online but a telephone service remains for reporting fatal and major injuries **only** - call the Incident Contact Centre on 0845 300 9923 (opening hours Monday to Friday 8.30 am to 5 pm).

REPORTING OUT OF HOURS

The HSE and local authority enforcement officers are not an emergency service. You should contact your enforcing authority out of hours in the following circumstances:

- fatal accidents at work
- accidents where several workers have been seriously injured
- accidents resulting in serious injury to a member of the public
- accidents and incidents causing major disruption, such as evacuation of people, closure of roads, large numbers of people going to hospital etc

If your incident fits these descriptions ring the duty officer on 0151 922 9235.

The Employer can also make a report to their Local Environmental Health Department, provided that their business falls into one of the following categories:

- office-based
- retail or wholesale

First Aid and Accident Reporting

- warehousing
- hotel and catering
- sports or leisure
- residential accommodation, excluding nursing homes
- concerned with places of worship
- pre-school child care
- mobile vending

The address and telephone number will be in the telephone book under the local authority's name.

For all other types of business it will be the HSE's area office and you as the employer can find the telephone number and address in the telephone book under the HSE.

Employers and members of the public seeking information and official guidance on health and safety can use the HSE's website - a huge knowledge bank where people can access and download information free of charge and use interactive web tools.

The HSE website features information on the most frequent health and safety enquiries such as those on RIDDOR reporting, First Aid and the health and safety responsibilities of new businesses. It currently receives 26 million visits every year and is regularly updated and improved to help businesses and members of the public quickly access the information they need.

The HSE continues to provide information and guidance to employers and workers in a range of other ways: through direct work with organisations and trade associations, face-to-face at workshops and safety training days and via books and e-bulletins. A comprehensive suite of health and safety advice is also available via the Government's website for businesses: -

"Businesslink.gov" -
http://www.businesslink.gov.uk/bdotg/action/layer?r.s=tl&topicId=1073858799

and

"Direct Gov." - http://www.direct.gov.uk/en/Employment/HealthAndSafetyAtWork/index.htm

SIMPLY SAFETY

ACCIDENT INVESTIGATION AND REPORTING

It is important that following any accident/incident that an investigation takes place and that a full report is written.

The purpose of the report and investigation is not to apportion blame – merely to establish the facts surrounding the incident's causes, in order to prevent recurrence. The report sets out a record of who, what, where, when and how the accident / incident occurred. It should be remembered, however, that independent bodies and insurance companies may see the report at a later stage, and that it may potentially be used as evidence in any later civil claims or court proceedings.

The report should be written in the past tense. The reasoning behind this is that the report will be read and reread after the incident has long since passed, and it will seem odd if written in the present tense. It is important to resist the temptation to allocate blame directly to named individuals; it is better to state that, for example, 'the Office Manager failed to follow the laid down procedure' rather that to state that it was the Office Managers fault.

There is no set way that you as the employer must follow to write up an investigation; however, they may like to adopt the following suggested format. The front page should include the following information:

- details of the injured person (ie name and department (for employees)/address (for non-employees))
- the name and postal address of where the accident/incident occurred
- day, date and time of accident/incident;
- name and job title of the person writing the report
- contents/index page

It is recommended that the format of the report should be as follows. Details of the suggested contents of the report are given below along with suitable headings.

General introduction:

This section of the report should give a general introduction to the report and a description of the accident location. For example – The main boiler room in basement of 'XYZ building', a 15-storey office building etc. (Remember to include descriptions of machinery, access, egress, lighting etc.)

Report on incident:

This section of the report should give a detailed description of what the situation was before the incident, actions that led to the incident, the event itself (including details of injuries, damage etc) and any immediate action taken after the incident occurred. This should include the training and competency of the injured party or team and type of equipment being used at the time of the accident.

First Aid and Accident Reporting

Additional information:

This section of the report should include any other relevant information not necessarily included in the immediate cause of the incident (e.g. previous reports on unsafe conditions, improvement notices, minutes of meetings etc).

Conclusions:

This section of the report should be a balanced view of what caused the accident/incident based on the evidence collected. It is important to clearly identify the primary cause and any secondary causes. At all times the information given in the report must be kept factual.

Actions taken since the incident:

This section of the report should detail any follow-up actions taken as a result of the incident but before more formal procedures are put in place. For example, details in any alterations in method of working, isolation of areas, etc. These are usually primary cause remedies.

Recommendations:

This section of the report should detail any suitable improvements to procedures, methods of working etc that will improve the prevailing conditions that led to the incident occurring and to prevent similar incidences in the future. Both primary and secondary cause remedies should be included with time scales recommended for implementation. The author should then sign the report off. Perhaps include advice re an action plan for this section including what is to be completed by who and by when...?

Statements:

This section of the report should include copies of statements taken and verbal explanations given by witnesses and injured parties. Where they are available, typed copies should be placed first with any manuscripts behind in the same order as the typed copies. Included in the statements should be the employee's details (name, department, position etc) or in the case of non-employees their name and address, occupation and employer's details along with their date of birth. The witnesses should be asked to sign the statement with the person recording the statement witnessing the signatures. It should be remembered that the witnesses/injured persons are entitled to have a copy of the statement – it is after all their statement.

Photographs:

Where possible photographs should be taken showing the area where the accident/incident occurred. Copies of these photographs should be included within this section, suitably annotated with captions under photos. It is important to include both detailed, close-up views and general views showing the location etc. Remember a picture can speak a thousand words!

Appendices:

This should include copies of the following:
- layout drawing showing the location of the accident/incident, folded to A4 size if larger;
- copies of the Accident Book entry;
- copies of F.2508 (*RIDDOR*) report;

SIMPLY SAFETY

- copies of pertinent risk assessments, method statements, permits to work etc;
- copies of any training records etc;
- copies of any previous audit/inspection reports that may have a bearing on this accident/incident and any follow-up reports.

KEEPING ACCIDENT / INCIDENT INVESTIGATION RECORDS

It is important that appropriate records are kept. This can be achieved for example by keeping copies of the completed RIDDOR report forms. Equally, the information about the accident / incident can be entered onto suitable computer software. An aid to investigation for you as the employer is the form shown TABLE (5.04).

Copies of any and all accident/incident investigation reports should also be kept along with any other documentation referring to the accident/incident and any follow-up action taken.

For more information on RIDDOR the employer should now refer to www.hse.gov.uk/riddor/index.htm.

TABLE 5.04: - SAMPLE ACCIDENT / NEAR-MISS REPORT

ACCIDENT / NEAR MISS REPORT				Form: AR10	
Copy sent to: Manager ☐ H&S Dept. ☐ Personnel File ☐			Report number:	Date	
A	Details of person making the report	Name	Job Title	Extension	
B	Details of Injured person				
	Name		Age	Sex	
	Home address and postcode		Job Title	Extension	
			Employee ☐	Contractor ☐	Visitor ☐	Public ☐
			Date of accident / incident		
			Time of accident / incident		
			Location (Building/Floor/Location)		
C	Details of Employer if not the Company				
	Name		Contact	Telephone	
	Address			Postcode	
D	Was the injury *(please tick the one that applies)*				

First Aid and Accident Reporting

	A fatality?	☐	A major injury or condition?	☐
	An injury, which prevented them doing their normal work for more than 7 days?	☐	An injury to a member of the public, which meant they had to be taken from the scene of the accident to a hospital for treatment?	☐
	An injury that required first aid treatment	☐	None of the above?	☐
E	Did the injured person *(please tick the one that applies)*			
	Become unconscious?	☐	Remain in hospital for more than 24 hrs?	☐
	Need resuscitation?	☐	None of the above	☐
F	Please tick the one box that best describes what happened			
	Contact with moving machinery	☐	Drowned or asphyxiated	☐
	Hit by a moving, flying or falling object	☐	Exposed to, or in contact with, a harmful substance	☐
	Hit by a moving vehicle	☐	Exposed to fire	☐
	Hit something fixed or stationary	☐	Exposed to an explosion	☐
	Injured while handling, lifting or carrying	☐	Contact with electricity or an electrical discharge	☐
	Slipped, tripped or fell on the same level	☐	Physically assaulted by a person	☐
	Fell from a height. How high was the fall in metres ?	☐	Cut or pierced by a sharp object	☐
	Trapped by something collapsing	☐	Another kind of accident	☐
G	State fully what happened: *Give as much detail as you can. Please include where relevant the names of any substance involved, name and type of any machinery involved, events that lead to the incident, part played by any people and the names and addresses of any witnesses. If it involves personal injury, please give details of what the person was doing.*			

SIMPLY SAFETY

CHAPTER 6
FIRE

FIRE RISK ASSESSMENT

REGULATORY REFORM (FIRE SAFETY) ORDER 2005 (*RR(FS)O 2005*)

The Regulatory Reform (Fire Safety) Order 2005 came into effect in October 2006 and replaced over 70 pieces of fire safety law.

The Regulatory Reform (Fire Safety) Order 2005 applies to all non-domestic premises in England and Wales, including the common parts of blocks of flats and houses which are in multiple occupation. The law applies to you if you are:

- responsible for business premises
- an employer or self-employed with business premises
- responsible for a part of a dwelling where that part is *solely* used for business purposes
- a charity or voluntary organisation
- a contractor with a degree of control over any premises
- providing accommodation for paying guests

Under this legislation a 'responsible person' must carry out a fire safety risk assessment and implement and maintain a fire management plan.

What were the main changes for the employer?

- A 'responsible person' has the role of compliance with the new legislation. This will generally be the employer in a workplace or in fact anyone person who may have control of all or part of the premises.
- Fire certificates are no longer be issued.
- Emphasis is on risk reduction and fire prevention.
- The responsible person must carry out a fire risk assessment of their premises and action all of the findings identified as a result of this fire risk assessment.

The 'responsible person' must as far as is reasonably practical make sure that everyone on the premises, or nearby, can escape safely if there is a fire.

Authors Note:

This is different from previous legislation in that you must consider everyone who might be on your premises, whether they are employees, visitors or members of the public, for example, at an open-air entertainment venue. You should also pay particular attention to people who may have a disability or anyone who may need special help. Don't forget to consider staff who may have a temporary disability e.g. a broken leg following a weekend sporting accident. How will you get them out of the building safely without impeding other members of staff? Consider using a personal evacuation plan for this purpose.

Although the core duties remain the same as above, different legislation applies to Northern Ireland and Scotland as follows:

- *Fire and Rescue Services (Northern Ireland) Order 2006 (SI 2006/1254) (FRS(NI)O 2006).*
- *Fire Safety (Scotland) Regulations 2006 (SI 2006/456) (FS(S)R 2006)* and *Fire Safety (Scotland) Act 2005 (FS(S)A 2005).*
- In addition the *Building Regulations* apply for each country.

WHAT ARE THE KEY DUTIES FOR YOU AS THE EMPLOYER?

This section seeks to summarise the key duties for the employer from a health and safety point of view.

Clearly, in maintaining the overall obligation to maintain a safe workplace, addressing the issue of fire prevention and fire risk assessment is a key task for you as an employer and your management team.

For the purposes of this chapter the key legislation is:

- *Regulatory Reform (Fire Safety) Order 2005 (SI 2005/1541) (RR(FS)O 2005).*
- *Health and Safety at Work etc. Act 1974 (HSWA 1974).*
- *Management of Health and Safety at Work Regulations 1999 (SI 1999/3242) (MHSWR 1999).*

Applying to most types of premises that are likely to be of concern to employers, these regulations explicitly provide that a general risk assessment must be carried out for their premises (see Chapter 3: Risk assessment – requirements and definitions),which should be supplemented by a specific risk assessment for fire (*SI 1999/3242, Reg 3*).

The *RR(FS)O 2005* places responsibility for complying with the new fire legislation with the 'responsible person'. In a workplace, this is the employer and any other person who may have control of any part of the premises, such as the occupier or owner. In all other premises the person or people in control of the premises will be responsible, eg employer. If there is more than one responsible person in any type of premises, all must take all reasonable steps to work with each other. In reality the 'responsible person' will no doubt be the employer who will have the task of completing out a risk assessment to demonstrate that the fire safety precautions are adequate. Principles of prevention are identified in the *RR(FS)O 2005* that are similar to generic risk assessment guidance – avoidance, replacing dangerous by less dangerous materials, provision of protective measures etc. Some of the important aspects are summarised here:

A full definition of **general fire precautions** is given in Article 4 of the Regulatory Reform (Fire Safety) Order 2005 as follows:

(a) measures to reduce the risk of fire on the premises and the risk of spread of fire on the premises:

(b) measures in relation to the means of escape from the premises;

SIMPLY SAFETY

    (c)   measures for securing that, at all material times, the means of escape can be safely and effectively used;

    (d)   measures in relation to the means for fighting fires on the premises;

    (e)   measures in relation to the means for detecting fire on the premises and giving warning in the case of fire on the premises; and

    (f)   measures in relation to the arrangements for action to be taken in the event of fire on the premises, including –

        (i)   measures relating to the instruction and training of employees; and

        (ii)   measures to mitigate the effects of the fire.

The *RR(FS)O 2005* does not detail how the actual fire risk assessment should be undertaken however by applying the key stages of a general risk assessment the fire risk would look no different from those outlined in the five stages of preparation of a general risk assessment in Chapter 3: Risk Assessment and Management.

What is the Objective of a Fire Risk Assessment?

The Responsible Person e.g. Employer must:

- Identify fire hazards and people at risk and eliminate or control the risk of those hazards causing harm to as low as is reasonably practicable.
- to determine what fire safety measures and management policies are necessary to ensure the safety of people in the building should a fire break out; by
- Reducing the probability of a fire starting.
- Ensuring that all occupants are alerted and can leave the premises safely in the event of a fire.
- Limiting the effects should a fire occur.

Providing the premises have been built and maintained in accordance with building regulations and are of normal risk or lower, then this should be fairly straight forward.. However if the premises are not in accordance with the building regulations or are very complex with high risk processes carried out on site then further guidance and action will be necessary. In such cases then it is recommended that the employer seeks the appropriate skills and expertise to assist.

THE FIVE STAGES FOR THE PREPARATION OF A FIRE RISK ASSESSMENT ARE AS FOLLOWS:

1. Identify potential fire hazards in the workplace.
2. Decide who, in the event of a fire, might be in danger in the workplace or while trying to escape from it, and note their location.
3. Evaluate the risks arising from the hazards and decide whether existing fire precautions are adequate or whether more should be done to eliminate the hazard or to control the risks, eg by improving the fire precautions.
4. Record the findings and details of the action taken as a result, create a plan to deal with emergencies and tell employees about the findings.
5. Keep the assessment under review and revise it when necessary.

Fire

DEPARTMENT FOR COMMUNITIES & LOCAL GOVERNMENT

The Department for Communities and Local Government (DCLG) supports the work of the Fire and Rescue Service (FRS) in reducing the incidence of accidental and deliberate fires in the home and in commercial premises and other public buildings by providing fire safety risk assessment guidance to those who are seeking advice on how to comply with the provisions of the Fire Safety Order - usually employers or owners/occupiers of commercial premises and buildings to which the public have access.

To assist the employer a set of fourteen guides has been developed to tell you what you have to do to comply with fire safety law, help you to carry out a fire risk assessment and identify the general fire precautions you need to have in place.

The guides are available for download from the Communities web site at:

http://www.communities.gov.uk/fire/firesafety/firesafetylaw/

Identification of Potential Fire Hazards

In the case of fire, this means identifying means by which a fire can start. Fire requires three things – a source of ignition (Heat), eg from a faulty or damaged electrical cable, fuel, eg combustible materials left in an area due to poor housekeeping and oxygen (see Triangle of fire below). You are unlikely to be able to do much about oxygen, but you can minimise and control fuel and ignition sources and break the triangle of fire.

Do not consider these in isolation. It is particularly where a source of fuel and a source of ignition (Heat) occur close together that the risk factor may be magnified.

Table 6.01 Triangle of Fire

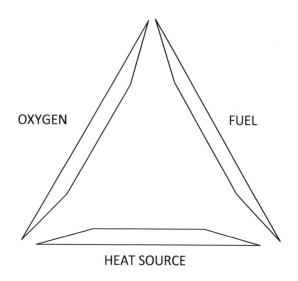

SIMPLY SAFETY

Assess Personnel Affected

You will need to consider how your staff will be warned of a fire and then how they will be evacuated from the building to a place of safety. As already highlighted above you, as the employer, should give special consideration to disabled persons and also staff with a temporary disability from, for example, a weekend sports injury. You will also need to consider how to handle visitors, contractors and others who may be affected by a fire incident.

Evaluate Risks and Current Control Measures

Once you have carried out your assessment, you will need to identify the areas where further remedial work is required to reduce the risks of fire in your workplace. If you have taken over an existing workplace with a current fire certificate, it may be that all that is required is to maintain existing systems and procedures. However if you are setting up systems from scratch, then you will need to consider several areas:

- reducing sources of fuel
- reducing sources of ignition
- detecting a fire and warning occupants
- means of escape
- fire fighting
- information and training for staff
- appointment and training of fire wardens

Potential Sources of Fuel and Unsafe Situations:

- Combustible Materials – These can be sub divided into two main groups; organic fuels such as paper, wood, cardboard, etc.; highly combustible fuels such as thinners, solvents, polyurethane foam, etc.
- Unsafe procedures or acts – Persons undertaking unsafe acts such as smoking next to combustible materials, use of non-intrinsically safe electrical equipment adjacent to chemicals giving off vapor etc.
- Unsafe conditions – Hazards that may assist a fire to spread in your workplace, e.g. if there are large areas of hardboard or polystyrene tiles etc., or open stairs that can cause a fire to spread quickly, trapping people and involving the whole building.
- Poor housekeeping. Storage of combustible materials under desks causing plugs and sockets to overheat, flammable chemicals not stored away properly, storage of combustible materials under stairs or within fire exit routes. (This last point should be picked up within the audit program of the building but Fire Wardens should be trained to spot such hazards on an ongoing daily basis and to ensure such items are cleared.)

Possible Sources of Ignition are:

- Defective electrical fittings and defective or misuse of electrical apparatus – light bulbs and fluorescent tubes too close to combustible materials, misuse or defective electrical extension leads and adapters, faulty or damaged wiring. (Ensure that

Fire

Electrical and PAT testing of equipment is carried out as part of the planned maintenance regime.)
- Matches, Lighters, Candles and Smoking materials.
- Flame or sparks from a work process such as welding, cutting, grinding or the use of a hot air gun.
- Arson - malicious ignition of combustible materials left around your building
- Electrostatic discharges.
- Ovens, kilns, open hearths, furnaces or incinerators.
- Boilers, engines and other oil burning equipment.
- Portable/Temporary heaters. (Ensure that PAT testing and pre user checks are completed before use.)
- Cooking equipment, including deep fat fryers.

Authors Note: *The above list is by no means exhaustive and is intended purely as a guide only.*

Record your Findings and Actions

Having carried out your fire risk assessment for the premises the new *Regulatory Reform (Fire Safety) Order 2005 (SI 2005/1541)* requires the 'responsible person' to record your findings and create an emergency plan to deal with any fire related emergency. This record should be retained and made available, on request, to the enforcing authority

As with any risk assessment it is important that a full record be kept of your activities. In particular you should do the following:

- Date the assessment was made
- Record the results of your risk assessment including hazards identified
- The actions that need to be taken as a result
- Identify any staff or other people at risk
- Record all maintenance activities including testing of fire alarm system, emergency lighting and fire appliances
- Record all training, including results of practice evacuations and fire marshal training
- Log all checks on means of escape
- Conclusions ascertained from the assessment

Revise Your Procedures as Necessary

You should review your procedures on a regular basis. They may need to be changed if your work processes change or if your workplace does, for example after a refurbishment project. Resist the temptation to make unnecessary changes to procedures as this may confuse staff unnecessarily. Remember also that if you do make alterations to your workplace that affect the means of escape or fire precautions you must take this into account and revise your fire risk assessment.

FIRE LOG BOOK

It is best practice for the responsible person / employer to collate all records of maintenance, testing, training and drills in one location within a fire log book. This will provide one focal point

SIMPLY SAFETY

for maintenance of fire records and will enable audit/inspections to be more easily effected by auditors or the local fire brigade.

Typical headings in a fire log book should include:

- Fire risk assessment.
- Details, location and maintenance of:
    o   fire fighting equipment (portable)
    o   emergency lighting
    o   fire detection systems
    o   sprinklers
    o   dry/wet risers
    o   smoke vents
- Means of escape (routes, doors, signage).
- Fire drills, records and reports.
- Weekly call point tests (fire alarm test).
- Instruction and training.

FIRE WARDENS AND GENERAL STAFF TRAINING

If a workplace or building is relatively small then the fire risk assessment may identify that a simple roll call system could be used to account for staff following any evacuation. However, for larger, more complex situations then the appointment of fire wardens and deputies will have to be used and it is important that, if this system is utilised, the role must be covered at all times during absenteeism caused through sickness, training or holidays. One way of covering this situation is to combine the fire warden's role with that of a security guard or other role that has to be present.

The appointment of fire wardens may be identified as a control measure within the fire risk assessment itself and in most cases form a key part of the ongoing fire prevention element. A principal fire warden may be appointed and in practice this may well be the employer. There must be at least one fire warden for each floor or designated area and these numbers will need to be increased for large or complex buildings. It is essential that the fire wardens are proactive all of the time and maintain a careful eye on what is happening around them and if they see the potential for problems, eg items gradually encroaching into a fire exit, then they must feel empowered to report such problems to the employer or principal fire warden.

The fire wardens must be provided with proper training and refresher training to be able to carry out the task.

General duties of a fire warden are:

- Identification of fire hazards in their workplace.
- Ensure that fire escape routes are maintained and kept clear at all times.
- Escalate issues identified above to management.
- In a fire situation they must ensure that the alarm is raised. (This may be through breaking a call point.)
- Ensure that all staff is evacuated safely.
- Ensure that disabled staff is evacuated.
- Fight the fire but only if trained to do so and if the escape route is clear.

ENFORCEMENT

The Regulatory Reform (Fire Safety) Order is enforced by periodic inspections or audits by the enforcing authority usually the local Fire and Rescue Authorities who are empowered to issue alterations, enforcement or prohibition notices under the Fire Safety Order.

DEFINITIONS OF NOTICES

Alterations Notice

An alteration notice may be served on the responsible person if the Fire and Rescue Authority is of the opinion that any structural alterations being made to the premises will constitute a serious risk to relevant persons (whether due to features of the premises, their use, and any hazard present or any other circumstances).

Enforcement Notice

Where the Fire and Rescue Authority is of the opinion that the responsible person or other person mentioned in Article 5(3) has failed to comply with any provision of the Fire Safety Order.

Prohibition Notice

Where the Fire and Rescue Authority is of the opinion that the risk to persons in case of fire, is so serious it will be necessary for the Authority to prohibit or restrict the use of parts of the premises until the specified matters have been remedied.

THE DANGEROUS SUBSTANCES AND EXPLOSIVE ATMOSPHERES REGULATIONS 2002

Certain provisions of The Dangerous Substances and Explosive Atmospheres Regulations 2002 (DSEAR) has been included into the RR(FS)O and has extended the requirement to mitigate the detrimental effects of a fire to all premises covered by the RR(FS)O. Employers are advised that when conducting your Fire Risk Assessment, if you use or store dangerous substances you must also consider DSEAR and how it will affect your general fire precautions.

Further Information

Further information may be found in:

- The *Regulatory Reform (Fire Safety) Order 2005 (SI 2005/1541)*, which can be downloaded from: www.opsi.gov.uk/si/si2005/20051541.htm.
- The fire safety risk assessment guides, available from: www.communities.gov.uk/fire/firesafety/.
- The Fire Protection Association: www.thefpa.co.uk.
- The Fire Services College: www.fireservicescollege.ac.uk
- Your local authority/fire brigade website.

CHAPTER 7
WORKPLACE WELFARE PROVISION

Welfare Provision – Overview

All workplaces must provide a minimum level of facilities in order to be compliant with health and safety law. Facilities concerned include lighting, temperature, sanitary and washing facilities, space standards and workstations. There are other issues too, necessitating policies on security, smoking, stress, alcohol and drugs, and lone working. Many of these areas will require you to liaise effectively with senior management and human resources, as an overall company policy will need to be agreed.

The main legislation that refers specifically to workplace environment is the *Workplace (Health, Safety and Welfare) Regulations 1992 (SI 1992/3004) (W(HSW)R 1992)*, as amended September 2002 by the Health and Safety (Miscellaneous Amendment) Regulations 2002) (SI 2002/2174) (HS(MA)R 2002). These regulations and the associated Approved Code of Practice (ACOP) L24 prescribe specific standards in support of these regulations. For more information on these regulations, see the *Appendices*.

In addition, the HSE have published a short guide for managers relating to workplace health, safety and welfare, IND(G) 244, which is available for download from the HSE website: www.hse.gov.uk.

These regulations apply to all workplaces with the exception of workplaces involving construction sites, those in or on a ship, or those below ground in a mine. In these cases the *Quarries Regulations 1999 (SI 1999/2024) (QR 1999)*, the *Health and Safety (Miscellaneous Amendments) Regulations 2002 (SI 2002/2174) (HS(MA)R 2002)*, the *Work at Height Regulations 2005 (SI 2005/735) (WAHR 2005)* and the *Construction (Design and Management) Regulations 2007 (SI 2007/320) (C(DM)R 2007)* would apply.

The employer (employer) will most likely be affected by a range of the regulations in the management of the workplace and should therefore be aware of the main requirements which are as follows:

- To ensure workplaces have stability and solidity appropriate to the nature of the work being undertaken.
- The provision of toilets, washing and drying facilities, accommodation for clothing, drinking water and eating area.
- The provision of safe workstations and seating. (Also covered by the *Health and Safety (Display Screen Equipment) Regulations 1992 (SI 1992/2792) (HS(DSE)R 1992)*: see ?.???.)
- To maintain the workplace and all associated workplace equipment by way of planned maintenance.
- The provision of adequate heating, lighting and ventilation. (Further guidance is provided in the HSE guidance document *Lighting at Work* HSG38.)
- To ensure the workplace is adequately cleaned and waste bins emptied.
- To ensure that persons and objects are prevented from falling any distance.

Workplace Welfare Provision

- The provision of traffic and pedestrian routes that are free of potholes, slopes, obstructions, uneven or slippery surfaces.
- To ensure that traffic and pedestrian routes are segregated to enable safe passage. (Further guidance is provided in the HSE guidance document *Workplace Transport Safety* HSG136.)
- To ensure that windows are made of safety materials to prevent breakage and injury.
- To ensure that windows operate correctly to facilitate safe opening and may be cleaned in a safe manner and will not pose a risk when open.
- To ensure that gates, doors and escalators are suitable for intended purpose and fitted with safety devices.

The following topics are covered in more detail, because they are most likely to impact on the decisions made by the employer.

Toilets and Washing Facilities

Toilets should be provided for male and female staff. If there are unisex toilets then these should be lockable from the inside. Toilets should be clean and well ventilated and have adequate lighting and hot and cold running water. In female toilets feminine hygiene facilities should be provided. Then numbers of toilets are prescribed in the ACOP L24 mentioned above and in the Appendices, Facilities for mixed use or women only are as listed in Table 7:01 below

Table 7:01 - Mixed Use (or Women Only)

People	Number of toilets	Wash basins
1–5	1	1
6–25	2	2
26–50	3	3
51–75	4	4
76–100	5	5

If you have only male staff then different provisions apply. Also bear in mind that you must make some provision for disabled access.

If staff are required to wash in the course of their work, for example if they are using hazardous substances, then you must provide adequate washing facilities. These should be clean, well lit and ventilated, and soap and towels should be provided. Separate male and female facilities should be provided unless a single unit can be locked from the inside. Prescribed numbers of units for use by men only are listed in Table 7:02

SIMPLY SAFETY

Table 7:02 - Toilets for Use by Men Only

Men	Toilets	Wash basins
1–15	1	1
16–30	2	1
31–45	2	2
46–60	3	2
61–75	3	3
76–90	4	3
91–100	4	4

Changing facilities must follow the same format; you should also provide secure lockers to avoid theft and if hazardous substances are involved in the work activities it should be possible to separate work clothes from employees' own clothes. Changing facilities should be easily accessible from washing facilities. You should provide seating and a means of hanging clothes.

Remember that for toilets, washing areas and changing areas it is not enough simply to provide them. You must have in place a system to ensure that they are adequately cleaned and maintained; for example that consumables are regularly replenished, lights are replaced as necessary and damage, such as broken tiles, is repaired as soon as possible.

Food and Water

You must provide an adequate source of clean drinking water. This must be either from the public water supply or from suitable bottled dispensers. Adequate supplies should be provided for the numbers of staff and to suit the demands of the work activity. They must be clearly labelled as drinking water and cups should be provided.

If food is eaten at work you should provide an area where it can be eaten with minimum disruption; this may require a separate designated area, and it certainly will do if there is any risk of food being contaminated by workplace activities. In many cases existing seating areas will be sufficient. You should provide a means for workers to make hot drinks. If there is no opportunity for them to obtain hot food, for example if the workplace is at some distance from shops, cafés and so on and if you have no staff canteen of your own, then you should provide facilities for their own food to be heated, for example a microwave.

Workplace Welfare Provision

Temperature in the Workplace

This is a subject that causes much discussion and debate. Often this is because a temperature that is entirely satisfactory for one member of staff is the cause of perceived discomfort to another working in the same office. As all employers will agree, you will never please everyone but the actual legal guidance is relatively straightforward.

The temperature of the workplace must be reasonable. The ACOP states that the minimum temperature should be at least 16°C, unless there is significant physical activity, in which case it should be at least 13°C. In assessing what is reasonable, beyond this guideline, due regard should be paid to the activity in the particular workplace. For example in a general office area where most work involves prolonged sedentary activity it is unlikely that a temperature of 16°C would be regarded as acceptable, and would indeed lead to serious complaints from staff. For light sedentary occupations such as office work the employer should aim for a temperature of 22°C plus or minus 2 degrees. In the summer a temperature of 24.5°C plus or minus 1.5 degrees is deemed to be acceptable.

There is no prescribed maximum temperature for the workplace.

Work in Hot or Cold Environments

The risk to the health of workers increases as conditions move further away from those generally accepted as comfortable. Risk of heat stress arises, for example, from working in high air temperatures, exposure to high thermal radiation or high levels of humidity, such as those found in foundries, glass works and laundries. Cold stress may arise, for example, from working in cold stores, food preparation areas and in the open air during winter.

The employer will need to complete an assessment of the risk to workers' health from working in either a hot or cold environment needs to consider both personal and environmental factors. Personal factors include body activity, the amount and type of clothing, and duration of exposure. Environmental factors include ambient temperature and radiant heat; and if the work is outside, sunlight, wind velocity and the presence of rain or snow.

Actions arising from your assessment may include:

- Introduction of engineering measures to control the thermal effects in a workplace environment, for example heat effects, may involve insulating any plant which acts as a radiant heat source, thereby improving air movement, increasing ventilation rates and maintaining the appropriate level of humidity. The radiant heat effects of the sun on indoor environments can be addressed either by orientating the building so that it doesn't suffer from the effects of solar loading, or where this is not possible, by the use of blinds or shutters on windows. Where workers are exposed to cold and it is not reasonably practicable to avoid exposure you should consider, for example, using cab heaters in fork-lift trucks in cold stores;
- Restricting exposure by, for example, re-organising tasks to build in rest periods or other breaks from work. This will allow workers to rest in an area where the environment is comfortable and, if necessary, to replace bodily fluids to combat dehydration or cold. If work rates cause excessive sweating, workers may need more frequent rest breaks and a facility for changing into dry clothing;
- Medical pre-selection of employees to ensure that they are fit to work in these environments;

SIMPLY SAFETY

- Use of suitable personal protective clothing (which may need to be heat resistant or insulating, depending on whether the risk is from heat or cold);
- Acclimatisation of workers to the environment in which they work, particularly for hot environments;
- Training in the precautions to be taken; and
- Supervision, to ensure that the precautions identified by the assessment are taken.

For further advice on thermal comfort in the workplace may be found on the HSE website at: www.hse.gov.uk/temperature/thermal

Smoking

Smoking is a leading cause of premature death in the UK. It is now also generally believed that passive smoking can lead to serious health problems for non-smokers. Under the *Health Act 2006* smoking has been banned in virtually all 'enclosed' and 'substantially enclosed' public places and workplaces. This includes both permanent structures and temporary structures such as tents and marquees as well as company vehicles. It also means that smoking rooms in both public and workplaces are not permitted. The law also states that the person with management responsibility for the premises or vehicle (the employer) is legally responsible for preventing smoking.

The effects upon the employer are as follows:

- Work vehicles used by more than one person will have to be smokefree.
- No-smoking signs will have to be displayed in all smokefree premises and vehicles.
- Employee smoking rooms and indoor smoking areas will no longer be allowed and therefore smokers will have to go outside.
- There are now legal duties to prevent people smoking in smokefree premises and vehicles.
- There are new penalties for failure to display no-smoking signs and failure to prevent smoking in a smokefree place.

Definitions

Premises

Premises will be considered 'enclosed' if they have a ceiling or roof and (except for doors, windows or passageways) are wholly enclosed either on a permanent or temporary basis.

Premises will be considered 'substantially enclosed' if they have a ceiling or roof, but have an opening in the walls, which is less than half the total area of the walls. The area of the opening does not include doors, windows or any other fittings that can be opened or shut

There is no requirement for the employer to provide outdoor smoking shelters for employees or members of the public.

If you as the employer decide to build a shelter, it is suggested that you discusses any plans you may have with your local council, as there may be a range of issues which need to be

Workplace Welfare Provision

considered. These might include planning permission, licensing, building control, noise and litter.

As the employer you should note that the Department of Health does not provide advice on the design or construction of smoking shelters.

If you want to provide a permanent smoking shelter for your staff or customers what should you do?

Contact the Council Planning Services for their advice and the necessary forms to apply for planning approval, because in most cases any permanent structure that is erected for smoking will require planning permission.

Check to see if the shelter will require Building Regulation approval. In most instances, provided the shelter is detached and of a modest size, no Building Regulation permission will be required. If however the floor area of the shelter exceeds 15m² there may be restrictions if the shelter is within 1m of a boundary. Any shelter over 30m² will require Building Regulation Approval. Also contact Building Control if your intended shelter is to be attached to another building.

To avoid a costly mistake, carefully check that the design of the smoking shelter will comply with the requirements of the Smoke-free (Premises and Enforcement) Regulations 2006. To comply with these Regulations the smoking shelter must not be wholly enclosed, or substantially enclosed. In practice this means that for a smoking shelter to comply with the law, it must not have sides that enclose more than 50% of the shelter.

Smokefree Vehicles

It should be noted that legislation states that It is the legal responsibility of anyone who drives, manages or is responsible for order and safety on a vehicle to prevent people from smoking. This includes the employer who has responsibility for company vehicles.

The law requires vehicles to be smokefree at all times if they are used:

- to transport members of the public
- in the course of paid or voluntary work by more than one person – regardless of whether they are in the vehicle at the same time

The employer will need to ensure that smokefree vehicles display a no-smoking sign in each compartment of the vehicle in which people can be carried. This must show the international no-smoking symbol no smaller than 70mm in diameter (see section on signage below).

The employer should note that:

- When carrying persons, smokefree vehicles with a roof that can be stowed or removed will not be required to be smokefree when the roof is completely removed or stowed.
- Vehicles that are used primarily for private purposes will not be required to be smokefree.

SIMPLY SAFETY

Ships and Waterborne Vessels

Ships and waterborne vessels will be covered by specific regulations that are being considered and consulted upon by the Department for Transport. More information is available for the employer from the Department for Transport by emailing **smokingonships@dft.gsi.gov.uk** or telephone 020 7944 5427.

Private Dwellings

In general, the new law does not cover private dwellings. However, as the employer you should note that any enclosed or substantially enclosed part of a premises shared with other premises, such as a communal stairwell or lift in a block of flats, will be required to be smokefree if:

- it is open to the public
- it is used as a place of work, for example, by a cleaner, postman or security guard

The law does not require self-contained residential accommodation for temporary or holiday use (for example, holiday cottages or caravans) to be smokefree. As the employer, however, you may choose to make the accommodation smokefree.

As the employer who is responsible for anyone who visits private dwellings as part of their work, for example delivering goods, or providing services such as plumbing, building or hairdressing, you should download further guidance at www.smokefreeengland.co.uk/resources.

Working from Home

Where, as the employer, you are responsible for anyone working from home you should note that the law covers this area as well. Any part of a private dwelling used solely for work purposes will be required to be smokefree if:

- it is used by more than one person who does not live at the dwelling
- members of the public attend to deliver or to receive goods and/or services

Signage

The employer must ensure that all smokefree premises and vehicles display no-smoking signs that meet the requirements of the law. Signs will make it clear which premises and vehicles are smokefree and demonstrate that the employer is taking the necessary steps to meet the requirements of the new law.

Signage for SmokeFree Premises

The employer needs to ensure that no-smoking signs are displayed in a prominent position at every entrance to smokefree premises.

These signs must meet the following minimum requirements:

- Be a minimum of A5 in size (210mm x 148mm)
- Display the no-smoking symbol, at least 70mm in diameter
- Display the following wording: "NO SMOKING. IT IS AGAINST THE LAW TO SMOKE IN THESE PREMISES"

Workplace Welfare Provision

As the employer you are also free to personalise their signs by changing the words 'these premises' to refer to the name or type of premises – such as 'this gym', 'this salon' or 'this restaurant' etc.

A smaller sign consisting of the international no-smoking symbol at least 70mm in diameter may instead be displayed at entrances to smokefree premises that:

- are only used by members of staff – providing the premises displays at least one A5 area sign
- are located within larger smokefree premises, such as a shop within an indoor shopping centre

Signage for Smokefree Vehicles

Smokefree vehicles are required to display the no-smoking symbol, which must be a minimum of 70mm in diameter and be displayed in every compartment in which people travel.

The new law requires certain vehicles to be smokefree; this includes work vehicles and all forms of public transport such as buses and coaches, taxis and private hire vehicles.

Work vehicles must be smokefree if they are used by more than one person in the course of any paid or voluntary work, regardless of whether they are in the vehicle at the same time or not.

Public service vehicles are similar e.g. if a person smokes in a taxi not only can the person smoking receive a fine but also the driver for allowing the offence to take place.

Vehicles that are primarily used for private purposes are not be covered by the legislation

Signs can be downloaded and printed by the employer from
www.smokefreeengland.co.uk/resources/guidance-and-signage.html

However Signs can no longer be ordered from Smokefree England. Instead, the employer can approach their local council, who may have signage and therefore may be able to help.

Penalties

The employer should note that the penalties and fines for the smokefree offences set out in the Health Act 2006 are as follows:

- Smoking in a smokefree premises or vehicle: a fixed penalty notice of £50 (discounted to £30 if paid within 15 days from the issue of a notice) or a fine by a court not exceeding level 1 on the standard scale (up to £200).
- Failure to display no smoking signs in smokefree premises and vehicles as required by the new law: a fixed penalty notice of £200 (discounted to £150 if paid within 15 days from the issue of a notice) or a fine by a court not exceeding level 3 on the standard scale (up to £1,000).
- Failing to prevent smoking in a smokefree premises or vehicle: a fine by a court not exceeding level 4 on the standard scale (up to £2,500).

SIMPLY SAFETY

Additional Information for the Employer

Smoking Help Lines:

- Pregnancy: For specialist advice and support for staff when going smokefree during pregnancy, call 0800 169 9 169 between 12pm and 9pm.
- Northern Ireland Smoking Helpline: If you live or work in Northern Ireland, call 0800 85 85 85.
- Scotland Smoking Helpline: If you live or work in Scotland, call 0800 84 84 84.
- Wales Smoking Helpline: If you live or work in Wales please call 0300 1000 069.
- NHS Asian tobacco helpline: Choose a helpline below to speak to an adviser in your preferred language. Lines are open every Tuesday 1pm–9pm.
    - Urdu: 0800 169 0 881
    - Punjabi: 0800 169 0 882
    - Hindi: 0800 169 0 883
    - Gujarati: 0800 169 0 884
    - Bengali: 0800 169 0 885

Alcohol and Drugs

Apart from the legal implications in the case of drugs the use of drugs and alcohol in the workplace should form part of your overall risk assessment. Staff acting under the influence of either are at risk of causing harm to themselves or colleagues, especially if their role involves the use of any machinery or if they are working in an area which has specific additional risks (plant rooms, roofs and so on).

You have a duty to have in place a policy that addresses these risks; how you treat them will depend upon your particular organisation. For example although a number of workplaces may find it easy to ban alcohol entirely, you may find this more difficult if you carry out much client entertainment. Whatever the case the component parts of your policy will remain the same:

- an acknowledgment of the risks caused by alcohol and drugs
- a clear outline of the occasions (if any) when it is permissible to use alcohol in the workplace
- the status of alcohol abuse within the company's disciplinary structure (in other words, how staff who are found to be under the influence of alcohol will be treated)
- a description of any support systems that are in place for dealing with staff who wish to seek assistance for drink/drug-related problems

The Health and Safety (Safety Signs and Signals) Regulations 1996.

These regulations, implement a European Council Directive on the minimum requirements for the provision of workplace safety signs. The Directive is standardised throughout EU member states and thus ensure that particular signs such as emergency exit, No Smoking, provide the same message wherever seen.

The regulations apply to all workplaces and all activities where people are employed and require employers to provide signage where other methods are unable to properly deal with the risk.

Workplace Welfare Provision

To obtain a copy of the Guidance document L64 please visit the HSE website:
http://www.hse.gov.uk/pubns/priced/l64.pdf

Security

Security issues fall within the competence of employers where they have an impact on the physical well-being of staff. For example, your risk assessment should consider whether, for example, your receptionists are vulnerable to abuse and whether your physical or electronic security measures are sufficient to address this.

There may be specific roles within your organisation that lead to increased vulnerability. These may include roles dealing with members of the public in stressful situations or when there is a risk of crime; doctors, nurses, transport staff, bank staff and many others all face such risks. You should consult with your security advisers and ensure that these risks are adequately dealt with and that staff in situations where such issues are likely to arise are adequately trained in appropriate responses.

Lone Working

Many business operations throw up situations where staff have to work on their own. This may be staff on night shifts, staff working late or at weekends, or staff on one-man sites or dealing with one-person processes. These situations throw up particular risks and these should be addressed. The guiding principle should be that lone workers should not be at any greater risk than any other worker.

You should carry out a risk assessment for lone working in the same way as your other work activities. Some of the issues you should consider are as follows:

- Is the activity one which can be legally carried out alone? Two people must carry out some work processes and activities, such as some work on plant and machinery, in confined spaces or on electrical switchgear, by law.
- Can you avoid the work entirely, meaning that someone does not have to work on his or her own? For example if it is a maintenance activity, can it be combined with other works meaning that other people are on site at the same time?
- Are the emergency procedures in place for the site capable of being carried out by a lone worker or do some adjustments have to be made?
- Does the lone worker have a means of asking for help if things go wrong?
- How will they be supervised? Even for a lone worker there must be some form of supervision, even if this is by planned visits during the course of the work, or over the telephone.
- Is the person themselves competent to work on their own? Have they received the necessary training for the particular work activity, and also for how to summon aid if an emergency situation arises?
- Is the person physically fit to work on his or her own? Have they made you aware of any medical condition that makes them unsuitable?

Overall merely because someone is working on their own you cannot delegate to them responsibilities for health and safety. They have a responsibility for looking after their own welfare, but you must provide them with a safe environment in which to work. An environment, which is perfectly safe when the workplace is fully occupied, may throw up a whole different set of hazards when someone is working on their own; you must address these.

SIMPLY SAFETY

In Case of Emergency (ICE)

This is a standard procedure all paramedics now follow at the scene of an accident when they come across your mobile phone and as a result it is recommended that employers introduce this into their work organisations especially if they have staff who regularly travel in the course of their work.

We all carry our mobile phones with names and numbers stored in its memory but nobody, other than ourselves, knows which of these numbers belong to our closest family or friends.

If we were to be involved in an accident or were taken ill, the people attending us would have our mobile phone but wouldn't know who to call.

Yes, there are hundreds of numbers stored but which one is the contact person in case of an emergency? Hence this 'ICE' (In Case of Emergency) Campaign.

The concept of 'ICE' is catching on quickly. It is a method of contact during emergency situations. As mobile phones are carried by the majority of the population, all you need to do is store the number of a contact person or persons who should be contacted during emergency under the name 'ICE' (In Case Of Emergency).

The idea was thought up by a paramedic who found that when he went to the scenes of accidents, there were always mobile phones with patients, but no indication of which number to call in an emergency.

In an emergency situation, Emergency Service personnel and hospital Staff would be able to contact the right person quickly by simply dialling the number you have stored as 'ICE'.'

For more than one contact name simply enter ICE1, ICE2 and ICE3 etc.

Ventilation

The employer needs to ensure that workplaces are adequately ventilated. Fresh, clean air should be drawn from a source outside the workplace, uncontaminated by discharges from flues, chimneys or other process outlets, and be circulated through the workrooms.

Ventilation should also remove and dilute warm, humid air and provide air movement which gives a sense of freshness without causing a draught. If the workplace contains process or heating equipment or other sources of dust, fumes or vapours, more fresh air will be needed to provide adequate ventilation.

Windows or other openings may provide sufficient ventilation but, where necessary, mechanical ventilation systems should be provided and regularly maintained.

Lighting

This should be sufficient to enable employees to work and circulate safely and in larger organisations may include the provision of local lighting at workstations and high-risk areas such as traffic routes. Lighting and light fittings should not create any hazard in their own right

If a workplace does not have natural daylight or for example during winter months, when it is dark, a sudden loss of lighting by way of power failure or other fault would likely cause a hazard. In such areas automatic emergency lighting should be provided.

CHAPTER 8
ASBESTOS MANAGEMENT

Introduction

Asbestos is the common name given to a number of naturally occurring, inorganic silicates, with complex compositions and fibrous, crystalline structure. Asbestos is likely to be present if a building was constructed or refurbished between 1950 and 1980. Asbestos is the greatest single cause of work-related deaths as asbestos-related diseases such as mesothelioma, asbestosis and lung cancer are thought to kill up to 2,000 people in the UK each year.

That's every week on average

- 4 plumbers die
- 20 tradesmen die
- 6 electricians die
- 8 joiners die

from what is essentially a hidden killer.

There are four main types:

- **chrysotile** (known as white asbestos): a fine, silky, flexible, white to grey/green fibre
- **amosite** (known as brown asbestos): a straight, brittle fibre, light grey to pale brown
- **crocidolite** (known as blue asbestos): a straight, flexible, blue fibre
- **anthophyllite**: a brittle, white to brown fibre

Exposure to and inhalation of asbestos fibres can result in a range of potentially fatal asbestos related diseases, as follows:

- asbestosis
- lung cancer
- mesothelioma
- diffuse pleural thickening

Asbestos is most commonly found in the following forms in buildings:

- as a spray coating on steel work, concrete walls and ceilings, for fire protection and insulation
- as insulation lagging in buildings and factories, on pipe work, and for boilers and ducts
- as asbestos insulating board, such as Asbestolux and Marinite, used as wall partitions, fire doors, ceiling tiles etc
- as asbestos cement products such as sheeting on walls and roofs, tiles, cold water tanks, gutters, pipes and in decorative plaster finishes

SIMPLY SAFETY

- some ceiling and vinyl floor tiles
- asbestos board/paper products in electrical equipment

CONTROL OF ASBESTOS REGULATIONS 2012.

The Control of Asbestos Regulations 2012 (SI 2012/632) came into force on 6 April 2012, updating previous asbestos regulations to take account of the European Commission's view that the UK had not fully implemented the EU Directive on exposure to asbestos (Directive 2009/148/EC).
In practice the changes are fairly limited and call for some types of non-licensed work with asbestos to have additional requirements, i.e. notification of work, medical surveillance and record keeping.

Note: All other requirements as outlined within the Control of Asbestos Regulations 2006 remain unchanged.

What has stayed the same?

- If existing asbestos containing materials (ACM's) are in good condition and are not likely to be damaged, then they may be left in place; their condition monitored and managed to ensure they are not disturbed as part of your asbestos management plan.
- If you're responsible for maintenance of non-domestic premises, you have a "Duty to Manage the asbestos in them and to protect anyone using or working in the premises from the risks to health that exposure to asbestos causes.
- If you want to do any building or maintenance work in premises, or on plant or equipment that might contain asbestos, you need to identify where it is and its type and condition; assess the risks, and manage and control these risks.
- The requirements for licensed work remain the same: in the majority of cases, work with asbestos needs to be done by a licensed contractor. This work includes most asbestos removal, all work with sprayed asbestos coatings and asbestos lagging and most work with asbestos insulation and Asbestos Insulating Board (AIB).
- If you are carrying out non-licensed asbestos work, this still requires effective controls;
- The control limit for asbestos is 0.1 asbestos fibres per cubic centimetre of air (0.1 f/cm3). The control limit is not a 'safe' level and exposure from work activities involving asbestos must be reduced to as far below the control limit as possible.
- Training is mandatory for anyone liable to be exposed to asbestos fibres at work. This includes maintenance workers and others who may come into contact with or disturb asbestos (e.g. cable installers), as well as those involved in asbestos removal work.

What has changed?

- From 6 April 2012, some non-licensed work needs to be notified to the relevant enforcing authority.
- From 6 April 2012, brief written records should be kept of non-licensed work, which has to be notified e.g. copy of the notification with a list of workers on the job, plus the level of likely exposure of those workers to asbestos. This does not require air monitoring on every job, if an estimate of degree of exposure can be made based on experience of similar past tasks or published guidance.

Asbestos Management

- By April 2015, all workers/self employed doing notifiable non-licensed work with asbestos must be under health surveillance by a Doctor. Workers who are already under health surveillance for licensed work need not have another medical examination for non-licensed work, BUT medicals for notifiable non-licensed work are not acceptable for those doing licensed work.

THE DUTY HOLDER EXPLAINED

Within the Control of Asbestos Regulations 2006 (SI 2006/2739) (CAR 2006), regulation 4 imposes a duty upon a duty holder, to manage asbestos containing materials, **so just who is the duty holder?**

In many cases, the duty holder is the person or organisation that has clear responsibility for the maintenance or repair of non-domestic premises through an explicit agreement such as a tenancy agreement or contract.

The extent of the duty will depend on the nature of that agreement. In a building occupied by one leaseholder, the agreement might be for either the owner or leaseholder to take on the full duty for the whole building; or it might be to share the duty. In a multi-occupied building, the agreement might be that the owner takes on the full duty for the whole building. Or it might be that the duty is shared - for example, the owner takes responsibility for the common parts while the leaseholders take responsibility for the parts they occupy. Sometimes, there might be an agreement to pass the responsibilities to a managing agent.

In some situations, there may be no tenancy agreement or contract or indeed, if there is, it may not specify who has responsibility for the maintenance or repair of the non-domestic premises. In this type of scenario, or where the premises are unoccupied, the duty is placed on whoever has control of the premises, or part of the premises. Often this will be the owner.

So essentially you as an employer may well be the Duty Holder.

CONTROL OF ASBESTOS REGULATIONS 2012

The *Control of Asbestos Regulations 2012 (SI 2012/632) (CAR 2012)* updates the *CAR 2006* which brought together the three previous sets of Regulations covering the prohibition of asbestos, the control of asbestos at work and asbestos licensing.

The *CAR 2012* prohibits the importation, supply and use of all forms of asbestos. They continue the ban introduced for blue and brown asbestos in 1985 and for white asbestos in 1999. They also continue to ban the second-hand use of asbestos products such as asbestos cement sheets and asbestos boards and tiles; including panels which have been covered with paint or textured plaster containing asbestos.

The HSE remind employers and duty holders that the ban applies to the new use of asbestos. If existing asbestos containing materials are in good condition, they may be left in place; their condition monitored and managed to ensure they are not disturbed.

The *CAR 2012* continues the duty for the employer (Duty Holder) to manage asbestos in premises *(SI 2012/632, Reg 4)*. This important legislation tackles the biggest occupational health killer in the UK, asbestos-related disease.

SIMPLY SAFETY

Guidance on the 'Duty to Manage' Asbestos may be found in the Approved Code of Practice (ACoP), *The Management of Asbestos in Non-Domestic Premises* L127 ISBN 978 7176 6209 8 as well as in the 'Duty to Manage' section of the HSE website.

The duty to manage requires the employer (Duty Holder) to undertake the following:

- take reasonable steps to find out if there are materials containing asbestos in non-domestic premises and if so, its amount, where it is and what condition it is in eg an asbestos survey
- assume materials contain asbestos unless there is strong evidence that they do not
- make and keep an up-to-date record of the location and condition of the asbestos-containing materials (ACM) – or presumed ACMs in the premises
- assess the risk of the likelihood of anyone being exposed to fibres from these identified materials
- prepare a plan setting out how the risks from the materials are to be managed
- take the necessary steps to implement the plan
- periodically review and monitor the plan and the arrangements to act on it so that the plan remains relevant and up to date
- have a plan to ensure that information is provided on the location and condition of the asbestos materials to anyone who is liable to work on or disturb them

There is also a requirement on anyone to co-operate as far as is necessary to allow the employer (duty holder) to comply with the above requirements.

The regulations also require the employer to ensure the:

- provision and cleaning of protective clothing
- cleanliness of premises and plant
- demarcation of designated 'asbestos areas'
- monitoring of air for concentrations of asbestos
- maintenance of health records and medical surveillance
- provision of washing and changing facilities and
- labelling of raw asbestos and asbestos waste.

How to Manage Asbestos

Asbestos is a very versatile product that was used extensively in the construction of buildings and a range of other products as it has good insulation properties, is totally inert and has good tensile strength. However, asbestos is deadly to humans as, if disturbed, it breaks into small fibres which can get into the lungs and cause the following diseases:

- Asbestosis – fibrosis of the lung tissue caused by asbestos. The lung tissue itself is damaged.
- Lung cancer – tumours grow in the lungs and may develop in other parts of the body.
- Mesothelioma – a cancer that can grow in the lining of the lung (pleura) or abdominal cavity (peritoneum). While some cases may be caused naturally, the vast majority are directly caused by exposure to asbestos fibres.

Asbestos Management

- Pleural plaques – can be formed in the lung lining and become calcified.

The employer (Duty Holder) should be aware of the HSE 'Asbestos – Hidden Killer' campaign

The employer (Duty Holder) has a duty to manage asbestos that may be present if the building was constructed or refurbished between the years 1950 to 1999 but can also affect buildings constructed or refurbished after this date as there have been examples of gaskets taken from old stock and also original features of the original building. This may be more likely if the building also has a steel frame protected by way of a spray coating and/or boilers with thermal insulation.

If there is asbestos present, the employer (Duty Holder) will need to know the location of the material as well as its form and condition and to then develop an asbestos management plan to determine how to prevent exposure of people to the known asbestos. If the employer (Duty Holder) suspects that a material in use within his/her building contains asbestos, he/she will need samples to be taken and analysed by a suitably accredited company that is accredited by the United Kingdom Accreditation Service (UKAS). On no account must the employer (Duty Holder) allow anyone to break or damage such material.

The employer (Duty Holder) should also be aware that the *CAR 2012* requires mandatory training for anyone liable to be exposed to asbestos fibres at work (*CAR 2012, reg 10*). This includes maintenance workers and others who may come into contact with or who may disturb asbestos (eg cable installers) as well as those involved in asbestos removal work.

When work with asbestos or work which may disturb asbestos is being carried out, the *CAR 2012* require the employer (Duty Holder) to prevent exposure to asbestos fibres. Where this is not reasonably practicable, they must make sure that exposure is kept as low as reasonably practicable by measures other than the use of respiratory protective equipment. The spread of asbestos must be prevented. The employer (Duty Holder) needs to check the *CAR 2012*, as they specify the work methods and controls that should be used to prevent exposure and spread.

The employer (Duty Holder) is also responsible for ensuring that worker exposure must be below the airborne exposure limit (control limit). The *CAR 20126* has a single control limit for all types of asbestos of 0.1 fibres per cm^3. A control limit is a maximum concentration of asbestos fibres in the air (averaged over any continuous four-hour period) that must not be exceeded.

In addition, short-term exposures must be strictly controlled and worker exposure should not exceed 0.6 fibres per cm^3 of air averaged over any continuous ten-minute period using respiratory protective equipment if exposure cannot be reduced sufficiently using other means.

Unless the employer (Duty Holder) is competent to undertake the above work, a specialist contractor should be sought and retained.

Most asbestos removal work must be undertaken by a licensed contractor but any decision taken by the employer (Duty Holder) as to whether work is subject to a license will be based upon the risk assessment. See Asbestos Risk Assessment in this chapter, below page 122.

Respiratory protective equipment is an important part of the control regime but it must not be the sole measure used to reduce exposure and should only be used to supplement other measures. Work methods that control the release of fibres, such as those detailed in the HSE Document *Asbestos Essentials Task Sheets* (www.hse.gov.uk/asbestos/essentials/index.htm) for non-licensed work should be used. The employer (Duty Holder) must ensure that any and all respiratory protective equipment (RPE) is suitable, fits properly and that worker exposure is reduced as low as is reasonably practicable.

SIMPLY SAFETY

If the work is licensable the employer (Duty Holder) has a number of additional duties and he / she needs to:

- notify the enforcing authority responsible for the site where the work is being undertaken (eg HSE or the local authority)
- designate the work area (see *CAR 2012, Reg 18* for details)
- prepare specific asbestos emergency procedures
- pay for their employees to undergo medical surveillance

The *CAR 2012* requires any analysis of the concentration of asbestos in the air to be measured in accordance with the 1997 World Health Organisation (WHO) recommended method.

From 6 April 2007, a clearance certificate for re-occupation may only be issued by a body accredited to do so. At the moment, such accreditation can only be provided by the United Kingdom Accreditation Service (UKAS): www.ukas.com.

HSE System for 'Managing my Asbestos'

The management of asbestos is very complex and can take some time to carry out effectively and as a result the HSE has produced a scheme of web pages that will assist the employer (Duty Holder) in complying with the 'Duty to Manage Asbestos'.

These web pages can be found at:
http://www.hse.gov.uk/asbestos/managing/index.htm

It is recommended that you as an employer or duty holder use these pages and the checklist contained therein, to mark your progress through a systematic approach to the management of asbestos. A simplified version of the HSE scheme is shown, as below:

Table 8.01 - Managing my Asbestos Checklist

	CHECKLIST FOR 'MANAGING MY ASBESTOS'	
	The web pages to help you to carry out your 'duty to manage asbestos' can be found at http://www.hse.gov.uk/asbestos/managing/index.htm	
	Use this checklist to mark your progress	
1	**Introduction** *Overview of the scheme, Checklist*	
2	**Are you responsible for maintenance or repair?** *Does the duty to manage apply to you and your premises?*	
3	**When was it built?** *Was it built before 2000, are you on a brownfield site or do you use old equipment?*	
4	**What information do you have already?** *Look at building plans, previous asbestos surveys and any other relevant documents.*	
5	**Inspect your building** *Create an asbestos register to list where asbestos may be present.*	
6	**Determining priorities for action**	

	Use a scoring tool to work out what needs doing first.	
7	**Decide how to deal with the different types of asbestos** *Use the online tool on how to treat the different types of asbestos, e.g. sprayed asbestos, asbestos cement*	
8	**Write your asbestos management plan** *The plan brings together your asbestos register, plans of work and schedule.*	
9	**Testing for asbestos** *If work is required, you need to test for asbestos first*	
10	**Tell people what you're doing** *You need to tell employees, contractors and maintenance workers about your findings*	
11	**Getting work done** *Does the work need a licensed contractor?*	
12	**Keep your records up to date** *If any work is done on asbestos, your records need updating, and you need regular checks on the state of the asbestos*	

HOW TO USE THIS FORM

STEP 1 - INTRODUCTION

This section provides an overview of the scheme and it is recommended *that you use the HSE Checklist, shown below, to help you through the systematic stages of managing your asbestos.*

If you are responsible for premises such as a shop or small industrial unit, following this scheme helps you to carry out your legal duty to manage asbestos.

This system helps you to do an **asbestos risk assessment** and produce an **asbestos management plan**. It involves:

1. Finding out and recording where asbestos might be.
2. Deciding what is most important.
3. Deciding what action to take and how to plan any work.

Important things to remember

- Asbestos is only dangerous when disturbed - **avoid unnecessary disturbance**.
- If unsure, **presume that material contains asbestos**.
- The duty to manage does not require asbestos removal.
- You don't always need a specialist but if you do then make sure that they are competent to provide advice or work on asbestos.
- **If you find anything wrong while following the scheme, get help.**

STEP 2 - ARE YOU RESPONSIBLE FOR MAINTENANCE OR REPAIR?

Does the duty to manage apply to you and your premises?

If you are responsible for maintenance or repair of premises or equipment, you are the duty

SIMPLY SAFETY

holder and will need to follow the next steps. But remember this duty only applies to:

- Non-domestic premises
- Common parts of domestic premises e.g. Boiler Room, Electrical Distribution rooms, Lift Shaft etc.

STEP 3 - WHEN WAS IT BUILT?

If you know for sure that the building was built in or after 2000:

It is unlikely to have any asbestos.

Authors notes: Do check with the Construction Design & Management (CDM) Safety File as principle contractors will usually provide a letter or certificate to state that no asbestos containing materials were used in the construction.

In addition if the building is of post 2000 construction but was built on an original basement area then check this, as we have experienced asbestos being discovered in such areas

It was built before 2000, or you are unsure:

Presume that the building contains asbestos unless you know for sure it doesn't e.g. documentary evidence of a management type of asbestos survey.

STEP 4 - WHAT INFORMATION DO YOU HAVE ALREADY?

Look at building plans, previous asbestos surveys and any other relevant documents.

Is there any existing information about asbestos in the building?

You should try to collect as much information as you can about any previous asbestos record as it will help with the next step, 'Inspect your building'

Try to get a copy of any reports or plans relating to the building. The building plans may not have any information about asbestos but a copy is useful for noting down your findings.

In addition you can:

- look for any records of previous asbestos work;
- check with the previous owners or tenants of the building;
- ask the facilities management company, if there is one;
- ask equipment suppliers or repairers;
- check with the building designer, architect or builder.

If you can't find the information don't worry. It is useful but not essential.

Key point Do note any previous asbestos surveys, but don't rely on them unless they are recent and have been carried out by a competent consultant.

Asbestos Management

STEP 5 - INSPECT YOUR BUILDING

Create an asbestos register to list where asbestos may be present.

This is known as a 'management survey'. The aim is to produce an 'asbestos register' which says where asbestos is located or where there might be asbestos.

For small premises e.g. workshop, trading estate unit, office, shop.

If you follow the below listed steps correctly, your own inspection is normally sufficient to create an asbestos register.

Inspecting Your Building:

Note: The HSE web site contains useful examples of site plans, asbestos register and a checklist of places & materials that can contain asbestos.

- Copy or draw a plan of the building.
- Walk round and look.
- Get some help - a second pair of eyes is always useful.
- Mark on the plan what contains, or might contain asbestos.
- Print a blank asbestos register.
- Note down each material that might contain asbestos. Note how much there is and its condition (good/poor)
- Where you can't get access, eg a roof void, wall cavity, presume that this contains asbestos. Note this down in the register.
- When your inspection has finished, complete your asbestos register.
- Add the date and sign it.

Key point Do not disturb any material that may contain asbestos

In the case of larger premises e.g. more than 25 employees, more than a few workrooms, or if you are unsure.

You may decide to employ a competent asbestos surveyor.

STEP 6 - DETERMINING PRIORITIES FOR ACTION

It is advisable to use a scoring system to work out Which materials need action first?

In essence this means completing a risk assessment on the material using the following as guide. Further guidance and an online material and priority scoring tool may be found on the HSE web address as above.

For each entry in your asbestos register you need a **material score** and a **priority score**.

- If the asbestos material is in **good condition**, use a **score of 1** for **both** material and priority.

SIMPLY SAFETY

- If it is **not in good condition** use the 'Material and priority scoring tool' to get material and priority scores.

Write the scores for each asbestos material in your asbestos register. You may also want to print the results page for each material for your records.

The highest priority score shows which work to carry out first.

If two items have the same priority score, go by the higher material score.

STEP 7 - DECIDE HOW TO DEAL WITH THE DIFFERENT TYPES OF ASBESTOS

Use the online HSE tool on how to treat the different types of asbestos, eg sprayed asbestos, asbestos cement.

Some examples of asbestos containing materials are listed below - **but don't start any work yet!** Put the result in your asbestos register. You may want to print the result pages for your records

- Sprayed asbestos e.g. 'limpet'
- Lagging e.g. pipes, boilers
- Asbestos insulating board
- Asbestos cement
- Textured coating

If you are unsure get advice from:

- an asbestos surveyor
- a licensed asbestos contractor

STEP 8 - WRITE DOWN YOUR ASBESTOS MANAGEMENT PLAN

The plan brings together your asbestos register, plans of work and schedule.

Before arranging for any work to be done you should start by writing an **'asbestos management plan'**. This should include:

- who is responsible for managing asbestos;
- the asbestos register you have just made;
- plans for work on asbestos materials;
- the schedule for monitoring the materials' condition; and
- telling people about your decisions.

The plan must say who is responsible for what. It can be written or held as a computer based record. Make it easy to read and easy to find when you, or anyone else, needs it. It must be easy to update.

Key point

Asbestos Management

- Update your plan whenever work affects asbestos materials.
- Record your regular monitoring of the condition of asbestos materials.

STEP 9 - TESTING FOR ASBESTOS

If work is required, you need to test for asbestos first. If you are not planning any work, you don't need to test for asbestos.

Before doing any work which may disturb asbestos materials, you must either:

- get expert help to test if asbestos is present or absent
(See guidance below on types of survey, brownfield sites and old equipment); or
- apply full asbestos safety precautions for the work.
(This is described later, in 'Getting work done')

If you are planning work discuss your requirements with a suitably qualified surveyor

Types of Survey

There are two different types of survey that your surveyor may recommend.

- Asbestos Management Survey
- Refurbishment Survey

Both of these survey types may require samples to be taken.

Brownfield Sites

There are specific points to consider when carrying out a survey on a brownfield site. A 'Brownfield' site is an area of land that was previously developed, often but not always for industrial and commercial purposes. It may be contaminated - asbestos may lay buried.

If you need to find out whether you are on a Brownfield site, ask your local authority planning department.

Before digging on a Brownfield site, it is good practice to sample the ground first. Any suspicious material requires analysis for asbestos and even if no asbestos is found in the sample, the excavation may still reveal suspicious material.

For further information on dealing with a Brownfield site that may contain asbestos please refer to the guidance issued by the Health & Safety Executive at

http://www.hse.gov.uk/asbestos/managing/brownfield.htm

Old Equipment (pre 2000)

There are specific points to consider when carrying out a survey on old equipment however it should be noted that equipment bought new after the year 2000 contains no asbestos. However second-hand or old equipment may very well contain asbestos. This means that equipment such as ovens, insulating mats, fire blankets, oven gloves, ironing surfaces, etc and equipment

SIMPLY SAFETY

with soundproofing, thermal insulation, brakes, etc. will more than likely contain asbestos. You should not buy or sell equipment that contains asbestos.

For further guidance on asbestos and old equipment please refer to the HSE page:

http://www.hse.gov.uk/asbestos/managing/oldequipment.htm

There are two Key Points that you as the employer need to understand

1. You will need to get expert help to carry out these tests.
2. If not tested, materials are presumed to be asbestos. You must apply full asbestos safety precautions when doing any work.

STEP 10 - TELL PEOPLE WHAT YOU'RE DOING

You need to tell employees, contractors and maintenance workers about your findings.

With your asbestos management plan in place, you need to tell people about your findings and decisions.

- Tell your employees.
- Train your maintenance workers to ask about asbestos for every job.
- Make sure everyone knows how to report problems so you can remedy defects.

You should stick labels on anything that contains or might contain asbestos if it is located where people are likely to disturb or damage it. You may obtain these from safety sign companies.

Warn anyone who is going to work on the fabric of your building, e.g. those involved in

- **construction:** -
  builders, roofers, painters and decorators, joiners, plasterers, shop fitters;
- **installation:** -
  plumbers, gas fitters, electricians, phone, alarm and data-wire installers, heating and ventilation engineers;
- **maintenance:** -
  engineers, repairers;
- **Other Work**: -
  excavation and demolition contractors, surveyors

STEP 11 - GETTING WORK DONE

One of the key questions that you need to ask as the employer is does the work need a licensed contractor? There are two key points that you need to remember: -

1. Don't do it yourself. It is important to realise that the contractor who is to do the work needs all the right training and equipment.
2. If you don't have professional tests done to confirm the presence or absence of asbestos, materials are *presumed to be asbestos. You must apply full asbestos*

Asbestos Management

safety precautions when doing all work. This means getting either a licensed or a trained contractor to do the work - see below.

Is the Work Licensed?

Depending on the materials and type of work being done you may need to use an HSE-licensed asbestos contractor however if this is not needed you should use a contractor who is trained to deal with asbestos. The HSE have a tool to help you decide which you need: -

http://www.hse.gov.uk/asbestos/managing/flashtools/isitlicenced.htm

Licensed Work

See link on the HSE website for List of licensed contractors

Facilities Needed

Information for the contractor about the hazards on your site:

- space for the airlock, the hygiene facility - decontamination unit - as close as possible to the work;
- space for waste storage eg a lockable skip.
- electricity and water supplies, and a drain for waste water.
- some personal protective equipment for emergency use.
- access to facilities - toilets, etc;
- you may need enhanced security against vandalism.

What You Should Expect

- Smoke testing the enclosure before and during the work. Turn off smoke detectors during these tests - and turn them back on afterwards!
- Air sampling near the enclosure or work area.
- Air extraction units, running continuously after the first smoke test until clearance of asbestos.
- Contractor carries out daily checks of the enclosure and keeps records for your inspection.
- To hear reports of anything that is wrong.
- Formal clearance, before you can reoccupy the area. You must have a copy of this certificate.

Legal Points to Consider

- The Construction (Design and Management) Regulations 2007 (CDM) apply to this work. . (See the Chapter on CDM)
- The contractor's detailed method statement should cover all health and safety risks, not just asbestos. (See the Chapter on risk assessment)

Non-Licensed Work

Employ a **contractor who is trained to work with asbestos** and should use methods like those outlined in 'Asbestos essentials' – see the HSE page at
http://www.hse.gov.uk/asbestos/essentials/index.htm

Asbestos Essentials

Asbestos Essentials is a task manual for building, maintenance and allied trades on how to

SIMPLY SAFETY

safely carry out non-licensed work involving asbestos and consists of a series of guidance documents, as follows:

- Work with asbestos cement (AC) (Non-Licensed)
- Work with textured coatings (TC) containing asbestos (Non-Licensed)
- Strictly controlled minor work on asbestos insulating board (AIB)
- Safe work on undamaged asbestos materials
- Removal and replacement of other asbestos containing materials
- Fly-Tipped waste
- Equipment and method sheets

Asbestos Essentials does not apply to licensed work and you should only go ahead if you are sure the work does not require a licence and you are trained to work on asbestos.

Please refer to the HSE page at - http://www.hse.gov.uk/asbestos/essentials/index.htm

STEP 12 - KEEP YOUR RECORDS UP TO DATE

If any work is done on asbestos, your records need updating, and you need regular checks on the state of the asbestos.

You should always keep your records up to date.

- Update the asbestos register whenever you have work done on asbestos materials;
- Check materials **at least once a year** to make sure they haven't deteriorated;
- Check against your asbestos register and identify;
    - who is going to make these checks;
    - when, and
    - why they are able to do the work, eg training;
- Update your asbestos management plan and date it;
- Warn everyone - employees and contractors - to check the asbestos register whenever work may disturb asbestos materials. They must ask the manager or supervisor.

You have all the documentation necessary to fulfil your duty to manage the asbestos in your premises.

ASBESTOS RISK ASSESSMENT

Where the employer (Duty Holder) knows there is asbestos within a building, he/she needs to ensure that an assessment is undertaken of the condition of the asbestos and in particular he/she needs to consider the risk of asbestos fibres being released into the air. Several factors need to be considered:

- Is the material being/likely to be disturbed?
- Is the surface damaged, frayed or scratched?
- Are surface sealants peeling or breaking off?
- Is the material becoming detached from its base?
- Are protective coverings missing?
- Is there asbestos dust or debris in the immediate surrounding area?

Depending upon the condition and type of the material, the employer (Duty Holder) will be advised what to do by the asbestos surveyor:

Asbestos Management

- If the material is in good condition, it is not likely to be damaged and if it is not likely to be worked on, then it is safest to leave the material in place and introduce a management system.
- If the material is in poor condition or it is likely to be damaged or disturbed, then the employer (Duty Holder) will need to decide whether to repair, seal, enclose or remove the material.

You as the employer (Duty Holder) must exercise control over access by workers, contractors and so on and will need to do the following:

- set up a register of where the asbestos is to be found
- label materials with warning signs or colour coding so that those who need to know are alerted to its presence
- keep records of all testing and test results upon suspected material

THE BASIC PRINCIPLES FOR THE EMPLOYER (DUTY HOLDER) TO CONSIDER

- Asbestos is only dangerous when disturbed. If it is safely managed and contained, it does not present a health hazard.
- Do not remove asbestos unnecessarily – removing it can be more dangerous than leaving it in place and managing it.
- Not all asbestos materials present the same risk. The measures that need to be taken for controlling the risks from materials such as pipe insulation are different from those needed in relation to asbestos cement.
- Do not assume you need to bring in a specialist in every case; for example, you can inspect your own building rather than employ a surveyor.
- If you are unsure about whether certain materials contain asbestos, you can presume they do and treat them as such.
- Remember that the duty to manage is all about putting in place the practical steps necessary to protect maintenance workers and others from the risk of exposure to asbestos fibres. It is **not** about removing all asbestos, as this in itself carries inherent risks.

TYPES OF SURVEY TO DETERMINE THE PRESENCE OF ASBESTOS

Before the employer (Duty Holder) attempts to commission an asbestos survey, they should acquaint themselves with the HSE publication 'Asbestos: The Survey Guide', HSG 264, which replaced the old MDHS 100 at the beginning of 2010. This document sets out how to survey a typical workplace for the presence of asbestos containing materials (ACMs) and how to record the results in a usable and practical format.

MANAGEMENT SURVEY

A management survey is now the standard survey and its purpose is to locate, so far as reasonably practicable, the presence and extent of any suspect asbestos containing materials (ACMs) in the building which could be damaged or disturbed during the normal occupancy of a building. This is taken to include foreseeable maintenance and installation, as well as to assess the condition of the ACMs.

A management survey will often necessitate minor intrusive works and potentially some disturbance. The true extent of any intrusion will vary between buildings and will depend on what

SIMPLY SAFETY

is reasonably practicable for each individual property. For example, the amount of intrusion will depend on such factors as to the type of building, the nature of construction and the accessibility to areas, etc.

The HSE state in their document HSG 264 that a management survey should include an assessment of the condition of the various ACMs and, their ability to release fibres into the air if they are disturbed in anyway. This 'material assessment' will give a good initial guide to the employer (Duty Holder) as to the priority for the management of any ACMs, as it will identify the materials which will most readily release airborne fibres if they are disturbed.

The survey will normally involve some sampling and analysis to confirm the presence or absence of ACMs. However, it can also involve presuming the presence or absence of asbestos in some cases. A management survey can be completed using a combination of sampling and presuming ACM's however it can be completed by just presuming the presence or absence of asbestos. If any materials are presumed to contain asbestos then the Employer (Duty Holder) must have the condition of the assumed asbestos assessed prior to any work taking place or any disturbance.

REFURBISHMENT AND DEMOLITION SURVEYS

The second type of survey is a refurbishment and demolition survey and the employer (Duty Holder) is required to have one undertaken prior to any refurbishment or demolition work being carried out. The aim of this type of survey is to locate and describe, so far as reasonably practicable, all ACMs in the area where the refurbishment work will take place or, if demolition is planned, within the whole building. The survey will naturally be fully intrusive and involve destructive inspection, as necessary, to gain access to all areas, including those that may be difficult to reach. The employer (Duty Holder) may also be required to commission a refurbishment and demolition survey in other circumstances, for example when more intrusive maintenance and repair work needs to be carried out or when plant is being removed or dismantled.

Refurbishment and demolition surveys are intended to locate all the asbestos in the building (or the relevant part of the building), so far as reasonably practicable. The employer (Duty Holder) needs to be aware that it is a disruptive and fully intrusive survey which may need to penetrate all parts of the building structure. Aggressive inspection techniques will be needed to lift carpets and tiles, break through walls, ceilings, cladding and partitions, and open up floors. In these situations the employer (Duty Holder) will need to establish controls to prevent the spread of debris and dust, which may include asbestos. Generally, refurbishment and demolition surveys should only be conducted in unoccupied areas to minimise risks to the public or employees on the premises. Ideally, the employer (Duty Holder) should ensure that the building is not in service and that all furnishings have been removed.

Further information is available from the HSE website and copies of HSG 264 can be downloaded from HSE Books free of charge at:
http://books.hse.gov.uk/hse/public/saleproduct.jsf?catalogueCode=9780717663859

The Health and Safety Executive have put together a schematic diagram showing the link between the asbestos survey and the management plan and this is detailed in Figure 8.02.

Figure 8:02

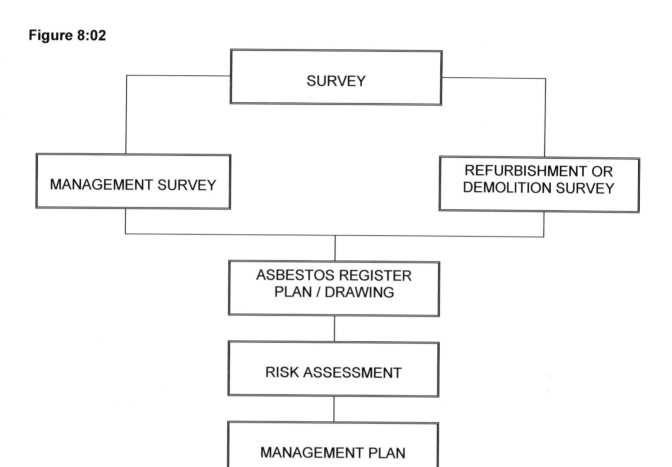

SIMPLY SAFETY

Asbestos Management Checklist

Question	Yes	No
Are you responsible for the maintenance and repair of your building/s?		
Was your building/s constructed before 2000? (Unlikely to contain asbestos if built after this date.)		
Do you have any previous asbestos information such as Asbestos Survey, Photographs, plans and drawings?		
Have you inspected your building/s to see where asbestos may be located? (You may consider using the services of a competent asbestos surveyor for this activity.)		
Is the asbestos surveyor that you intend to use UKAS accredited and will they adhere to HSG264?		
Have you carried out a risk assessment to prioritise which asbestos work need to be done first? e.g. a scoring system.		
Have you used the online HSE tool to decide how to deal with the various types of asbestos?		
Do you have an asbestos management plan? And does it contain: • Who is responsible for management of the asbestos? • An asbestos register for the site. • Plans for any works on the asbestos. • Monitoring schedule to periodically check the condition of the asbestos. • Details of how information regarding asbestos will be communicated to staff, contractors etc. • Plans for regular review of the plan.		
Are you planning any intrusive works that may disturb the asbestos in your building/s? (If Yes then you must test for the presence of asbestos by carrying out a Refurbishment Survey on the area of the intended works as a minimum.)		
Have you informed your employee's, contractors and maintenance workers of the intended asbestos works?		
Have you established if the intended asbestos works need to be carried out by an HSE licensed contractor? (Use the HSE tool to find out at http://www.hse.gov.uk/asbestos/managing/flashtools/isitlicenced.htm		

Asbestos Management

| Have you updated your records following any asbestos works? | | |

ACCREDITATION/CERTIFICATION OF SURVEYORS

Employer (Duty Holders) need to remember they have a Duty to Manage and not a duty to survey. It is important to source a competent surveyor to undertake the required asbestos survey.

To be competent, the 'surveyor' must:

- have sufficient training, qualifications, knowledge, experience and ability to carry out their duties in relation to the survey and to recognise their limitations;
- have sufficient knowledge of the specific tasks to be undertaken and the risks which the work will entail;
- be able to demonstrate independence, impartiality and integrity;
- have an adequate quality management system; and
- carry out the survey in accordance with recommended guidance.

The employer (Duty Holder) can check whether an organisation has the appropriate training, experience and can demonstrate that they are technically competent to undertake surveys for ACMs through accreditation to ISO/IEC 17020.9 The United Kingdom Accreditation Service (UKAS) is the sole national accreditation body in the United Kingdom (UKAS, 21–47 High Street, Feltham, Middlesex TW13 4UN Tel: 020 8917 8400 www.ukas.com). Accreditation gives an assurance that an independent and authoritative body has assessed the technical competence of an organisation, including its underpinning management system. The scheme should ensure that the organisation can provide a valid service for the services specified on its schedule of accreditation.

Individual surveyors can also demonstrate that they are technically competent to undertake specified surveys through holding 'personnel' certification from a Certification Body accredited by UKAS for this activity under ISO/IEC 17024.10 Personnel certification provides assurance that an individual has achieved a defined level of competence to carry out specific activities. Currently there is one accredited scheme: 'ABICS' (Asbestos Building Inspectors Certification Scheme) which is operated by the Faculty of Occupational Hygiene, part of the British Occupational Hygiene Society (BOHS) (see www.abics.org) (BOHS, 5/6 Melbourne Business Court, Millennium Way, Pride Park, Derby DE24 8LZ, Tel: 01332 298101 www.bohs.org). A number of people have also been certificated under a previous scheme 'NIACS' (National Individual Asbestos Certification Scheme). Certificated surveyors should also work within a general Quality Assurance framework provided by ISO/IEC 17020 (or ISO 900111 as a minimum).

HOW TO REMOVE ASBESTOS

The removal of asbestos is a challenge that a great number of employer (Duty Holder)s will probably face at some time.

Most asbestos removal work must be undertaken by a licensed contractor but any decision made by the employer (Duty Holder) on whether particular work is licensable is based on the risk. The employer (Duty Holder) needs to be aware that work is only exempt from licensing if:

SIMPLY SAFETY

- The exposure of employees to asbestos fibres is sporadic and of low intensity (but exposure cannot be considered to be sporadic and of low intensity if the concentration of asbestos in the air is liable to exceed 0.6 fibres per cm^3 measured over ten minutes).
- It is clear from the risk assessment that the exposure of any employee to asbestos will not exceed the control limit.
- The work involves:
  - Short, non-continuous maintenance activities. Work can only be considered as short, non-continuous maintenance activities if any one person carries out work with these materials for less than one hour in a seven-day period. The total time spent by all workers on the work should not exceed a total of two hours. It is important that the amount of time the employer (Duty Holder) permits their employees to spend working with asbestos insulation, asbestos coatings or asbestos insulation board (AIB) is managed to make sure that these time limits are not exceeded. This includes the time for activities such as building enclosures and cleaning.
  - Removal of materials in which the asbestos fibres are firmly linked in a matrix, such materials include: asbestos cement; textured decorative coatings and paints which contain asbestos; articles of bitumen, plastic, resin or rubber which contain asbestos where their thermal or acoustic properties are incidental to their main purpose (eg vinyl floor tiles, electric cables, roofing felt) and other insulation products which may be used at high temperatures but have no insulation purposes, for example gaskets, washers, ropes and seals.
  - Encapsulation or sealing of asbestos-containing materials which are in good condition.
  - Air monitoring and control, and the collection and analysis of samples to find out if a specific material contains asbestos.

Under the *CAR 2012*, anyone carrying out work on asbestos insulation, asbestos coating or asbestos insulating board (AIB) needs a licence issued by HSE unless they meet one of the exemptions above.

REMEMBER: - Although you may not need a licence to carry out a particular job, you still need to comply with the rest of the requirements of the Asbestos Regulations.

When you as the employer (Duty Holder) is responsible for the disposal of asbestos waste, you should note that it should be double-bagged in heavy-duty polythene bags and clearly labelled with the prescribed label before it is transported to an appropriately licensed place for disposal.

Further guidance on asbestos may be found in publications, such as:

- The 'Duty to Manage' Asbestos may be found in *The Management of Asbestos in Non-Domestic Premises – Approved Code of Practice* (AcoP), HSE, L127 ISBN 978 7176 6209 8.
- The 'Duty to Manage' section of the HSE website at www.hse.gov.uk.
- *Asbestos: the Licensed Contractors Guide*, HSE, HS(G)247.
- Asbestos Essentials: task manual: task guidance sheets for the building and maintenance trades, HSE 2001, HSG210, ISBN 0717618870.

The employer (Duty Holder) should be aware of the HSE 'Asbestos – Hidden Killer' campaign details of which may be found on the HSE asbestos microsite at www.hse.gov.uk/asbestos/.

Asbestos Management

ASBESTOS ESSENTIALS FOR UNLICENSED WORK.

What you need to do

Before starting work, as the employer, you need to check what asbestos is present, in commercial properties as previously stated there should be a plan / register and you need to ask to see it. You need to check that the plan covers the area of the building that you will be working in and if you are doing refurbishment work that it includes a survey that tells you what types of asbestos is present and what is it's condition. If there is no register or survey or the report is not clear you must not start work. Alternatively, you can assume that any material you need to disturb does contain asbestos. The client also needs to see your plan of work to understand what work you are going to do, and how it is planned to be done.

Your Workers

Everyone who works with, or may disturb asbestos, must be properly trained (including the self-employed).

What the premises owner (client) needs to tell you

The Client needs to let you know where any asbestos containing materials (or materials presumed to contain asbestos) are, that you are likely to meet or encounter in the work you are doing. It is essential that the information provided is specific.

Main points:

- You need training to work safely with ACMs.
- Asbestos Essentials does not apply to licensed work. You should only go ahead if you are sure the work does not require a licence.
- Work with, or disturbance of, any type of ACM can be dangerous.
- Second-hand equipment may not be asbestos-free.
- If you work on ACMs and you smoke, you are at much greater risk of lung cancer.
- Consider those around you. Don't put your workmates in danger or take fibres home on your clothes and put your family at risk.
- Carry out the work and dispose of contaminated materials safely.

Does the work need a licence?

Most work with asbestos needs to be carried out by a licensed contractor. This includes work on asbestos coating and asbestos lagging; and work on asbestos insulation or asbestos insulating board (AIB) where the risk assessment demonstrates that the fibre release will be high, eg the material is badly damaged, or the work is not short duration work.

'Short duration' means any one person doing this type of work for less than one hour, or more people doing the work for a total of less than two hours, in any seven consecutive days. The total time spent by all workers must not exceed two hours. This includes time spent setting up, cleaning and clearing up.

Non-licensed work includes work on asbestos-containing textured coatings and asbestos cement.

SIMPLY SAFETY

Is it notifiable non-licensed work?

From April 2012, some non-licensed work, where the risk of fibre release is greater, is subject to three additional requirements – notification of work, medical examinations and record keeping (the requirement for medical examinations does not come into force until April 2015).

This work is known as notifiable non-licensed work (NNLW).

To decide if the work is NNLW, you will need to consider the type of work you are going to carry out, the type of material you are going to work on and its condition:

- Decide what type of work you are doing:
    - Maintenance – e.g. drilling holes to attach fittings or pass cables through, painting, cleaning etc. Maintenance includes some removal where it is incidental to the main task, eg removing an asbestos ceiling tile to allow inspection;
    - Removal – e.g. as part of a refurbishment or redesign project; or
    - Encapsulation – e.g. work to enclose or seal asbestos materials in good condition; or
    - **Air monitoring and control, and the collection and analysis of samples.**

- Consider the asbestos type:
    - Is it friable? – the more friable a material is, the more likely it will release asbestos fibres when worked on and the greater the risk of exposure. Materials such as asbestos insulation are more friable than materials such as asbestos cement; and
    - How firmly is the asbestos bonded in a matrix? (For removal work only) – Asbestos containing materials (ACMs) where the asbestos is coated, covered or contained within another material, such as cement, paint or plastic are considered to be firmly bonded in a matrix; and

- Consider the material's condition:
    - Has the material been damaged or is it in poor condition? – e.g. badly flood or fire-damaged; and
    - Will the materials' matrix be destroyed when worked on? – e.g. deteriorating textured decorative coatings ('Artex') with gel or steam.

Once you've considered these three elements, the decision flow chart below will help you to decide which category your work with asbestos is, or check the HSE website for more help before you start.

In summary, most work with firmly bonded materials in good condition such as asbestos cement, bitumen, plastic, resin, rubber, roofing felt, paper linings, cardboard, textiles, gaskets, washers and rope etc will not need to be notified. Short duration 'maintenance' work involving AIB which is in good condition will also not normally need to be notified, NNLW will normally include short duration maintenance and removal work with asbestos insulation, removal of textured decorative coatings where the material is destroyed e.g. by scraping it off, and short duration removal of AIB as part of refurbishment.

Asbestos Management

Planning

Before carrying out any work:

- Ask the premises owners for their records of asbestos; what was checked, what was found, and what was not checked.
- If there is no record and you have reason to suspect asbestos, ask for an asbestos survey to be done before accepting the contract (you will have to check yourself in domestic properties).
- Check if the work could require a licence. See 'More help'.
- When a licence is not needed for the work, check if the work is NNLW and if so, follow the requirements and then follow the task sheets or other HSE guidance.
- If there is no task sheet for the work, get help from a competent health and safety advisor.
- When you seek advice, ensure that the person providing that advice is competent.
- If asbestos-containing material needs replacement, the replacement must be asbestos-free.

Prepare a short plan of work. If the work is NNLW, your copy of the notification may help you. Make sure the plan includes the following:

- what the work is and how long it is likely to last;
- the address and description of the job;
- when the work will be done;
- the procedures to follow to reduce exposure and prevent the spread of asbestos, ie by following the Asbestos essentials task sheets;
- the equipment needed, including personal protective equipment (PPE);
- decontamination and waste disposal arrangements; and
- emergency procedures.

See equipment and method (em) sheets for useful advice to help you prepare this plan.

Make sure that everyone involved is fully aware of the plan and knows:

- what they need to do;
- how to wear their PPE and RPE correctly;
- why each action is being taken; and
- what to do in the case of emergencies and accidents.

Manage the Work

- Monitor the work to ensure it is being carried out with the appropriate controls.

Caution: Emergency call-out is no excuse for low standards or cutting corners.

Disposal of Asbestos Materials and Waste

'Hazardous' or 'Special' Waste needs safe disposal. This includes:

- asbestos;

SIMPLY SAFETY

- materials containing asbestos; and
- anything contaminated with asbestos unless fully decontaminated.

Make sure you double-bag and label asbestos waste.

For advice on disposal contact the Local Authority, the Environment Agency

ASBESTOS LICENSING UNIT (ALU)

From April 2012, the Health and Safety Executive's (HSE) Asbestos Licensing Unit (ALU) changed the method of payment for asbestos licence fees and introduced an online revised FOD ASB1 application form.

Changes to the method of payment for asbestos licence fees

When an ASB1 application form, re-assessment request or amendment to a licence is received in ALU, based in Edinburgh, HSE's Financial Operations, based in Bootle, Merseyside will raise an invoice for the relevant amount, which will be sent directly to you for payment.

Online revised FOD ASB1 Application Form

The FOD ASB1 application form has now been replaced by an online Business Form.

The ASB1 should be completed online and submitted electronically.

New applicants, on request for an ASB1, will be sent an electronic link to access the form. Renewal applicants will still be notified, in writing, three months in advance of their licence expiry and sent an electronic link to access the form.

Transitional period

The new procedures commenced in April 2012 but the ALU appreciates that they will take time to be fully implemented. ALU will therefore accept the previous ASB1 and method of payment for a short period of time.

ALU stated that the new procedures will be fully operational by October 2012.

CHAPTER 9
BUILDING SERVICES

CONSTRUCTION (DESIGN AND MANAGEMENT) REGULATIONS 2007

The HSE state at the beginning of the Construction (Design and Management) Regulations 2007 (SI 2007/320) (C(DM)R 2007) that:

- 'All those who work in the construction industry have their part to play looking after their own health and safety and in improving the industry's health and safety record.'

DEFINITIONS

CONSTRUCTION WORK

'Construction work' is defined in C(DM)R 2007 as meaning the carrying out of any building, civil engineering or engineering construction work and includes:

- The construction, alteration, conversion, fitting out, commissioning, renovation, repair, upkeep, redecoration or other maintenance (including cleaning which involves the use of water or an abrasive at high pressure or the use of corrosive or toxic substances), de-commissioning, demolition or dismantling of a structure.

- The preparation for an intended structure, including site clearance, exploration, investigation (but not site survey) and excavation, and the clearance or preparation of the site or structure for use or occupation at its conclusion.

- The assembly on site of prefabricated elements to form a structure or the disassembly on site of prefabricated elements which, immediately before such disassembly, formed a structure.

- The removal of a structure or of any product or waste resulting from demolition or dismantling of a structure or from disassembly of prefabricated elements which immediately before such disassembly formed such a structure.

- The installation, commissioning, maintenance, repair or removal of mechanical, electrical, gas, compressed air, hydraulic, telecommunications, computer or similar services which are normally fixed within or to a structure.

It does not include the exploration for or extraction of mineral resources or activities preparatory thereto carried out at a place where such exploration or extraction is carried out.

'Construction project' will fall into one of two categories, 'notifiable' and 'non-notifiable', and these are defined below.

NOTIFIABLE PROJECTS

Except where the project is for a domestic client notification will be required to the HSE if the project, commonly referred to as a 'construction project' is likely to:

SIMPLY SAFETY

- last longer than 30 days or
- involve more than 500 person days of construction work, for example 50 people working for over 10 days

Any day on which construction work is carried out (including holidays and weekends) should be counted, even if the work on that day is of short duration. A 'person day' is one individual, including supervisors or specialist trades, carrying out construction work for one normal working shift.

Construction work for a domestic client is not notifiable and although a domestic client does not have duties under C(DM)R 2007, those who work for them on construction projects will.. A domestic client is someone who lives, or will live, in the premises where the work is carried out. The premises must not relate to any trade, business or undertaking.

NON-NOTIFIABLE PROJECTS

Are all those projects that do not meet the above criteria.

CONTRACTORS AND SELF-EMPLOYED

It should be noted that the C(DM)R 2007 have defined the term 'contractor' to include many groups that were originally felt by many persons to fall without the definition of contractor. The regulations state that anyone who directly employs, engages construction workers or control or manages construction work (as defined above) is a contractor for the purposes of these regulations.

This includes companies that use their own workforce to do construction work on their own premises. The duties on contractors apply whether the workers are employees or self-employed and to agency workers without distinction.

Thus the employer undertaking in-house projects employing their own staff definitely fall under the C(DM)R 2007 and must comply with the duties detailed below

DUTY HOLDERS

The employer is liable to be at the forefront of all projects both notifiable and non-notifiable and, as shown above, it is possible that he/she could end up as a multi-duty holder. As such and to enable the employer to fully discharge their duty, a brief description of the duties of all duty holders is detailed below.

THE CLIENT (EMPLOYER) – ROLES AND RESPONSIBILITIES

The client (Employer) will need to ensure that on ALL projects that he/she:

- checks the competence and resources of all appointees
- ensures there are suitable management arrangements for the project welfare facilities
- allows sufficient time and resources for all stages
- provides pre-construction information to designers and contractors

Where projects are notifiable under C(DM)R 2007, the employer must also:

Building Services

- appoint a CDM Co-coordinator
- appoint a Principal Contractor
- make sure that construction work does not start unless a construction phase plan is in place and there are adequate welfare facilities on site
- provide information relating to the health and safety file to the CDM Co-coordinator
- retain and provide access to the health and safety file

CDM Co-ordinators – Roles and Responsibilities

It is possible that in some cases the employer will be appointed as the CDM Co-coordinator. Whatever the case, the C(DM)R 2007 require that a CDM co-ordinator must be appointed to advise the employer on projects that last more than 30 days or involve 500 person days of construction work. The CDM Co-ordinator's role is to advise the employer on health and safety issues during the design and planning phases of construction work.

A CDM Co-ordinator is only required where the project is notifiable to:

- advise and assist the client with his/her duties
- notify details of the project to HSE
- co-ordinate health and safety aspects of design work and co-operate with others involved with the project
- facilitate good communication between the client, designers and contractors
- liaise with principal contractor regarding ongoing design work
- identify, collect and pass on pre-construction information
- prepare/update health and safety file

Designers – Roles and Responsibilities

The term 'designer' has a broad meaning and relates to the function performed, rather than the profession or job title. Designers are those who, as part of their work, prepare design drawings, specifications, bills of quantities and the specification of articles and substances. This could include architects, engineers and quantity surveyors as well as employers.

On all projects designers will need to:

- eliminate hazards and risks during design
- provide information about remaining risks
- Where projects are notifiable under the regulations, designers must also:
- check that the client is aware of their duties and that a CDM co-ordinator has been appointed
- provide information needed for the health and safety file

Principal Contractors – Roles and Responsibilities

A principal contractor is only required where the project is notifiable. The principal contractor's role is to plan, manage and co-ordinate health and safety while construction work is being undertaken. The principal contractor is usually the main or managing contractor for the work.

The principal contractor needs to:

SIMPLY SAFETY

- plan, manage and monitor construction phase in liaison with the contractors
- prepare, develop and implement a written plan and site rules (initial plan completed before the construction phase begins)
- give contractors relevant parts of the plan
- make sure suitable welfare facilities are provided from the start and maintained throughout the construction phase
- check competence of all appointees
- ensure all workers have site inductions and any further information and training needed for the work
- consult with the workers
- liaise with CDM coordinator regarding ongoing design
- secure the site

CONTRACTORS – ROLES AND RESPONSIBILITIES

A 'contractor' is a business who is involved in construction, alteration, maintenance or demolition work. This could involve the employer and his/her internal employees as well as other external contractors. In these cases on all projects the employer and all other contractors will need to:

- plan, manage and monitor their own work and that of their workers
- check the competence of all their appointees and workers
- train their own employees
- provide information to their workers
- ensure that there are adequate welfare facilities for their workers

In addition, where projects are notifiable under the C(DM)R 2007, contractors must also:

- check that the employer is aware of their duties, check that a CDM co-ordinator has been appointed and ensure that HSE has been notified before the work starts
- co-operate with the principal contractor in planning and managing work, including reasonable directions and site rules
- provide details to the principal contractor of any contractor engaged in connection with carrying out work
- provide any information needed for the health and safety file
- inform the principal contractor of any problems with the plan
- inform the principal contractor of reportable accidents, diseases and dangerous occurrences

WORKERS – ROLES AND RESPONSIBILITIES

A 'worker' is anyone who carries out work during the construction, alteration, maintenance or demolition of a building or structure. A worker could be, for example, a plumber, electrician, scaffolder, painter, decorator or steel erector, as well as those supervising the work such as the employer.

All employees or self-employed persons on construction sites should be better informed and have the opportunity to be more involved in health and safety. It is the duty of the employer as well as the worker to:

- ensure the worker only carries out construction work that they are competent to do
- report obvious risks

Building Services

- co-operate with others and co-ordinate work so as to ensure their own health and safety and that of others who may be affected by the work
- follow site health and safety rules and procedures

PARTICULARS TO BE NOTIFIED TO THE HSE

When the construction project meets the criteria to be a notifiable project, a F10 should be completed. A sample F10 can be found on the HSE web site at https://www.hse.gov.uk/forms/notification/index.htm.

Briefly, the information that needs to be provided to the HSE is as follows:

1. Date of forwarding of the F10.
2. Exact address of the construction site.
3. The name of the local authority where the site is located.
4. A brief description of the project and the construction work which it includes.
5. Contact details of the client (name, address, telephone number and email address, if available).
6. Contact details of the CDM co-ordinator (name, address, telephone number and email address, if available).
7. Contact details of the principal contractor (name, address, telephone number and email address, if available).
8. Date planned for the start of the construction phase.
9. The time allowed by the client to the principal contractor referred to in C(DM)R 2007, reg 15(b) for planning and preparation for construction work.
10. Planned duration of the construction phase.
11. Estimated maximum number of people at work on the construction site.
12. Planned number of contractors on the construction site.
13. Name and address of any contractor already appointed.
14. Name and address of any designer already engaged.
15. A declaration signed by or on behalf of the client that he/she is aware of his/her duties under these regulations.

THE HEALTH AND SAFETY FILE

When putting together the health and safety file, the employer should consider including information about each of the following where they are relevant to the health and safety of any future construction work. The level of detail should allow the likely risks to be identified and addressed by those carrying out the work:

Brief Description of The Work Carried Out.

Any residual hazards which remain and how they have been dealt with (e.g. surveys or other information concerning asbestos; contaminated land; water bearing strata; buried services etc).

Key structural principles (e.g. bracing, sources of substantial stored energy – including pre- or post-tensioned members) and safe working loads for floors and roofs, particularly where these may preclude placing scaffolding or heavy machinery there.

Hazardous materials used (e.g. lead paint; pesticides; special coatings which should not be burnt off etc).

Information regarding the removal or dismantling of installed plant and equipment (eg any special arrangements for lifting, order or other special instructions for dismantling etc).

SIMPLY SAFETY

Health and safety information about equipment provided for cleaning or maintaining the structure.

The nature, location and markings of significant services, including underground cables; gas supply equipment; fire-fighting services etc.

Information and as-built drawings of the structure, its plant and equipment (eg the means of safe access to and from service voids, fire doors and compartmentalisation etc).

The Employer should note that the ACOP to the regulations states that file does not need to include things that will be of no help when planning future construction work, for example:

- the pre-construction information, or construction phase plan;
- construction phase risk assessments, written systems of work and COSHH assessments;
- details about the normal operation of the completed structure;
- construction phase accident statistics;
- details of all the contractors and designers involved in the project (though it may be useful to include details of the principal contractor and CDM co-ordinator);
- contractual documents;
- information about structures, or parts of structures, that have been demolished – unless there are any implications for remaining or future structures, for example voids;
- information contained in other documents, but relevant cross-references should be included.

Some of these items may be useful to the client, or may be needed for purposes other than complying with the CDM Regulations, but the Regulations themselves do not require them to be included in the file. Including too much material may hide crucial information about risks.

WORK AT HEIGHT REGULATIONS 2005 (AS AMENDED)

DEFINITIONS

The employer should be aware that the Work at Height Regulations 2005 (SI 2005/735) (WHR 2005) state that a place is 'at height' if (unless these regulations are followed) a person could be injured falling from it, even if it is at or below ground level. The WAHR 2005 goes on to define 'work' as including

'... moving around at a place of work (except by a staircase in a permanent workplace) but not travel to or from a place of work. For instance, a sales assistant on a stepladder would be working at height, but we would not be inclined to apply the Regulations to a mounted police officer on patrol.'

Further information is available from the HSE publication Work at Height Regulations 2005 (as amended) a brief guide which may also be downloaded from the HSE web site at:

www.hse.gov.uk/pubns/indg401.pdf

Building Services

MANAGEMENT OF WORKING AT HEIGHTS

The WAHR 2005 came into force on 6 April 2005 and apply to all work at height where there is a risk of a fall, liable to cause personal injury, and they place duties on employers, (as well as the self-employed, and any person who controls the work of others, for example building owners who may contract others to work at height).

There is a simple hierarchy set out by the HSE for managing and selecting equipment for work at height. This means that the employers must:

- avoid work at height where they can
- use work equipment or other measures to prevent falls where they cannot avoid working at height
- where they cannot eliminate the risk of a fall, use work equipment or other measures to minimise the distance and consequences of a fall should one occur

To comply with the WAHR 2005, employers must ensure:

- all work at height is properly planned and organised;
- all work at height takes account of weather conditions that could endanger health and safety;
- those involved in work at height are trained and competent;
- the place where work at height is done is safe;
- equipment for work at height is appropriately inspected;
- the risks from fragile surfaces are properly controlled; and
- the risks from falling objects are properly controlled.

The WAHR 2005 include Schedules giving requirements for existing places of work and means of access for work at height, collective fall prevention (e.g. guardrails and working platforms), collective fall arrest (e.g. nets, airbags etc), personal fall protection (e.g. work restraints, fall arrest and rope access) and ladders. See below for additional information.

PLANNING

In planning the work, the employers must (SI 2005/735, Regs 4 and 6(1), (2)):

- Ensure that no work is done at height if it is safe and reasonably practicable to do it by any other way other than at height.
- Ensure that the work is properly planned, appropriately supervised, and carried out in as safe a way as is reasonably practicable.
- Plan for emergencies and rescue.
- Take account of the risk assessment carried out under the Management of Health and Safety at Work Regulations 1999 (SI 1999/3242) (MHSWR 1999), Reg 3.

SIMPLY SAFETY

Where he/she cannot eliminate the risk of a fall, he/she must use work equipment or other measures to minimise the distance and consequences of a fall should one occur.

- Use work equipment or other measures to prevent falls where they cannot avoid working at height.
- Avoid work at height where they can.

OTHER CONSIDERATIONS FOR THE EMPLOYER

In addition to the above, the employer must ensure that the following areas are taken into account:

Weather

Ensure that the work is postponed while weather conditions endanger health or safety (but this does not apply to emergency services acting in an emergency).

Emergency Procedures/Rescue

Ensure that emergency procedures and rescue are considered. This could include how you would rescue an operative who was taken ill whilst working at height or some failure of equipment being used. In practice, this would most probably involve use of emergency services such as the fire brigade, but you may have your own site-based emergency team.

Training

Ensure that everyone involved in the work is competent (or, if being trained, is supervised by a competent person). This will include involvement in organisation, planning, supervision, and the supply and maintenance of equipment.

Where other precautions do not entirely eliminate the risk of a fall occurring, you must (as far as it is reasonably practicable to do so) train those who will be working at height how to avoid falling, and how to avoid or minimise injury to themselves should they fall.

Place of Work

Ensure that the place where work is done at height (including the means of access) is safe and has features to prevent a fall, unless this would mean that it is not reasonably practicable for the worker to carry out the work safely (taking into account the demands of the task, equipment and working environment). Where this is not possible, the employer must provide equipment for preventing (as far as is reasonably practicable) a fall occurring. If this does not entirely eliminate the risk of a fall occurring, the employer must do all that is reasonably practicable to minimise the distance and effect of a fall.

Equipment

When selecting work at height equipment the employer must use the most suitable equipment, giving collective protection measures (e.g. guard rails) priority over personal protection measures (eg safety harnesses), as well as taking into account the working conditions and the risks to the safety of all those at the place where the work equipment is to be used

The employer must ensure that all equipment, temporary structures (e.g. scaffolding), and safety

Building Services

features comply with the detailed requirements of MHSWR 1999, Schedules 2–6, e.g. requirement for:

- Schedule 2   Guard rails, toe-boards, barriers, and similar collective means of operation.
- Schedule 3   Working platforms.
- Schedule 4   Collective safeguards for arresting falls.
- Schedule 5   Personal fall protection systems.
- Schedule 6   Ladders.

Inspections

The employer must ensure (as far as it is reasonably practicable to do so) that each individual place at which work is to be done at height is checked on every occasion before that place is used. This will involve checking the surface and every parapet, permanent rail etc.

The employer must also include any item that is mentioned within MHSWR 1999, Schedules 2–6 (see above) is inspected after it is assembled or installed (or after it has been assembled and installed if both are required), if its safety depends on how it is assembled or installed. It should be inspected as often as is necessary to ensure safety and, in particular, the employer should ensure that any deterioration can be detected and remedied in good time.

Before the employer uses any equipment which has come from another business, and before any equipment leaves their own business, he/she must ensure that it is accompanied by an indication (clear to everyone involved) that the last inspection required by the WAHR 2005 has been carried out.

The employer must ensure that any platform used for (or for access to) construction work (for the definition of 'construction work', see the Construction (Design and Management) Regulations 2007 at 2.187 above) and from which a person could fall more than 2 metres is inspected in place before use (and not more than seven days before use). Where it is a mobile platform, inspection at the site is sufficient without re-inspection every time it is moved.

The employer must ensure that the person inspecting a platform (see above) prepares a report before going off duty, giving the details listed below:

- the name and address of the person for whom the inspection was carried out
- the location of the work equipment inspected
- a description of the work equipment inspected
- the date and time of the inspection
- details of any matter identified that could give rise to a risk to the health or safety of any person
- details of any action taken as a result of any matter identified as giving rise to a risk to the health or safety of any person
- details of any further action considered necessary
- the name and position of the person making the report

The employer must ensure that he/she receives the report (or a copy) within 24 hours of

SIMPLY SAFETY

completing the inspection.

The employer must keep the report of a platform inspection made under the above instructions, safe from loss and unauthorised interference at the construction site until the work is completed and after that at the employer's office for further three months. The employer must be able to provide a printed copy when required.

The employer must keep all other records of inspection until the next inspection has been carried out.

Fragile Surfaces

The employer must ensure that no one working under their control goes onto or near a fragile surface unless that is the only reasonably practicable way for the worker to carry out the work safely, having regard to the demands of the task, equipment, or working environment.

If anyone does work on or near a fragile surface the employer must ensure (as far as it is reasonably practicable to do so) that suitable platforms, coverings, guard rails, and the like are provided (and used) to minimise the risk and must do all that is reasonably practicable, if any risk of a fall remains, to minimise the distance and effect of a fall.

If anyone working under the control of the employer may go onto or near a fragile surface, he/she must do all that is reasonably practicable to make them aware of the danger, preferably by prominent warning notices fixed at the approaches to the danger zone.

Falling Objects

Where it is necessary to prevent injury, the employer must do all that is reasonably practicable to prevent anything falling and, if it is not reasonably practicable, he/she must ensure that no one is injured by anything falling.

The employer must ensure that nothing is thrown or tipped from height if it is likely to injure anyone or stored in such a way that its movement is likely to injure anyone.

If the workplace contains an area in which there is a risk of someone being struck by a falling object or person, the employer must ensure that the area is clearly indicated and that (as far as reasonably practicable) unauthorised people are unable to reach it.

WORK AT HEIGHT (AMENDMENT) REGULATIONS 2007

The Work at Height (Amendment) Regulations 2007 (SI 2007/114) (WAH(A)R 2005), applies to those who work at height providing instruction or leadership to one or more people engaged in caving or climbing by way of sport, recreation, team building or similar activities in Great Britain.

CONFINED SPACES

A confined space is a place which is substantially enclosed (though not always entirely), and where serious injury can occur from hazardous substances or conditions within the space or nearby (e.g. lack of oxygen).

A number of people are killed or seriously injured in the UK each year in confined spaces. These occur across a wide range of industries, from those involving complex plant through simple storage vessels. Those killed include not only people working in the confined spaces but those

Building Services

who try to rescue them without proper training or equipment. There are a number of common maintenance tasks which the employer is most likely to manage and which can involve entry into a confined space and therefore they are advised to consider their duties and the risks involved, eg filter changes in large air handling units and internal inspection of tanks.

LEGISLATION

The Health and Safety at Work etc Act 1974 places duties upon the employer to ensure the health and safety of their employees as well as others who may be affected by the employers undertaking. This duty is further reinforced by the Confined Spaces Regulations 1997 (SI 1997/1713) (CSR 1997).

The CSR 1997 place key duties upon the employer as follows:

- Take all reasonable steps to avoid the need for entry into confined spaces. This should be done by the risk assessment process and it is recommended that all such assessments are recorded and reviewed on a regular basis.
- Where there is no alternative but to enter a confined space, the employer must ensure the health and safety of those whom he/she employs to enter a confined space:
- Appoint a competent person who has sufficient knowledge and training to undertake the necessary risk assessments and review/produce a detailed method statement for the proposed work prior to any work being carried out in a confined space.
- Operate a documented safe system of work for entry to and working within a confined space.
- Operate a permit to work system, which incorporates permits for entry to confined spaces.

Should entry to a confined space be required and where there is a danger of oxygen deficiency or a danger of other gases, vapours and so on then the employer must ensure the following:

- There are suitable numbers of maintained and working breathing apparatus and safety belts, harnesses and ropes.
- Suitable and sufficient training has been given to those employees who may be required to use such equipment in the use of the breathing apparatus and the safety belts/harnesses and ropes.

Where the employer employs a contractor to carry out work in confined spaces he/she must ensure:

- The equipment being used is in working condition and operates correctly so as to permit safe entry to a confined space where there is a danger of oxygen deficiency or a danger of other gases, vapours etc.
- Suitable and sufficient training has been given to those contractors in the use of the safety equipment.
- The equipment being used by the contractor is suitable, sufficient and is maintained correctly.

Further information may be found in the following guidance: Safe Working in confined spaces INDG 258 - http://www.hse.gov.uk/pubns/indg258.pdf

SIMPLY SAFETY

ELECTRICITY AT WORK REGULATIONS 1989

Under the Electricity at Work Regulations 1989 (SI 1989/635) (EWR 1989) the employer has a number of duties. Within these regulations many of the duties are absolute duties, which mean to say they must be undertaken (SI 1989/635, Reg 4(4)).

The employer must ensure the following:

- All electrical installations and equipment are installed in accordance with the Institute of Electrical Engineers IEE / IET Wiring Regulations 17th Edition (BS 7671:2008 Requirements for Electrical Installations). These regulations do not have statutory force; however, they are considered to be best practice and any installation adopting the IEE Wiring Regulations should satisfy the requirements under EWR 1989.
- All electrical installations in the UK must now conform to BS7671: 2008. Furthermore, most work on installations in dwellings in England and Wales now falls under the Building Regulations Part P.
- Faulty electrical installations cause around 12,500 electrical fires and an average of 81 deaths per year. These fires are frequently due to lack of testing and inspection, poor housekeeping, and often both.
- The fixed installations are maintained in a safe condition through regular routine safety testing and maintenance.
- All portable appliances are regularly maintained and that they are tested in accordance with the recommendations detailed within the risk assessment. A sample guide issued by the HSE is detailed below in Table 9:01.
- There is a safe system of work in operation that implements safe systems for working on electrical equipment as well as for maintenance, inspection and testing.
- Working on live electrical equipment is strictly forbidden. This work can then only be carried out when a suitable risk assessment has been undertaken, and that a method statement has been produced giving full details of how the work should be undertaken, the risks etc, and that a permit to work has been issued by a competent electrical person before any work commences.
- Only those employees who are competent electricians are permitted to undertake any electrical work.
- All work on the organisation's electrical system that is above 450v will be undertaken by approved specialist contractors who are considered to be competent, fully trained and equipped for this type of work. All work of this nature is forbidden to be undertaken by the employer's employees.
- The employer's safe system of work is passed on to any contractors working on his/her premises, that they fully understand the safe system and agree to work to it and conduct themselves accordingly whilst on the premises.
- Suitable and sufficient training has been provided to all employees, whose work involves working with electricity to enable them to carry out their work in a safe and sensible manner, thus not putting their health and safety at risk.
- Suitable personal protective equipment is provided where required, and that it is maintained in a good condition.
- Suitable detailed records are kept and maintained for the items given above.

Building Services

- Under the Building (Amendment) (No 3) Regulations 2004 (SI 2004/3210) (B(A)(No3)R 2004), employers must ensure that all domestic electrical wiring installation work complies with Approved Document P.

Table 9.01: Office and other low-risk environments only: Suggested initial intervals

Equipment/environment	User checks	Formal visual inspection	Combined inspection and testing
Battery-operated (less than 20 volts)	No	No	No
Extra low voltage: (less than 50 volts AC), eg telephone equipment, low voltage desk lights	No	No	No
Information technology: eg desktop computers, VDU screens	No	Yes, 2–4 years	No if double insulated – otherwise up to 5 years
Photocopiers, fax machines: NOT hand-held. Rarely moved.	No	Yes, 2–4 years	No if double insulated – otherwise up to 5 years
Double insulated equipment: NOT hand-held. Moved occasionally, eg fans, table lamps, slide projectors	No	Yes, 2–4 years	No
Double insulated equipment: HAND-HELD, eg some floor cleaners	Yes	Yes, 6 months–1 year	No
Earthed equipment (Class 1): eg electric kettles, some floor cleaners	Yes	Yes, 6 months–1 year	Yes, 1–2 years
Cables (leads) and plugs connected to the above Extension leads (mains voltage)	Yes	Yes, 6 months–4 years depending on the type of equipment it is connected to	Yes, 1–5 years depending on the type of equipment it is connected to

SIMPLY SAFETY

NOTE:- Experience of operating the maintenance system over a period of time, together with information on faults found, should be used to review the frequency of inspection.

It should also be used to review whether and how often equipment and associated leads and plugs should receive a combined inspection and test.

Further guidance may be found in the following HSE publications: -

- Maintaining Portable Electrical equipment in offices and other low risk environments, INDG236.
- Electrical Safety and you, INDG231.
- Maintenance priorities in catering, HSE information sheet (Catering information sheet 12).
- Industry Guidance can also be sought from the Institution of Engineering and Technology at www.theiet.org.

GAS SAFETY

LEGISLATION

To control the risk from the supply and use of flammable gas, there are three significant items of legislation:

- The Gas Safety (Management) Regulations 1996 (SI 1996/551), concerned with piped gas distribution.
- The Gas Appliances (Safety) Regulations 1995 (SI 1995/1629), concerned with new commercial and domestic (not industrial) gas appliances.
- The Gas Safety (Installation and Use) Regulations 1998 (SI 1998/2451), concerned with the safety of installations, maintenance and use of gas appliances.

THE GAS SAFE REGISTER

The Gas Safe Register operates under an agreement with the HSE. The gas industries previous scheme, CORGI Gas Registration, had been in place for more than 17 years and during that time the number of domestic gas related fatalities had fallen significantly

Gas Safe Register maintain the register of businesses and operatives who are competent to undertake both piped natural gas and liquefied petroleum gas (LPG) in Great Britain, Northern Ireland, the Isle of Man and Guernsey. Under the Gas Safety (Installation and Use) Regulations 1998 for a gas engineering business to legally undertake gas work that is within the scope of the Regulations they must be on the Gas Safe Register.

Gas Safe registered engineers carry an identity card which consumers are encouraged to ask an engineer for before they have gas work carried out in their home. The front of the card has a photograph, a registration number and an expiry date and the reverse shows the different categories of work that the engineer is qualified to undertake, e.g. cookers, boilers, gas fires.

New businesses and engineers with no previous history or those returning to the industry who have a history of complaints or a record of unsafe gas work will be subject to a time limited probationary period. During that period they will be required to report all gas work they carry out so it can be inspected by a Gas Safe Register Inspector.

The Gas Safe Register have a team of inspectors who monitor that gas work is being undertaken competently and safely. They deal with complaints and undertake risk based proactive inspections and work closely with regulators such as HSE and Local Authorities.

Gas engineers and consumers can contact the Gas Safe Register in any of these ways:

- Through the web at: - http://www.gassaferegister.co.uk/advice/gas_safety_in_the_home/doing_diy.aspx
- Phone - Consumers: 0800 408 5500; Engineers: 0800 408 5577
- Email - enquiry@gassaferegister.co.uk
- By post - PO Box 6804, Basingstoke RG24 4NB
- In an Emergency
- If you smell gas then call the free 24-hour National Grid Gas Emergency Helpline:
- England, Scotland and Wales: 0800 111 999
- Isle of Man: 01624 644 444
- Northern Ireland : 0800 002 001
- Jersey: 01534 755555
- Guernsey: 01481 749000

It is the responsibility of you, the employer, to ensure that any gas appliances within your premises are safe and without risk to the health and safety of employees. To enable you to discharge this duty there are various actions that must be undertaken:

- Ensure that appliances are installed and maintained properly. Appliances should be checked for safety at least every 12 months.
- Ensure that only companies that are registered with the Gas Safe Register are permitted to service and maintain equipment. The employer must always ask to see a current Gas Safe Register registration document.
- Ensure that there is sufficient fresh air available for any gas appliance.
- Ensure that there is a system in place to prevent the use of any appliance that is suspected or has been found to be unsafe.
- Ensure that there is an emergency procedure to turn off the gas in the event of a suspected leak and to notify the gas supplier, or to evacuate the premises if the gas cannot be turned off at the meter.

EMPLOYERS AS LANDLORDS

Employers who act as Landlords must arrange maintenance by a Gas Safe Registered engineer for all pipe work, appliances and flues, which they own and have provided for their tenants use.

Employers who act as Landlords must also arrange for an annual gas safety check to be carried out every 12 months by a Gas Safe Registered engineer

Employers who act as Landlords must keep a record of the safety check for 2 years and issue a copy to each existing tenant within 28 days of the check being completed and issue a copy to

SIMPLY SAFETY

any new tenants before they move in.

For more information on Landlords duties refer to the HSE website: -
http://www.hse.gov.uk/gas/domestic/faqlandlord.htm

WATER
CONTROL OF LEGIONELLA

INTRODUCTION

Legionnaires Disease is one of a group of diseases collectively known as legionellosis. 37 different species of bacteria are associated with legionellosis, the most dangerous being Legionella pneumophilia. Infection by L. pneumophilia can result in pneumonia and other potentially life-threatening effects. Legionellosis is associated with a fatality rate of approximately 12%.

SOURCE

Legionella organisms are widespread in natural water sources and have been found in rivers, lakes, mud and soil. However, legionella can also colonise man-made re-circulating hot and water systems such as storage tanks, calorifiers and air conditioning systems.

ROUTE OF INFECTION

Legionellosis is caused by the inhalation of airborne droplets, which contain legionella bacteria. However, infection can only occur under certain conditions that permit the growth and multiplication of the organism and involve the creation of droplets, which can be inhaled.

LEGAL REQUIREMENTS

The Approved Code of Practice for 'The control of Legionella bacteria in water systems' (L8) applies to the control of Legionella bacteria in any undertaking involving work activity and to premises controlled in connection with a trade, business or other undertaking where water is used or stored and where there is a means of creating and transmitting water droplets which may be inhaled, thereby causing a reasonably foreseeable risk of exposure to Legionella bacteria.

A water system includes all plant/equipment and components associated with that system, eg all associated pipe-work, pumps, feed tanks, valves, showers, heat exchangers, quench tanks, chillers etc. It is very important that the system is considered in its entirety and not, for example, just a cooling tower in isolation.

The employer needs to ensure that a competent person carries out a suitable and sufficient risk assessment to identify and assess the risk of legionellosis from the company's work activities and water sources and any necessary precautionary measures.

The employer needs to ensure that the risk assessment identifies all systems that are susceptible to colonisation by Legionella and which incorporate a potential means for creating and disseminating water droplets shall be identified and that the risks they present are addressed. Risks need to be assessed not just for the routine operation or use of the system, but also in relation to maintenance, breakdown, abnormal operation, and commissioning or unusual circumstances.

Where the assessment demonstrates that there is no reasonably foreseeable risk or that risks are insignificant and unlikely to increase, it is likely that the employer need not take any further measures. It is important, however, that all such risk assessments are reviewed periodically.

Where the assessment shows that there is a reasonably foreseeable risk, the employer needs to ensure that use of the water systems, plant or systems of work that lead to exposure are avoided so far as is reasonably practicable. Where it is found that this is not reasonably practicable, the employer needs to ensure that a written scheme is produced for minimising the risk from exposure.

The employer needs to ensure that any written scheme produced is sufficiently specific and detailed to enable him/her to implement and manage it effectively. In particular, the scheme needs to contain such information about the plant and system as is necessary to minimise the risk from exposure:

- an up-to-date plan showing the layout of the plant or system, including parts that are temporarily out of use (a schematic plan will suffice)
- a description of the correct and safe operation
- the precautions to be taken

The primary objectives of any written scheme are to avoid conditions that permit Legionella to proliferate and to avoid creating a spray or aerosol. Where this is impractical, the risk may be controlled by minimising the release of droplets and by preventing water conditions that permit Legionella to proliferate.

In general, proliferation may be avoided in the following ways:

- avoiding water temperatures between 20°C and 46°C
- avoiding water stagnation
- avoiding the use of materials in the system that can harbour or provide nutrient for bacteria and other organisms
- keeping the system clean so as to avoid the build up of sediments etc which may harbour bacteria or provide a nutrient source for them
- the use of a suitable water treatment programme where it is appropriate and safe to do so and
- ensuring that the system operates safely and correctly and is well maintained

OPERATION OF COOLING TOWERS

The employer shall ensure that the local authority is notified of all installations of wet cooling towers and evaporative condensers under his/her control in accordance with the requirements of the Notification of Cooling Towers and Evaporative Condensers Regulations 1999 (SI 1999/2225) (NCTECR 1999). A copy of the notification needs to be kept in the water services log for the building in which they are located.

The employer needs to ensure that the risk of legionnaire's disease from cooling tower systems is controlled:

- maintaining the system in a clean and sound condition
- controlling water quality
- carefully monitoring precautions

SIMPLY SAFETY

It is important that cooling tower systems are kept in regular use wherever possible. Where a system is used intermittently or may be needed at short notice, the employer should ensure that it is run approximately once each week. The employer should also ensure that the system is dosed with water treatment chemicals at the same time and that the water quality is carefully monitored. The whole system needs to be run for long enough to thoroughly distribute the treated water.

If a system is out of use for a week or longer the employer needs to ensure that the water is treated with biocide immediately upon reuse.

If a system is out of use for a month or longer the employer needs to ensure that a competent person undertakes the following actions when the system is isolated:

- it is drained down
- all supplies are isolated
- it is cleaned and chlorinated

When the employer intends to re-commission a system he needs to ensure that the following tasks are undertaken prior to re-commissioning:

- the system needs to be repainted where necessary
- the system needs to be serviced and calibrated
- a review treatment regime needs to be undertaken
- the system needs to be refilled and chlorinated
- the system needs to be tested to ensure that the calibration is correct every five days for approximately one month, or until the tower is under control

As the employer you need to ensure that details of all maintenance and treatment of the cooling tower systems are kept within the water log.

OPERATION, MAINTENANCE AND INSPECTION OF DOMESTIC WATER SERVICES

The employer needs to ensure that water services are operated at temperatures that prevent the proliferation of Legionella:

- hot water storage (calorifiers) are operated at a temperature of at least 60°C
- hot water distribution is operated at a temperature of 50°C attainable at taps furthest from the storage device within one minute of running
- cold water storage and distribution is operated at a temperature of 20°C or below
- all storage tanks comply with all water bylaws

You as the employer need to ensure so far as is reasonably practicable that pipe work is as short and direct as possible, especially where it serves intermittently used taps and appliances. you should make sure that there are no dead legs are left when undertaking any alterations to the services, and that any dead legs discovered during routine inspections or maintenance are removed.

You also need to make sure that all pipe work has been suitably lagged so as to maintain temperatures.

You as the employer need to ensure that there is a suitable and sufficient maintenance and inspection procedure in place to ensure safe delivery of water to the building. A sample system run by maintenance operatives could be as follows:

- Daily: check the water temperatures at all calorifiers, report any failures to the employer, keeping a record of the time and results.
- Weekly: flush showerheads and spray taps at full operating temperature for at least 10 minutes, and keep a record of the time to confirm the operation.
- Monthly:
    - descale and disinfect all showerheads and spray taps, keeping records on the showerheads' chlorination to confirm that the maintenance was carried out
    - check water temperatures of domestic water services at taps after one minute's running, recording the time and results to confirm the test was carried out
    - check the condition of any on-line water treatment systems, remedy any defects, and record the time and results.
- Six monthly:
    - before carrying out the monthly tests, raise the temperature of the hot water system to at least 70oC, and ensure that each tap is run at a temperature of 60oC for at least one minute. The results of the test need to be recorded.
- Annually:
    - check the conditions in tanks, for the presence of organic materials, vermin etc
    - check the conditions in calorifiers, for organic materials and unduly heavy build-up of scale
    - check the condition of accessible pipe work and insulation
    - test all domestic water services for the presence of Legionella, keeping a record of all results.

You as the employer need to ensure that all defects identified during maintenance and inspection of the domestic water services are remedied as soon as is reasonably practicable, unless there is a risk to health, in which case action must be taken immediately. Details of all defects and action taken need to be recorded and kept for future reference/inspection.

FURTHER INFORMATION MAY BE FOUND AT:

HSE website at www.hse.gov.uk within the Legionnaires disease microsite.

The publication Legionnaires Disease a guide for employers. IAC 127 (rev2) ISBN 0 7176 1773 4.

APPROVAL OF CONTRACTORS

Before any contractor is appointed to carry out work the employer needs to ensure that the company proposed for the work is not only capable to undertake the work but is compliant with current health and safety legislation. The best way to ascertain if the prospective contractors do comply is to issue to them, as a pre-tender document, a pre-qualification questionnaire based upon their health and safety experience, record and compliance.

PRE-QUALIFICATION QUESTIONS

An example of such a pre-qualification questionnaire would be to include questions on the following topics:

- Do they have a health and safety policy and is it up to date?
- Who is responsible for health and safety within the company and what are their qualifications?

SIMPLY SAFETY

- Do they have a professional health and safety adviser (in-house or contract)?
- Provide details of all insurances.
- Provide details of their health and safety training for operatives and management.
- Provide details of their accident statistics for the last three years.
- Provide details of their dealings and any notices/prosecutions by the enforcing authorities over the last three years.
- Provide details of any safe systems of work that they operate including permits to work etc
- Provide details of any memberships of professional bodies, especially health and safety organisations.

It is strongly recommended that as the employer you do not place any order or allow the contractor to start work until you have received the contractor's completed pre-qualification questionnaire and supporting documentation, and that you have verified that the contractor is competent to carry out the work for which they will be appointed; and until they have established a safe system of work. Once this has been done the employer can then issue site authorisation / approval for work documentation, authorising nominated persons from the vetted contractor to carry out work on his/her premises.

SITE AUTHORISATION / APPROVAL FOR WORK

No contractor should be permitted access to an organisation's premises until they have been given a valid site authorisation by the employer.

This authorisation should not be issued until:

- All named individuals from the contracting company have received site induction training from the employer or an authorised person appointed by the employer.
- The contractors have provided the employer with a confidentiality agreement signed by each individual contractor employee.
- The contractor has submitted a completed Job Safety Risk Assessment and method statement for the works that they will be carrying out, to the employer and that it has been approved by the employer or their nominated representative.

The individual contractor can then be issued with the necessary security pass and can be added to the list of personnel authorised to work within the employer's premises. This must not be confused with a Permit To Work (PTW), which is discussed in depth below.

SAFE SYSTEM OF WORK

A safe system of work has been defined by the Health and Safety Executive as follows:

'A safe system of work is the formal procedure which results from the systematic examination of a task in order to identify all the hazards. It defines safe methods to ensure that hazards are eliminated and risks minimised.'
(HSE, 1991)

Taking the above definition it can be seen that part of your general duties as the employer has to be to ensure that all work carried out on your premises is safe and without risk to health. You need to ensure that before any work is carried out within your buildings that it is 'systematically examined' and that hazards etc are minimised. It is recommended therefore that this can be achieved by the production of a detailed method statement. You need to ensure that all method statements and risk assessments are prepared by the contractor undertaking the work and that the contractor does the following:

- identify the work to be carried out and its location
- explain in detail how the work will be carried out
- identify safe access and egress routes for personnel, plant and materials
- identify any mechanical plant, access plant and lifting equipment that will be used, along with details of where it will be sited and how it will be used
- name the person responsible for supervising the work
- name all those who will be involved in the work
- identify all recognised risks to health and safety associated with the work
- identify how any risks identified on the checklist will be controlled
- identify any necessary permit to work that may be required
- set out the steps to be taken to remove or control all other risks to health and safety identified
- identify the effect of the activity on the company's business continuity and the steps that will be taken to minimise any disruption
- identify what, if any, services will be disrupted
- set out the action to be taken in case of emergency
- give the name and telephone number of the person to be contacted in case of emergency

PERMIT TO WORK

A permit to work is a formal document that forms a written authorisation for specific work to be carried out and is designed for the safety of persons at work during the carrying out of high-risk work activities where the failure of one control measure is likely to result in a serious accident or fatality.

The permit to work should detail the specific area in which the work is to be carried out, it should fully detail the plant/equipment that is to be worked upon and it should give a specific time frame within which the work is to be carried out. Permits to work are normally required for the following, although it is not an exhaustive list:

- asbestos
- confined spaces
- electrical work (high voltage or multi fed systems)
- lifts
- roofs and elevations
- hot works
- excavations
- hazardous areas

In most cases the employer will find it easier to use permits that have been specifically designed for the high-risk activity and generally these would be as follows:

- Confined Space
- Electrical Work
- Work at Height
- Hot Work

SIMPLY SAFETY

GENERAL PERMIT (TO COVER HIGH-RISK ACTIVITIES)

It is imperative that competent employees issuing permits are trained in the correct method for completing a permit and larger organisations will most likely employ an 'Authorised Person' (AP) for such a task.

In some organisations permits to work are issued to all contractors coming onto site no matter what the job involves and this tends to be used more as a security measure rather than a process to control high-risk activities. The danger here is that such a system will dilute the Permit to Work system and in such cases then it is recommended that a separate system such as an 'Authority to Work' system is used.

The employer needs to ensure that when a permit is issued that a competent person issues it and that the method statement and risk assessments produced is fully comprehensive and that the work activities are monitored on a periodic basis and records maintained during the life of the permit. Once everything is agreed, then a permit can be issued; it is important, though, that each permit identify the following:

- a unique permit identity number and the work to which the permit applies
- the number of the job safety risk assessment record that applies to the work
- the exact location where the work is being carried out
- the precise start and end date and time for which the permit will be valid
- details of isolations made
- the precise start and end date and time for which the permit will be valid
- the name of the competent supervisor
- the names of the competent persons who will be carrying out the work
- the safety requirements including control measures/precautions and the provision of personal protective equipment
- any other permits that are applicable
- details of how and when the works covered under the permit were monitored
- the hand back / cancellation procedure on the completion or suspension of work

Once issued it is important that the work being undertaken under a Permit to Work is monitored to ensure that the work is being undertaken in accordance with the permit and accompanying documentation. Such monitoring should be completed at regular intervals cognisant of the risks involved and the work location and records should be maintained for inspection if required.

Further details of how to operate a Permit to Work system may be found in the following HSE publications:

- HS(G)250 – Guidance on Permit to Work Systems.
- HS(G)253 – The Safe Isolation of Plant and Equipment.

SICK BUILDING SYNDROME

Sick Building Syndrome (SBS) is a term that relates to 'illnesses' that are suffered by employees and which normally manifest themselves through various recognisable symptoms. Everyone at work will suffer occasional headaches, dry throats and sore eyes at some time and these could

Building Services

be due to a variety of factors that are attributable to the workplace. However, the employer needs to be on the alert for symptoms that are persistent whilst at work but diminish when away from work and could be an indicator of possible Sick Building Syndrome.

There are occasions when people in particular buildings can experience the above type of symptoms more often than is usual within other buildings. It has been found that symptoms tend to increase in severity with the time spent in the building and improve over time or disappear when the person is away from the building. Although the symptoms are generally fairly mild they can affect not only the individual's performance but also that of their colleagues. The symptoms include the following:

- eye, nose and throat irritation
- stuffy or runny nose
- dry or itchy skin or skin rash
- headaches, lethargy, irritability, poor concentration
- nausea and dizziness

Sick Building Syndrome is not a recognised illness that can be diagnosed precisely and thus the employer must rely upon improving the environment of the workplace rather than having medical aid to cure the illness.

LEGAL DUTIES

The employer has legal duties under several pieces of legislation to ensure that the workplace is safe and without risks to health for those at work and although there is no specific legislation referring to Sick Building Syndrome (SBS) he/she must still take the situation very seriously.

The employer needs to be aware that most cases of SBS will occur due to the presence of several factors being in combination rather that a single issue. Each case or 'outbreak' of SBS needs to be viewed separately as the factors involved in the outbreak will be unlikely to be the same for two buildings.

The employer, in trying to understand the factors that have come together and have brought about a suspected incident of SBS, needs to look at two main topics: building issues and work issues.

Taking the Building Issues, the employer needs to consider the state of the following within the building:

- building and office design
- building services and maintenance
- indoor environment and air quality

Taking the work issues, the employer will have to consider that certain factors may be beyond his control and action from other departments may be required to rectify the items listed below:

- employees unsure of job roles
- routine work
- work with display screen equipment
- unhelpful management practices
- lack of management training

SIMPLY SAFETY

- the culture within the company/department

HOW TO ENSURE OPERATION WITHOUT SICK BUILDING SYNDROME

As explained above there is no absolute cause of Sick Building Syndrome (SBS) and, therefore, you will not be able to take a single action to cure the problem, you will need to undertake your own investigation into the building-related areas and will need to satisfy yourself that everything is operating to optimum efficiency.

As the employer you will need to look at some of the areas below in an effort to at least eliminate a possible cause of trouble:

- Does air conditioning operate in the building and is it working?
- Is the heating and ventilation operating correctly?
- Does the ventilation require cleaning and is it maintained correctly?
- Is the lighting sufficient, does it cause glare and is there any flicker?
- What is the level of user control?
- Is the equipment within the workplace correctly maintained and repaired?
- Is the cleaning effective?
- Does the workplace suffer from dust from old paper/carpets etc?

As the employer you will need to keep your employees of the area affected informed of progress. However it is possible that a solution will be without your experience and you will then need to consult specialists within certain fields in an effort to solve this particular problem – such persons as building service engineers, occupational health practitioners, occupational hygienists, ergonomists and management specialists.

PRESSURE SYSTEMS SAFETY REGULATIONS 2000

The Pressure Systems Safety Regulations 2000 (SI 2000/128) and the Pressure Equipment Regulations 1999 (SI 1999/2001) apply to all plant and systems that contain a relevant fluid. A relevant fluid is defined as steam or gas under pressure and liquids under pressure which become gases upon release to the atmosphere, at a pressure greater than 0.5 bar (about 7psi) above atmospheric (except for steam).

Typical examples of pressure systems and equipment are:

- Boilers and steam heating systems.
- Pressurised process plant and piping.
- Compressed air systems (Fixed and portable).
- Pressure cookers, autoclaves and retorts.
- Heat exchangers and refrigeration plant.
- Valves, steam traps and filters.
- Pipe work and hoses.
- Pressure gauges and level indicators.

The principal causes of incidents are:

- Poor equipment and system design.
- Poor maintenance of equipment.
- Unsafe system of work.
- Operator error, poor training and supervision.

Building Services

- Poor installation.
- Inadequate repairs or modifications.

The employer has specific duties under these regulations:

- When installing new equipment ensure that it is suitable for its intended purpose and installed correctly.
- The pressure system should be designed and manufactured from suitable materials.
- Establish the safe operating limits of the plant.
- Fit suitable protective devices and ensure they function properly.
- Have a suitable written scheme drawn up or certified by a competent person for the examination at appropriate intervals of the following:
  - pressure vessels included in the regulations
  - all safety devices
  - all pipe work that is potentially dangerous
- Arrange for a competent person to carry out examinations within the intervals set down in the scheme.
- Provide adequate operating instructions (including emergency instructions) to any person operating it by way of an operation manual.
- Provide suitable on the job training as well as supervision for all new employees.
- Ensure the pressure system is maintained in good repair.
- Keep adequate records of the most recent examination and any manufacturer's records supplied with the new plant.

Further Information is available from the following HSE publications:

- L22 (rev 1998) Safe Use of Work Equipment. Provision and Use of Work Equipment Regulations 1998. Approved Code of Practice and Guidance.
- L24 Workplace (Health, Safety and Welfare) Regulations 1992 — Approved Code of Practice.
- L82 A Guide to the Pipelines Safety Regulations 1996.
- L122 Safety of Pressure Systems: Pressure Systems Safety Regulations 2000: Approved Code of Practice.

TRANSPORTABLE GAS CONTAINERS (GAS CYLINDERS)

The current legislation that applies is the Pressure Systems and Transportable Gas Containers Regulations 1989 (SI 1989/2169).

It is worth noting that the definition of 'transportable gas container' as opposed to a 'mobile pressure system' as covered in the Pressure Systems Safety Regulations 2000 (SI 2000/128) has been defined as a container, e.g. gas cylinder, that can be removed from its appliance when empty and transported to a place where it can be refilled.

As the employer your responsibilities under these regulations are mainly limited to safety when using gas cylinders that is unless you are involved in the manufacture, filling and importation of all existing gas containers.

SIMPLY SAFETY

Generally your duty as the employer is to ensure that they have suitable and sufficient information on the following areas:

- the cylinders, their design, construction and identification
- the gases contained within the cylinders, for example propane, oxygen, nitrogen, acetylene, carbon dioxide etc
- how the cylinders should be transported, carried and lifted
- the correct storage for each type of cylinder
- what segregation is required
- how to make safe connections
- the correct equipment that is required, for example gauges, hoses, end connections, flashback arrestors, use of correct personal protective equipment
- how to keep the equipment safe
- what emergency procedures are required

Further information may be obtained from:

- The British Compressed Gases Association at their website www.bcgs.co.uk.
- Or the HSE publications:
- The safe use of compressed gases in welding, flame cutting and allied processes. HS(G)139.
- The safe use of gas cylinders. HS(G)308.

CHAPTER 10
TOOLS AND EQUIPMENT

PROVISION AND USE OF WORK EQUIPMENT REGULATIONS 1998 – OVERVIEW

LEGAL REQUIREMENTS

The Regulations require risks to people's health and safety, from equipment that they use at work, to be prevented or controlled. In addition to the requirements of PUWER, lifting equipment is also subject to the requirements of the Lifting Operations and Lifting Equipment Regulations 1998.

WHAT DOES PUWER DO?

In general terms, the Regulations require that equipment provided for use at work is:

- suitable for the intended use;
- safe for use, maintained in a safe condition and, in certain circumstances, inspected to ensure this remains the case;
- used only by people who have received adequate information, instruction and training; and
- accompanied by suitable safety measures, eg protective devices, markings, warnings.

The introduction of the *Provision and Use of Work Equipment Regulations 1998 (SI 1998/2306) (PUWER 1998)* saw the introduction of some important health and safety laws for the provision and use of work equipment. It also saw the rationalisation of many old and potentially obsolete regulations relating to machine guarding and such matters. *PUWER 1998* cover the following:

- the definition of who has duties
- the general duties which can apply to the employer in respect of suitable equipment, as well as the maintenance, inspection, information and instructions and training of operatives on the equipment
- that the equipment is able to control selected hazards

Within the regulations the words 'use' and 'work equipment' are liberally used and it is worth taking a moment to understand (within the terms of the regulations) what these words mean:

- use – This term means any activity that involves work equipment. This means starting, stopping, programming, setting, transporting, repairing, modifying, maintaining, servicing and cleaning (*SI 1998/2306, Reg 2(1)*).
- work equipment – This term means any machinery, appliance, apparatus or tool or assembly of components that function as a whole (*SI 1998/2306, Reg 2(1)*).

The regulations give a non-exhaustive list of work equipment that is covered by these regulations; as can be seen by the sample below the equipment is far-reaching:

- company car
- bunsen burner
- car ramp
- scaffolding

SIMPLY SAFETY

- computer
- portable drill
- lifting slings
- pressure water cleaners
- forklift truck
- soldering iron
- vehicle hoist
- meat cleaver
- ladder
- handsaw
- photocopies

(SI 1998/2306, Reg 2 Guidance 2 Work Equipment 62)

It is important for the employer to remember that *PUWER 1998* should be linked in with the *Management of Health and Safety at Work Regulations 1999 (SI 1999/3242)*.

TO WHOM DO THE REGULATIONS APPLY?

If you are an employer or self-employed person and you provide equipment for use at work, or if you have control of the use of equipment, then the Regulations will apply to you.

They do not apply to equipment used by the public, for example compressed-air equipment used in a garage forecourt. However, such circumstances are covered by the Health and Safety at Work etc Act 1974 (HSW Act).

While the employers staff do not have duties under PUWER, they do have general duties under the HSW Act and the Management of Health and Safety at Work Regulations 1999 (MHSWR). For example to take reasonable care of themselves and others who may be affected by their actions, and to co-operate with their employer.

The Regulations cover places where the HSW Act applies – these include factories, offshore installations, offices, shops, hospitals, hotels, places of entertainment etc. PUWER also applies in common parts of shared buildings and temporary places of work such as construction sites. While the Regulations cover equipment used by people working from home, they do not apply to domestic work in a private household.

LEGAL REQUIREMENTS OF PUWER 1998 – SUITABILITY, MAINTENANCE AND INSPECTION

SUITABILITY

The suitability of the work equipment is the focal point of the regulations and addresses the safety of the work equipment from three separate directions (*SI 1998/2306, Reg 4*):

- the initial integrity of the work equipment
- the place where the work equipment will be used
- the purpose for which it will be used

The regulations require that any work equipment must be suitable by design, construction or adaptation for the actual work it is provided to do. The employer must take into account any ergonomic risks, that is that the design of the task has taken into account the shape, size and limitations of the operator.

Tools and Equipment

MAINTENANCE

This regulation is very broadly based and requires that work equipment is maintained safe to use through both planned preventive maintenance and repair. The employer should keep an up-to-date maintenance log for all equipment and they must ensure that a competent person maintains the equipment (*SI 1998/2306, reg 5*).

INSPECTION

Where during the installation or even while the machinery is in operation a significant risk has been identified, and where it is possible that deterioration would be likely to lead to a dangerous situation, you as the employer must ensure that a suitable and sufficient inspection is carried out. The inspection may vary from a simple visual inspection right through to a fully detailed and comprehensive inspection, which may have to include some dismantling and/or testing (*SI 1998/2306, Reg 6*).

As the employer you will need to ensure that those who decide what type of inspection should be carried out and how frequently, are competent to make such a decision.

The following are examples of where an inspection will be required:
- Following installation where the guarding is dependent upon presence-sensing devices such as pressure-sensitive mats or light beams or curtains.
- Where deterioration leads to a significant risk, for example on fairground equipment, paper-cutting guillotines, die-casting machines, horizontal injection-moulding machines, complex automated equipment.
- Where exceptional circumstances may jeopardise safety such as during major modifications or repairs, where there is known or suspected serious damage and where there is a change of use following a long period of disuse.

As the employer you must ensure that records of all inspections are kept. The law does not require that they are kept in any particular format so either paper or handwritten records are fine as well as computerised maintenance records.

INFORMATION, INSTRUCTIONS AND TRAINING

Where it is found that risks cannot be adequately controlled during normal operation (or while repairs, maintenance or any other such work is undertaken) by measures such as guarding or other protection devices, as the employer you must ensure that only those persons that have been designated as competent persons on that piece of machinery are permitted to work on that machinery.

A competent person in this case will mean a person who has received sufficient information, training, instruction and supervision.

As the employer you must ensure that adequate training, information and instruction is given to those employees who will be using the work equipment as well as to their supervisors. This training etc must be comprehensive and must at the end of the course prove that the operatives and supervisors are aware of how the equipment works as well as all the hazards etc (*SI 1998/2306, Regs 8, 9*). It is recommended that comprehensive notes of the training are given to each of the operatives and supervisors.

SIMPLY SAFETY

For certain groups, special training will need to be given, for example to young people, drivers and chainsaw operators.

The Conformity with Community Requirements Regulation means that the employer will need to check that adequate operating instructions have been provided with the equipment and that there is information about residual hazards, such as noise and vibration. You should ensure that the equipment is checked for obvious faults. If you are in any doubt as to how the equipment should be operated or what the equipment is designed to do you should contact the supplier and manufacturers for further advice. As the employer you need to ensure that the products you are taking control of carry a CE marking and that all the relevant certificates or declarations accompany them.

DANGEROUS PARTS OF MACHINERY

Under this regulation the duty for you as the employer is an Absolute Duty. This means that this duty MUST be undertaken at all costs and without fail. This is to ensure that access is prevented to dangerous parts of equipment and to ensure that the movement of any dangerous part of the machinery is stopped before any part of a person enters a danger zone. The regulations lay down a hierarchy of measures that should be taken (they are frequently used in some degree of combination) (*SI 1998/2306, Reg 11*):

- the provision of fixed enclosing guards
- the provision of other guards or protection devices
- the provision of protection appliances (eg jigs, holders, push sticks)
- the provision of information, instruction, training and supervision

The regulations go on to say that guards and protection devices must satisfy certain criteria:

- they must be suitable for their purpose
- they must be of good construction, sound material and adequate strength
- they must be properly maintained
- they must not be easily bypassed or disabled
- they must be situated at sufficient distance from the danger zone
- they must not unduly restrict the view of the operation of the machinery
- they must not increase risk to health and safety
- they must allow for fitting or replacing parts as well as maintenance work to be undertaken without having to remove guards or protection devices

While *PUWER 1998* still remains in force, certain amendments were introduced under the *Health and Safety (Miscellaneous Amendments) Regulations 2002 (SI 2002/2174),* which affected the employer's approach to work with dangerous machine parts. The HSE had been concerned that under the original regulations, there was too much leeway for employers to simply provide training and instruction to workers as a control measure when using dangerous machinery, instead of starting with the safest option of fitting fixed guards. Under the 2002 amending regulations, 'information, training, instruction, and supervision' are now seen as an additional requirement, and not as one of the principal control measures to manage risk when working with dangerous machine parts.

Tools and Equipment

GUARDS AND PROTECTION DEVICES

Types of Guard and Safety Device

There are a number of types of guard and control device to protect from dangerous machine parts, including the following:
- *Fixed guards.*
  These are always in position, and difficult to tamper with, but can restrict access and make cleaning difficult.
- *Adjustable guards.*
  These can be adjusted by the user, or automatically by the machine as work is passed through them. They allow better access, but increase accidental risk of contact with dangerous parts.
- *Interlocking guards.*
  These ensure that equipment can only be operated when a moveable part connects to the power source, so that they default to safe. A good example here is the door of a photocopier machine, which disconnects the power when opened.
- *Trip devices.*
  These detect the presence of an operator within a danger zone to shut off power, using trip switches, pressure pads or laser sensors.
- *Other measures.*
  These include two-handed control devices and hold-to-run controls, which default to safe (for example by isolating the equipment from its power source) if the operator releases them.

There are also various other requirements specific to guards and protection devices that you as as the employer need to take into account with regard to protection against specified hazards (*SI 1998/2306, reg 12*).

Protection against Failure

Employers have to ensure so far as is reasonably practicable that work equipment is protected, and where it is not practicable that the equipment is adequately controlled (without the need for PPE) against the risk to health and safety from the following:
- ejected or falling articles or substances
- rupture or disintegration of parts of the work equipment
- fire or overheating of the work equipment
- unintended or premature discharge or rejection of any article, gas, dirt, liquid, vapour or substance
- unintended or premature explosion of the work equipment or any article or substance produced, used or stored in it

High or Very Low Temperature

Employers need to ensure that there is protection against parts of the work equipment that could cause (*SI 1998/2306, reg 13*) the following:
- burns
- scalds
- sears

SIMPLY SAFETY

CONTROLS AND CONTROL SYSTEMS

This requires that you as the employer ensure that the equipment is provided with controls that allow the machine to do the following (*SI 1998/2306, Reg 14*):
- to start as well as being restarted
- to change speed, pressure or operating conditions

It must not be possible to perform any of the above actions except by deliberate action except in the case of an automatic device.

Stop Controls

In the same way the employer needs to ensure that stop controls are fitted and functioning to ensure the following (*SI 1998/2306, reg 15*):
- The equipment can be brought to a complete stop safely. A complete stop should be achieved where necessary for health and safety, otherwise machines may come to rest gradually/at the end of the cycle.
- If necessary the equipment should be disconnected from all sources of energy.

Emergency stop controls need to be provided where the other safeguards are not adequate to prevent a risk when some irregular event occurs. Emergency stop controls should be in addition to all other stop controls (*SI 1998/2306, Reg 16*).

Position of Controls

Operators need to be able to see the work equipment and therefore controls need to be clearly visible and identifiable as well as safely located. It is also important that audible, visible or other suitable warnings be present indicating when work equipment is about to start (*SI 1998/2306, Reg 17*).

Control systems should be safe, so far as is reasonably practicable, and should ensure the following (*SI 1998/2306, reg 18*):
- their operation does not create a risk to health and safety
- no fault in them can lead to an increased risk to health and safety
- they do not interfere with the stop or emergency stop controls

Isolation

Work equipment must be easy to isolate from its source of energy. Any such means must be clearly visible and identifiable. For portable powered work equipment a plug and socket disconnection would be considered satisfactory.

STABILITY

Work equipment needs to be stabilised by clamping or other means where necessary, for example by use of counterbalancing, outriggers, footing of ladders.

LIGHTING

This regulation requires that anywhere work equipment is used the area is adequately lit.

MAINTENANCE

This regulation requires that any maintenance or repairs to work equipment can be carried out safely whilst the equipment is shut down. Where this cannot be undertaken then appropriate protective measures can be taken.

Tools and Equipment

Markings / Warnings

Where risks cannot be reduced by hardware measures alone, and reliance is placed on safe systems of work, markings and warnings may form a part of such systems.

MOBILE WORK EQUIPMENT

These requirements relate to equipment when it is travelling. All new mobile work equipment that came into use after 5 December 1998 must comply with the requirements. Equipment existing before that had to comply after 5 December 2002.

Employees carried on mobile equipment

As the employer you need to ensure that no employee is carried on mobile work equipment unless it is suitable for carrying persons and that it incorporates features for reducing risks to their safety for example:

- seating
- side, front, rear barriers/guard rails
- secure handholds
- falling object protective structures (FOPS)
- restraining systems: full-body seat belts, lap belts
- adjustments to speed
- separation from wheels/tracks by guard rails, fenders

Roll-Over Protection

It is important that as the employer you ensure that risks from rolling over of equipment when moving are minimised. Roll-over can be due to uneven surfaces, variable or slippery ground conditions, excessive gradients, inappropriate speeds, incorrect tyre pressures as well as sudden direction changes. Risks can be reduced in several ways:
- Stabilising the equipment, eg using counterbalance weights, increasing track width by use of more or wider wheels, locking up moveable parts.
- Providing structures that allow equipment to all only to one side (known as roll-over protective structures (ROPS)).
- Providing structures to give sufficient clearance if overturned (ROPS).
- Providing restraining systems to prevent workers being carried from being crushed between any part of the work equipment and the ground or impacting with the inside of the cab/structure.
- Exemptions apply to: fork lift trucks already fitted with above structures, where risks to safety would be increased and where it would not be reasonably practicable.

Rollover Protection for Fork Lift Trucks

This regulation requires that risks need to be reduced as low as is reasonably practicable on fork lift trucks. It requires that fork lift trucks that have structures as described above and which carry an employee are adapted or equipped to reduce the risks to safety from overturning to as low as is reasonably practicable.

Self-propelled work equipment

This regulation covers the risks from the use of self-propelled work equipment and prevention strategies that as the employer you need to consider such as:

SIMPLY SAFETY

- preventing unauthorised start-up
- minimising collision of rail-mounted equipment
- stopping and braking devices
- secondary emergency braking provision
- ensuring driver's field of vision
- use of appropriate lighting
- provision of fire-fighting appliances

REMOTE CONTROLLED WORK EQUIPMENT

As the employer you need to understand this regulation as it covers the use of remote controlled or radio controlled work equipment. It covers the risks from the use of such equipment and the provision of certain features:

- prevent its operation when out of range
- to prevent crushing or impact
- use of alarms/flashing lights to alert to its presence
- sensing or contact devices
- stopping safely

DRIVE SHAFTS

The regulation requires employers ensure that where the seizure of the drive shaft between mobile work equipment and its accessories or anything towed is likely to involve a risk to the employee then the employer must ensure the following:

- the work equipment has a means of preventing such a seizure and
- where such a seizure cannot be avoided then the employer has taken every possible measure to avoid an adverse affect on the safety of an employee

The employer must also ensure that the work equipment has a system for safeguarding the shaft when in the following circumstances:

- work equipment has a shaft for the transmission of energy between it and other mobile work equipment
- the shaft could become soiled or damaged by contact with the ground when uncoupled

LIFTING OPERATIONS AND LIFTING EQUIPMENT REGULATIONS 1998 – OVERVIEW

The *Lifting Operations and Lifting Equipment Regulations 1998 (SI 1998/2307) (LOLER 1998)* came into force in December 1998. They apply in all work premises and work situations subject to the *Health and Safety at Work etc. Act 1974 (HSWA 1974)*. The regulations replaced most of the previously existing laws relating to the use of lifting equipment.

For the employer the requirements imposed by these regulations relate to lifting equipment provided for use or used by an employee at work. The types of equipment covered by these regulations as defined by the Health & Safety Executive are such as cranes, lifts and hoists, and their components including chains, ropes, slings, hooks, shackles and eyebolts. Examples of equipment covered include a passenger lift, a dumb waiter, a vehicle inspection hoist and a scissors lift. LOLER does not apply to escalators; these are covered by more specific legislation, ie the Workplace (Health, Safety and Welfare) Regulations 1992.

Tools and Equipment

As the employer you should note that If they allow employees to provide their own lifting equipment, then this too is covered by the Regulations.

As the employer should be aware that there is also an important link with these regulations and the *Provision and Use of Work Equipment Regulations 1998 (SI 1998/2306) (PUWER 1998)*, which apply to all work equipment, including lifting equipment.

TO WHOM DO THE REGULATIONS APPLY?

If you are an employer or self-employed person providing lifting equipment for use at work, or you have control of the use of lifting equipment, then the Regulations will apply to you. They do not apply if you provide equipment to be used primarily by members of the public, for example lifts in a shopping centre. However, such circumstances are covered by the Health and Safety at Work etc Act 1974 (HSW Act).

While the Employers staff do not have duties under LOLER, they do have general duties under the HSW Act and the Management of Health and Safety at Work Regulations 1999 (MHSWR), for example to take reasonable care of themselves and others who may be affected by their actions and to co-operate with others.

The Regulations cover places where the HSW Act applies - these include factories, offshore installations, agricultural premises, offices, shops, hospitals, hotels, places of entertainment etc.

LOLER 1998 – DESIGN, INSTALLATION AND MARKING

Strength and Stability

As the employer you need to ensure that lifting equipment has adequate strength for the proposed use, with an appropriate factor of safety against failure. Equipment must also have adequate stability for its proposed use (*SI 1998/2307, Reg 4*).

Lifting Equipment for Lifting Persons

Work equipment used for raising and lowering people needs to be specifically designed for the purpose. Whatever the equipment as the employer you must ensure that all necessary precautions to ensure the health and safety of the user have been taken (*SI 1998/2307, Reg 5*).

Positioning and Installation

As the employer you need to ensure that lifting equipment has been installed and/or positioned in such a way as to minimise the risk of a person being struck or the load moving in an uncontrolled manner (*SI 1998/2307, Reg 6*).

You also need to ensure that loads are not required to be lifted over people and that systems are in place to prevent crushing when the equipment is in its extreme position.

Path of Travel (where fixed) to be Protected by Suitable Enclosure

As the employer you need to ensure so far as is reasonably practicable that devices used for lifting such as hooks have been fitted with safety catches so as to avoid loads slipping and falling. You also need to ensure that interlocking gateways etc are provided to any shaft enclosure and that when there is more than one piece of lifting equipment in use both they and their loads must be prevented from coming into contact with each other.

SIMPLY SAFETY

Lifting Equipment Marking

As the employer you need to ensure that all lifting equipment is suitably marked with its safe working load (SWL) and that any carrier of persons has displayed visibly upon it the maximum number of persons to be carried in addition to the SWL (*SI 1998/2307, Reg 7*).

LOLER 1998 – ORGANISATION OF LIFTING OPERATIONS

As the employer you need to ensure that where lifting operations are taking place that they are properly planned appropriately supervised and carried out in a safe manner.

As the employer you need to ensure that the person planning the operation has adequate practical and theoretical knowledge and experience of planning such operations. The plan must address the following:

- the risks identified
- the resources required and
- the procedures and responsibilities involved

You should also ensure the following:

- lifting equipment is not used in the open air where weather conditions could affect the integrity of the equipment or expose persons to danger
- lifting equipment is not used in a manner likely to cause it to overturn
- lifting equipment is used so as to minimise any form of risk from 'proximity' hazards (eg overhead power lines, other equipment/structures, racking)
- employees are given appropriate training and instruction
- lifting accessories are compatible with the load and used in a safe manner
- lifting accessories are stored in conditions that do not lead to damage or deterioration

LOLER 1998 – EQUIPMENT TESTING AND EXAMINING

As the employer you need to assure yourself that the equipment has been thoroughly examined and inspected by a competent person who has the appropriate practical and theoretical knowledge and experience of the particular lifting equipment and that they are independent and impartial (*SI 1998/2307, reg 9*).

In addition:

- a thorough examination is required after substantial or significant modification or repair
- lifting equipment should be thoroughly examined at intervals that have been specified in the regulations (as detailed below) or shorter intervals if the competent person considers this appropriate, or in accordance with the intervals specified in the examination scheme for the equipment
- lifting equipment for lifting persons, or an accessory for lifting, as a minimum once every six months
- other lifting equipment, as a minimum once every 12 months

The examination scheme may be drawn up by any competent person and should identify and specify which parts of the equipment should be thoroughly examined, the intervals between examinations and, where appropriate, those parts that need to be tested.

Tools and Equipment

As the employer you need to ensure that the competent person is informed of any changes in the use of the equipment that may have an effect on the examination scheme.

Different items or parts of the lifting equipment may be thoroughly examined at different intervals. As the employer you need to ensure that the competent person reviews the time between thorough examinations periodically. Examples of lifting machinery which may require regular inspection are fork-lift trucks, hoists, automated stacking equipment etc.

Should any dangerous defects be noted during the thorough examination the competent person needs to inform the employer immediately. A written report must be made as soon as is practicable containing information specified in *SI 1998/2307, Sch 1*. This report should also be given to any person from whom the equipment has been hired or leased.

Where the defect involves an existing or imminent risk of serious personal injury, a copy of the report must be sent as soon as is practicable to the relevant enforcing authority.

As the employer you must ensure that the lifting equipment is not used before the defect is remedied.

LOLER 1998 – Documentation

As the employer you need to keep the following documentation with regards to lifting equipment (*SI 1998/2307, reg 11*):

- an EC declaration of conformity relating to lifting equipment (where received) for so long as the equipment is operated
- reports of thorough examination of lifting equipment (but not an accessory for lifting) must be kept until the equipment ceases to be used
- reports of thorough examination of an accessory for lifting should be kept for two years after the report has been made
- records of where the safety of lifting equipment depended on installation conditions and where there is exposure to conditions causing deterioration

As the employer you need to ensure that the reports, or copies, are stored at the premises where the lifting equipment is being used.

DANGEROUS SUBSTANCES AND EXPLOSIVE ATMOSPHERES REGULATIONS 2002 (DSEAR)

Dangerous substances can put peoples' safety at risk from fire and explosion. DSEAR puts duties on Employers and the self-employed to protect people from risks to their safety from fires, explosions and similar events in the workplace, this includes members of the public who may be put at risk by work activity.

What are Dangerous Substances?

Dangerous substances are any substances used or present at work that could, if not properly controlled, cause harm to people as a result of a fire or explosion. They can be found in nearly all workplaces and include such things as solvents, paints, varnishes, flammable gases, such as liquid petroleum gas (LPG), dusts from machining and sanding operations and dusts from foodstuffs.

SIMPLY SAFETY

WHAT DOES DSEAR REQUIRE?

As the employer you must:

- find out what dangerous substances are in their workplace and what the fire and explosion risks are;
- put control measures in place to either remove those risks or, where this is not possible, control them;
- put controls in place to reduce the effects of any incidents involving dangerous substances;
- prepare plans and procedures to deal with accidents, incidents and emergencies involving dangerous substances;
- make sure employees are properly informed about and trained to control or deal with the risks from the dangerous substances;
- identify and classify areas of the workplace where explosive atmospheres may occur and avoid ignition sources (from unprotected equipment, for example) in those areas.

WHEN DOES DSEAR APPLY?

Apart from certain activities involving ships, DSEAR applies whenever:

- there is work being carried out by an Employer (or self employed person);
- a dangerous substance is present (or is liable to be present) at the workplace;
- the dangerous substance could be a risk to the safety of people as a result of fires, explosions or similar energetic events.

Fires and explosions create harmful physical effects - thermal radiation, overpressure effects and oxygen depletion. These effects can also be caused by other energetic events such as runaway exothermic reactions involving chemicals or decomposition of unstable substances such as peroxides. These events are also covered by DSEAR.

(Definintion - An exothermic reaction is a chemical reaction that is accompanied by the release of heat-It gives out energy to its surroundings. The energy needed for the reaction to occur is less than the total energy released.)

The following examples illustrate the type of activities covered by DSEAR:

- storage of petrol as a fuel for cars, boats or horticultural machinery;
- use of flammable gases, such as acetylene, for welding;
- handling and storage of waste dusts in a range of manufacturing industries;
- handling and storage of flammable wastes such as fuel oils;
- welding or other 'hot work' on tanks and drums that have contained flammable material;
- work that could release naturally occurring flammable substances such as methane in coalmines or at landfill sites;
- use of flammable solvents in laboratories;
- storage and display of flammable goods, such as paints, in shops;
- filling, storing and handling aerosols with flammable propellants such as LPG;
- transporting flammable substances in containers around a workplace;
- deliveries from road tankers, such as petrol and bulk powders;

Tools and Equipment

- chemical manufacturing, processing and warehousing;
- the petrochemical industry, both onshore and offshore.

WHERE DOES DSEAR APPLY?

As the Employer you should be aware that DSEAR applies to workplaces where dangerous substances are present, used, or produced.

Workplaces are any premises or parts of premises used for work. This includes places such as industrial and commercial premises, land-based and offshore installations, mines and quarries, construction sites, vehicles and vessels, etc. Places such as the common parts of shared buildings, private roads and paths on industrial estates and road works on public roads are also premises – as are houses and other domestic premises, if people are at work there.

WHAT DOES DSEAR REQUIRE?

DSEAR places duties on the Employers (and the self-employed, who are considered employers for the purposes of the Regulations) to assess and eliminate or reduce risks from dangerous substances. Complying with DSEAR involves:

Assessing Risks

Before work is carried out, you as the employer must assess the fire and explosion risks that may be caused by dangerous substances. This should be an identification and careful examination of:

- the dangerous substances in the workplace;
- the work activities involving those substances; and
- the ways in which those substances and work activities could harm people.

The purpose is to help the employer to decide what they need to do to eliminate or reduce the risks from dangerous substances.

If there is no risk to safety from fires and explosions, or the risk is trivial, no further action is needed. If there are risks then you as the employer must consider what else needs to be done to comply fully with the requirements of DSEAR.

If you as the employer have five or more employees, you must record the significant findings of the risk assessment.

Preventing or Controlling Risks

As the employer you must put control measures in place to eliminate risks from dangerous substances, or reduce them as far as is reasonably practicable. Where it is not possible to eliminate the risk completely you must take measures to control risks and reduce the severity (mitigate) the effects of any fire or explosion

The best solution is to eliminate the risk completely by replacing the dangerous substance with another substance, or using a different work process. This is called substitution in the Regulations.

In practice this may be difficult to achieve – but it may be possible to reduce the risk by using a less dangerous substance; for example replacing a low flashpoint liquid with a high flashpoint one. In other situations it may not be possible to replace the dangerous substance at all; for example, it would not be practical to replace petrol with another substance at a filling station.

SIMPLY SAFETY

Control Measures

Where the risk cannot be eliminated, DSEAR requires control measures to be applied in the following priority order:

- reduce the quantity of dangerous substances to a minimum;
- avoid or minimise releases of dangerous substances;
- control releases of dangerous substances at source;
- prevent the formation of a dangerous atmosphere;
- collect, contain and remove any releases to a safe place (for example, through ventilation);
- avoid ignition sources;
- avoid adverse conditions (for example, exceeding the limits of temperature or control settings) that could lead to danger;
- keep incompatible substances apart.

These control measures should be consistent with the risk assessment and appropriate to the nature of the activity or operation.

STORAGE OF FLAMMABLE LIQUIDS IN PROCESS AREAS, WORKROOMS, LABORATORIES AND SIMILAR WORKING AREAS

The *Dangerous Substances and Explosive Atmospheres Regulations 2002 (SI 2002/2776) (DSEAR)* require risks from the indoor storage of dangerous substances to be controlled by elimination or by reducing the quantities of such substances in the workplace to a minimum and providing mitigation to protect against foreseeable incidents.

It is recognised that, for practical purposes where flammable liquids are used, there is likely to be a need for a limited quantity to be stored in the workroom/working area. It is the responsibility of you as the employer / duty holder to carry out a risk assessment for the amount of dangerous substances being stored. As the employer / duty holder you will need to justify the need to store any particular quantity of flammable liquid within a workroom/working area. The guiding principle is that only the minimum quantity needed for frequently occurring activities or that required for use during half-day or one shift should be present in the workroom/working area (DSEAR ACoP L135, para 39 refers). Clearly, actual quantities will depend on the work activity and also the organisational arrangements for controlling the fire risks in the workroom / working area.

When not in use, containers of flammable liquids needed for current work activities should be kept closed and stored in suitable cabinets or bins of fire-resisting construction and which are designed to retain spills (110% volume of the largest vessel normally stored in it). These bins or cabinets should be located in designated areas that are where possible away from the immediate processing area and do not jeopardise the means of escape from the workroom/working area. The flammable liquids should be stored separately from other dangerous substances that may enhance the risk of fire or compromise the integrity of the container or bin/cabinet; for example energetic substances, oxidizers and corrosive materials. It is recognised that these other dangerous substances may be flammable liquids in their own right or held in a flammable liquid. However, it is still inappropriate to store these in the same cabinets or bins with other flammable liquids. (Further guidance on Energetic and spontaneously combustible substances is contained in HS(G)131 published by HSE.)

It is recommended that the maximum quantities that may be stored in cabinets and bins are no more than 50 litres for extremely flammable, highly flammable and those flammable liquids with

Tools and Equipment

a flashpoint below the maximum ambient temperature of the workroom/working area; and no more than 250 litres for other flammable liquids with a higher flashpoint of up to 55°C (DSEAR ACoP L135, para 40 refers).

As the employer / duty holder you must realise that these quantities are intended to be viewed as recommended maxima representing good industry safe practice, rather than be taken as absolute limits. There is intended to be some flexibility with these limits, where it is recognised that the design of modern buildings and the pattern of work can sometimes make adherence to these quantities difficult to achieve; for example, in large or open-plan workrooms/working areas.

However, where you as the employer / duty holder do identify a need to store quantities in excess of the recommended maxima, a robust demonstration of this requirement would need to be made and in particular the risk assessment should take into account the following:

- The properties of the materials to be stored or handled in the workroom/working area. For mixed storage the worst case situation should be applied, ie all materials in the storage cupboard or bin should be considered as being the same material as the one that has the lowest flashpoint.
- The amount of flammable liquids being handled in the workroom/working area and the quantities of liquid that may be accidentally released or spilled.
- The size of the workroom/working area and the number of people working in it.
- Ignition sources in the workroom/working area and potential fire spread in the event of an ignition.
- Exhaust ventilation provision to the workroom/working area and/or the storage cupboard or bin.
- The fire performance of the storage cupboard or bin.
- The arrangements for closing the cupboard or bin doors/lid in the event of a fire.
- Means of escape from the workroom/working area.

The particular objective, in the event of an incident, is to ensure that people can safely escape from the workroom/working area. In this context, the purpose of storing Dangerous Substances in cupboards and bins of appropriate construction and design is to provide a physical barrier to delay the involvement of these materials in a fire and limit the passage of flame and hot gases should the Dangerous Substances subsequently become involved, for sufficient time for people's safe evacuation and the employers / duty holder's immediate emergency procedures supporting this to be implemented (DSEAR ACoP L136 par. 68 refers).

For additional information, the employer should refer to the HSE website:

www.hse.gov.uk/fireandexplosion/storageflammliquids.htm

FLAMMABLE LIQUIDS – RISKS

When considering flammable liquids the employer needs to be aware that the liquids concerned are those that have a flashpoint of 55C or below. This therefore includes all liquids that are classified as 'flammable', 'highly flammable' or 'extremely flammable' including petroleum spirit and petroleum mixtures. As the employer you will need to ensure that no works are permitted to be undertaken without a full risk assessment being undertaken covering all aspects of the proposed works.

The undertaking of the risk assessment should show up that the main hazards involved with these substances are fire and explosion, involving either the liquid or the vapour given off from it and a source of ignition. As the employer or duty holder you need to be aware that some of the general causes of incidents with flammable liquids are as follows:

SIMPLY SAFETY

- lack of training or general awareness of the situation
- hot works that take place on or in close proximity to flammable liquids
- exposure to heat from a nearby fire
- inadequate control of ignition sources
- dismantling or disposal of equipment that contains or had contained a flammable liquid

You also need to be aware of other areas that must be taken into consideration when dealing with flammable liquids. Some of these are as follows:

- the amount and spread of vapour release when exposed to the air
- the specific and individual characteristics of the flammable liquid being used
- the potential hazards of vapour and air mixtures
- the physical environment involved

It is vital that as the employer you ensure that sources of ignition are excluded from areas where flammable liquids are handled. These sources should be considered:

- smoking
- naked flames for example hot work operations such as welding
- work involving cutting equipment which can cause sparks
- static electricity
- hot surfaces
- electrical lighting
- electrical circuits and equipment which are not flameproof or intrinsically safe in their construction

FLAMMABLE LIQUIDS – PRECAUTIONS AND PROCEDURES

The employer needs to ensure that any 'hot work' being undertaken on any vessels that may contain a residue of a flammable substance must be subject to a full permit to work, which will ensure that the work is undertaken in a carefully controlled manner.

PRECAUTIONS

As the Employer you will need to ensure that there are suitable and sufficient precautions in use and these should become apparent from the risk assessment. These will follow the normal precautions, which the employer will find fully explained within Chapter 3: Risk Assessment and Management. However in brief with regards to flammable liquids these are as follows:

- Substitution: Where it is acceptable on health or environmental grounds, it is possible to use liquids which are either non-flammable or have a higher flashpoint. The use of these liquids may provide suitable alternatives.
- Separation:
  It is possible that by using fire-resisting partitions the employer can separate areas where flammable liquids are handled from other parts of the workroom. It is important to remember when doing this that suitable signage is placed within and without the area.
- Dispensing and Decanting:
  This should be undertaken in such a way as to reduce spills and releases of dangerous flammable vapours. Wherever possible the employer should ensure that

the operatives use an enclosed transfer system. If this cannot be undertaken then it is important to ensure that containers are designed so as to minimise spillage, release of vapours and the effects of fire.
- Ventilation:
  The employer needs to ensure that all areas where flammable liquids are handled are adequately ventilated (this means at least six complete air changes per hour).
- Housekeeping: It is essential that the employer ensures that good standards of housekeeping are maintained, for example by ensuring the following:
  - leaks and/or spills are dealt with promptly
  - larger spillages are adequately contained
  - contaminated material, cloths etc are placed within a suitable designed container (a metallic container with a suitable lid will suffice)
  - all waste containers are regularly and safely emptied
  - operatives or their clothing do not come into direct contact with any spillages
  - any spill does not enter into the drainage systems
  - the disposal of any waste liquids is done safely and does not create any pollution problems

EMERGENCY PROCEDURES

It is important to note that should there be any doubt as to the safety of any substance then as the employer you must seek the advice of the local fire prevention officer. It is also essential that the local fire prevention officer's advice should always be sought on fire safety matters.

As the employer you must always ensure that all operatives and other staff are aware of the established fire precautions and procedures to be followed in an emergency. These instructions should be written and made available to all employees. The instructions must also be taken into account when any risk assessments are being undertaken, when any work is being planned and in all training courses.

The fire-fighting equipment that should be provided within the area of concern will depend on the type of liquid being used as well as the conditions within which it is stored. As the employer you should seek advice from the local fire prevention officer on the best methods of fire prevention and what fire fighting equipment should be provided. It is important that when placing extinguishers in positions to deal with possible small outbreaks that all staff who are liable to work in these areas are trained in the correct usage of the fire-fighting equipment provided as well as not to put themselves at risk of injury.

INFORMATION AND TRAINING

As the employer you should ensure that all staff are informed of the flammable liquids in use at the premises as well as the hazards and general precautions that need to be taken. Specific training that is based upon the written procedures or method statements should be given to those handling flammable liquids. This training should include the following:

- general safety advice for dealing with flammable liquids
- any specific instructions on individual processes or activities
- the emergency procedures which have been established
- the use of any personal protective equipment (PPE) that has been provided

SIMPLY SAFETY

SCAFFOLDS AND LADDERS

Please also refer to the section on Work at Heights.

Information and statistics provided by the HSE show that falls from a height continue to be the biggest killer on construction sites and as the latest figures from 2010/2011 reveals that over 43,000 employees suffered a major injury as a result of a fall from height and that more than 14,000 employees suffered a major injury as a result of slips, trips and falls from a height. They go on to say that 'work at height should be carried out from a platform with suitable edge protection. Occasionally this may not be possible and a ladder may have to be used.' The employer needs to decide upon the type of equipment that should be used by undertaking a risk assessment and looking at what the job includes, where it is and how long the task will take. It is important that the employer understands that wherever possible scaffolding should be used and that very little work should be undertaken from a ladder.

DON'T LET A FALL SHATTER YOUR LIFE

The HSE has launched an initiative that will be most useful for the employer and can be found at: -

www.hse.gov.uk/**fall**s/wait/index.htm

The Work at Height, Access equipment Information Toolkit (WAIT) is a free on line toolkit of advice and guidance aimed at people who occasionally need to work at height. It helps you select the right access equipment for the planned work.

Further details of how to access and operate the WAIT system may be obtained from the HSE web site at:

http://www.hse.gov.uk/shatteredlives/index.htm

WORKING AT HEIGHTS

The employer (you), in so far as is reasonably practicable, needs to make sure that, prior to any working at height being authorised, you must:

- assess the risk to help decide how the work can be undertaken safely
- follow the hierarchy for safe work at height which is:
  - avoid
  - prevent
  - mitigate

  and give collective measures priority

- plan and organise the work properly taking into account the weather conditions and the possibility of emergencies
- ensure that those working at heights are competent
- manage the risks from working equipment to be used and inspect the place where the work is to be carried out (including access and egress)

It is also your responsibility as the employer to ensure that all employees are aware that they must:

Tools and Equipment

- ensure that they inform the employer of any medical conditions which may affect their ability to work at heights safely
- use the equipment provided by the employer safely and in accordance with any instructions and training given, and not to tamper or modify the equipment
- take positive steps to understand the hazards in the work place and to comply with safety rules and procedures

As the employer you should be aware of the HSE 'Shattered Lives' campaign, which is aimed at raising the awareness of the risks of slips, trips and falls and their prevention and useful posters and e-learning tools may found on the HSE website at: -

www.hse.gov.uk/shatteredlives/index.htm.

(See above for information on the *Work at Heights Regulations 2005*.)

SCAFFOLDING

When the employer is considering using scaffolding there are various areas that he/she needs to consider.

Protection of the public is paramount and there are various things that as the employer you need to ensure happen:

- the appropriate highway authority needs to be contacted before erecting a scaffold on a public highway
- when the scaffold is erected the employer needs to ensure there is a minimum amount of storage of materials and equipment on the scaffold
- the design of the scaffold must protect persons against falling materials
- the area under the scaffold and its immediate surroundings need to be cordoned off during erection or dismantling to avoid persons walking too close or under the scaffold whilst it is being built
- preventing unauthorised access to the scaffolding by removing all means of access when the scaffolding is unattended
- always use the correct mechanical hoists or rubbish chutes to move materials and waste

The erection of the scaffolding is an important function and the employer needs to ensure that the following points are covered:

- a competent person must supervise the erection of any scaffolding
- only competent persons may be used to erect scaffolding
- all scaffolds require bracing to help prevent them from collapsing. The platform of a general-purpose scaffold should be at least four boards wide
- all scaffolds that include 'independent' scaffolds should be securely tied, or otherwise supported
- additional ties will be required for scaffolding that is sheeted or uses netting, when the scaffolding is used as a loading platform for materials or equipment, and when hoists, lifting appliances or rubbish chutes are attached to it

As the employer you have the responsibility to ensure that scaffolds are used safely and it is worth considering including the following points in any instructions given to employees of contractors who will use scaffolding:

SIMPLY SAFETY

- do not take up boards, move handrails or remove ties to gain access for work
- only competent scaffolders are permitted to make changes in the scaffolding
- no work will take place from partially boarded scaffolds
- do not overload a scaffold

Scaffolds are required to be regularly inspected and the employer needs to ensure that these requirements are met:

- a competent person must inspect scaffolds usually at least every seven days: any faults found must be put right
- a competent person must inspect scaffolds following any alterations and adjustments to the structure
- a competent person must inspect scaffolds after weather that is likely to have affected the strength and stability of the scaffold

LADDERS, STEPLADDERS AND TRESTLES

When it has been decided to use a ladder, stepladder or trestle the employer needs to ensure that the equipment in question complies with the following:

- is in good condition and that it has been (and is) regularly inspected for damage
- is secured in such a way that it cannot slip
- when used as access, that ladders extend about 1 metre above the working platform
- is long enough and positioned so that workers do not have to overreach
- that no one climbs up a ladder or uses one to work off unless the ladder can be securely held by the worker e.g. at least 3 points of contact at all times
- that top platforms of stepladders are not used unless they are equipped with special handholds
- that trestle platforms and stepladders are not used for work above two metres in height

Ladders are work equipment and as such are subject to the requirements of the *Provision and Use of Work Equipment Regulations 1998 (PUWER 1998)*. As the employer you should therefore maintain a Ladder Register, which should contain the following information:

- Ladders should be numbered individually and placed on a Ladder Register which records:
    - make/type of ladder
    - duty/weight/class rating
    - date first put into use
- The ladder should be subject to suitable, regular documented management inspections, which take into account the degree of use and type of equipment. In practice, three-monthly inspections are recommended.
- Procedures should be in place for handling any defect found, which would include repair or removal of the ladder, stepladders and trestles from service.
- Ladders should be subjected to a daily pre-use check.
- Defects will include: cracked, bent or warped stiles; cracked, bent or missing rungs; loose, defective or missing feet, tie rods, brackets; and corrosion of fittings etc.

Tools and Equipment

LADDER EXCHANGE

This annual initiative provides UK businesses with an easy and simple way to replace broken, damaged or bent ladders and trade them in for safe new ones. Nearly 7000 'dodgy' ladders have been surrendered in the three years the Health and Safety Executive (HSE) has been running the ladder exchange initiative..

Further information may be obtained from the HSE web site at:

www.hse.gov.uk/falls/ladderexchange.htm

PERSONAL PROTECTIVE EQUIPMENT

Personal protective equipment (PPE) refers to all equipment that is worn to protect the wearer against risk to their health and safety

PPE is defined in the Regulations as 'all equipment (including clothing affording protection against the weather) which is intended to be worn or held by a person at work and which protects him against one or more risks to his health or safety', e.g. safety helmets, gloves, eye protection, high visibility clothing, safety footwear and safety harnesses.

Hearing protection and respiratory protective equipment provided for most work situations are not covered by these Regulations because other regulations apply to them. However, these items need to be compatible with any other PPE provided.

Cycle helmets or crash helmets worn by employees on the roads are not covered by the Regulations. Motorcycle helmets are legally required for motorcyclists under road traffic legislation.

In 1992 the introduction of the *Personal Protective Equipment Regulations 1992 (SI 1992/2966) (PPER 1992)* laid duties upon not only the employer but also the employee.

The duties of the employer require him/her to undertake a risk assessment to ensure that suitable PPE is provided to employees exposed to a risk to their health or safety. (This is not a replacement for the normal risk assessments that are undertaken for work activities, but is in addition.) The exception to this is where the risk has been adequately controlled by other equally or more effective means *(SI 1992/2966, Reg 4(1))*. This duty *(SI 1992/2966, Reg 4(3))* requires that the equipment is as follows:

- is appropriate to the risks and workplace conditions
- takes into account the ergonomics and state of health of the employee
- fits the wearer correctly
- is effective in preventing or adequately controlling the risk without increasing an overall risk

It is important that the employer understands that PPE is seen as a last resort in the hierarchy of control measures. It is also important to remember that it should be made readily available, generally on an individual basis, and that no charge can be made to the employee for any such equipment that is provided for health and safety.

As the employer youy must also ensure that the following areas are covered:

- that where more than one piece of PPE has to be worn at the same time that they are compatible *(SI 1992/2966, reg 5)*

SIMPLY SAFETY

- that PPE should be maintained (including replaced or cleaned as appropriate) in an efficient state, in efficient working order and in good repair (*SI 1992/2966, Reg 7*)
- that suitable accommodation is provided for the safe storage of PPE (*SI 1992/2966, Reg 8*)
- that contaminated or defective PPE is segregated (*SI 1992/2966, Reg 8,* Guidance 8, 51)
- that suitable and sufficient information, instruction and training is provided in a systematic way so that it covers users, managers, supervisors as well as repair, maintenance and test personnel (*SI 1992/2966, Reg 9*)
- that records of training etc are kept
- that employees are aware of their duties to the employer in reporting the loss or defect (*SI 1992/2966, Reg 11*)

CE Marking

The employer should ensure any PPE they buy is 'CE' marked and complies with the requirements of the Personal Protective Equipment Regulations 2002. The CE marking signifies that the PPE satisfies certain basic safety requirements and in some cases will have been tested and certified by an independent body.

OTHER REGULATIONS

The employer should note that the PPE at Work Regulations do not apply where the following six sets of regulations require the provision and use of PPE against these hazards. For example, gloves used to prevent dangerous chemicals penetrating the skin would be covered by the Control of Substances Hazardous to Health Regulations 2002 (as amended). The regulations are:

- The Control of Lead at Work Regulations 2002.
- The Ionising Radiations Regulations 1999.
- The Control of Asbestos Regulations 2006 & 2012.
- The Control of Substances Hazardous to Health Regulations 2002 (as amended).
- The Noise at Work Regulations 1989.
- The Construction (Head Protection) Regulations 1989.

APPENDIX 1 - HEALTH AND SAFETY LEGISLATION FOR EMPLOYERS

HEALTH AND SAFETY AT WORK ETC. ACT 1974

This is the key piece of health and safety legislation in the UK and is sometimes referred to as the 'umbrella act' as previously mentioned it allows regulations and approved codes of practice (AcoPs) to be made.

Whereas previous legislation had mainly addressed specific risks in specific workplaces and had been extremely prescriptive in describing the actions that should be taken to deal with that risk, the Health and Safety at Work etc. Act 1974 (HSWA 1974) was more general. It stated that employers had a duty to provide a safe workplace and that they were also responsible for the safety of all those who were affected by their work. It did not prescribe in detail how the employer should provide this safe workplace and in assigning this overall responsibility to the employer it used the words 'so far as is reasonably practicable'.

Subsequent legislation and regulation, together with a body of case law, has developed to provide interpretation and guidance on just what a safe workplace should consist of and the actions to be taken by those responsible for health and safety within the workplace to provide such an environment.

HSWA 1974 identified groups upon which were placed a broad set of general duties. These groups of persons are as follows:

- employers
- employees
- manufacturers and suppliers of industrial products
- persons in control of buildings, e.g. landlords, managing agents
- the self-employed
- occupiers of buildings in which persons work other than one's own employees

EMPLOYER'S DUTIES UNDER HASWA 1974

The employer's general duties under the Health and Safety at Work etc. Act 1974 (HSWA 1974) are as follows:

- The provision and maintenance of plant and systems of work that are without risk to health (HSWA 1974, s 2(2)(a)).
- To ensure the safety and absence of risks to health in connection with handling, storing and transporting articles and or substances (HSWA 1974, s 2(2)(b)).
- The provision of instruction, training, information and supervision to ensure the employees' health and safety at work (HSWA 1974, s 2(2)(c)).
- The maintenance of the workplace so that there is an absence of risk to health and safety; this includes means of access and egress (HSWA 1974, s 2(2)(d)).
- The provision and maintenance of the working environment that is free from risk to employees' health and safety, including adequate arrangements for facilities and the employees' welfare (HSWA 1974, s 2(2)(e)).
- (where there are five or more employees) the preparation of a health and safety policy setting out (HSWA 1974, s 2(3)):

- a general statement of policy intent
- the organisational responsibilities for health and safety
- the arrangements to carry out the policy
  (Further information may be found in Chapter 2 page 36 - Health and safety policy statement'.)
- The provision of health and safety equipment such as personal protective equipment without charge to employees (HSWA 1974, s 9).
- Conducting his/her undertaking to ensure that persons not in his/her employment are not exposed to risks to their health and safety.
- Allowing trade unions to appoint safety representatives to represent other employees in consultation with the employer.
- Allowing employees to elect fellow workers to act as safety representatives to represent them in consultation with the employer (HSWA 1974, s 2(4)).
- Consulting with his/her employees' safety representatives in matters pertaining to health and safety (HSWA 1974, s 2(6)).
- When requested, to establish a health and safety committee (HSWA 1974, s 2(7)).
- Occupiers of buildings in which persons other than one's own employees work need to ensure that anything that is provided is safe and without risk to health. This includes machinery and equipment as well as access and egress (HSWA 1974, ss 3, 4) (for more information on occupier liability, see 13.3 Property management).
- Controlling any emissions into the atmosphere for any building under their control.
- Ensuring that if they design, manufacture, import or supply any article for use at work then it must, so far as is reasonably practicable:
  - be free from risk when used correctly
  - have been tested to ensure its safety
  - have sufficient operating instructions to enable it to be used without risk to health and safety
- The employer cannot charge his/her employees for anything that is done or provided for the safety of the employee.

Employee's Duties Under HASWA 1974

Employees' duties are as follows (Health and Safety at Work etc. Act 1974 (HSWA 1974), s 7):

- To take reasonable care of him/herself and of others through his/her acts or omissions (e.g. what he/she does or does not do).
- To co-operate with the employer in the implementation of health and safety matters.
- To not intentionally or recklessly to interfere with or misuse anything provided in the interests of the employee's health, safety and welfare (HSWA 1974, s 8).

Self-employed and contractors' duties under HSWA 1974

Contractors and those who are self-employed have, when at work, all of the above duties as well as the following (HSWA 1974, s 3):

- Every contractor and self-employed person shall conduct his/her undertaking in such a way that, so far as is reasonably practicable, he/she and others who are not his/her employees are not exposed to risks to their health and safety through his/her work activity.

- He/she must provide information on any hazards and risks arising from his/her work to those who may be affected by his/her work but who are not his/her employees.

The Health and Safety at Work etc Act 1974 created a framework for developing regulations and approved codes of practice, the most notable being the set of European-derived regulations generally referred to as the 'six pack', as shown in Figure 11:01.

Figure 11.01 - Six Pack Illustration

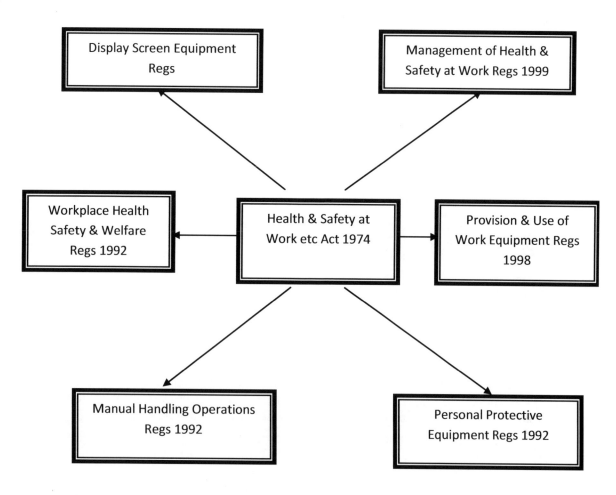

SIMPLY SAFETY

THE MANAGEMENT OF HEALTH AND SAFETY AT WORK REGULATIONS (MHSWR) 1999

The original regulations, from 1992, were revoked by the introduction of the Management of Health and Safety at Work Regulations 1999 (SI 1999/3242).

MHSWR 1999, which were derived from an EC framework directive, described, in more detail than the Health and Safety at Work etc. Act 1974 (HSWA 1974), the ways in which employers must set out the health and safety arrangements for the workplace. In particular they expanded the role of risk assessment to apply to the workplace in general, rather than to address particular issues, as had previously been the case. Principal points of the regulations can be listed as follows:

- The employer must carry out suitable and sufficient risk assessments of the workplace, which consider all the reasonably foreseeable hazards of tasks carried out within the workplace and provide adequate controls and monitoring to ameliorate those risks (SI 1999/3242, reg 3). All these assessments must be recorded, and they must be updated at least annually or when there are significant changes.
- The employer must have health and safety arrangements in place which include planning for safety and control of risk in a documented form, and which are included in the company's overall management systems (SI 1999/3242, reg 5).
- Employers must carry out appropriate health surveillance of employees (SI 1999/3242, reg 6). (Obviously this will be a more significant duty in workplaces where identifiable health conditions may arise because of the materials used or the tasks carried out. e.g. High Risk or specialist processes.)
- Employers must appoint a competent person to assist in the discharge of their health and safety duties (SI 1999/3242, reg 7). (The definition of what constitutes a competent person is discussed in 2.114.)
- The employer must have emergency procedures in place, which describe actions to be taken in the event of serious incidents and identify those responsible (SI 1999/3242, reg 8). A means of communicating these arrangements to staff must be provided.
- The employer must provide information to others working in the workplace (eg contractors) on the risks within the workplace and the emergency procedures in place (SI 1999/3242, reg 12). Equally contractors must provide employers with details of the risks associated with the tasks they are carrying out.
- The employer must ensure that staff are competent to carry out their tasks safely and must provide them with the training and equipment to enable them to do so (SI 1999/3242, reg 13). This includes temporary workers.
- Employers must specifically address the risks to expectant mothers and young people (SI 1999/3242, reg 19).
- Employees must use equipment correctly and must report any health and safety breaches (potential or actual) to the employer (SI 1999/3242, reg 14).

These regulations describe how the employer must set up the arrangements for health and safety in their workplace and manage them. The regulations specifically require that risk assessments be undertaken for all work processes, in addition to the specific risk assessments previously required under health and safety legislation

The risk assessment must do the following:

- consider all hazards and risks, which are reasonably foreseeable, associated with each work task
- draw reasonable conclusions from the above
- prepare workable risk control strategies
- be appropriate to the work and worker
- not be out of date too quickly

For more information refer to Chapter 3 - Risk Assessment and Management

SIX PACK SUBSIDIARY DIRECTIVES

As well as the issues listed above, the same framework directive also produced five other implementing regulations in the UK, which together with M(HSW)R, to make up the six pack. These regulations, which have all come into force, are as follows:

- Provision and Use of Work Equipment Regulations 1998 (SI 1998/2306) (PUWER).
- Manual Handling Operations Regulations 1992 (SI 1992/2793) (MHOR).
- Workplace (Health, Safety and Welfare) Regulations 1992 (SI 1992/3004) (W(HSW)R).
- Personal Protective Equipment at Work Regulations 1992 (SI 1992/2966) (PPER).
- Health and Safety (Display Screen Equipment) Regulations 1992 (SI 1992/2792) (HS(SCE)R).

PROVISION AND USE OF WORK EQUIPMENT REGULATIONS (PUWER) 1998

For more information on PUWER in practice, see Chapter 8.

These regulations were designed to pull together and tidy up the laws governing equipment used at work. They replaced a vast amount of legislation already covering particular kinds of equipment in different industries.

The regulations require that work equipment be chosen with a view to its safe working and that the equipment be well maintained (SI 1998/2306, Regs 4, 5). They also require that information, training, instruction and supervision is given and that periodic inspection of the equipment is undertaken (SI 1998/2306, reg 6).

Within the regulations there is the term use – This term means any activity that involves work equipment. This means starting, stopping, programming, setting, transporting, repairing, modifying, maintaining, servicing and cleaning (SI 1998/2306, reg 2).

Within the regulations there is the term work equipment – This term means any machinery, appliance, apparatus or tool or assembly of components that function as a whole (SI 1998/2306, reg 2).

MANUAL HANDLING OPERATIONS REGULATIONS (MHOR) 1992

For more information on MHOR risks, see 2.164–2.168 and for MHOR in practice see 2.170–

SIMPLY SAFETY

2.176.

These regulations define manual handling as the lifting, lowering, pushing, pulling, carrying or moving of loads, whether by hand or by other form of bodily force (SI 1992/2793, reg 2). The main thrust of the legislation is to prevent manual handling injuries from occurring.

The regulations require (SI 1992/2793, reg 4) that the employer must avoid hazardous manual handling tasks so far as is reasonably practicable and where they are unable then an assessment must be undertaken of manual handling which must look specifically at the following to ascertain how the job can be done without any risk to health and safety of the employee:

- the task
- the individual
- the load
- the environment
- any other factors that may have an effect

It is recommended that a written record of it will be required unless the assessment is very simple.

WORKPLACE (HEALTH, SAFETY AND WELFARE) REGULATIONS 1992

For more information on the workplace regulations see Chapter 7.

These regulations replaced a total of 35 pieces of old law, including part of the Factories Act 1961 (FA 1961) and parts of the Offices, Shops and Railway Premises Act 1963 (OSRPA 1963). They had the effect of making the law clearer and making it easier to understand what is expected of the employer.

The regulations apply to all places of work except (SI 1992/3004, Reg 3):

- means of transport
- construction sites
- mines and quarries
- fishing boats
- workplaces on agricultural or forestry land that is away from the main buildings are also exempt from most requirements (SI 1992/3004, Reg 3(4))

People connected with the workplace, such as the owner of a building that is leased to one or more employers or self-employed people, have to make sure that requirements falling within their control are satisfied (SI 1992/3004, Reg 4).

The regulations require the following of employers:

- To ensure adequate maintenance of the workplace, systems, equipment, etc (SI 1992/3004, Reg 5).
- To ensure that indoor workplaces be sufficiently ventilated by a source of fresh or purified air (SI 1992/3004, Reg 6).
- To maintain a reasonable temperature (normally 16°C minimum or 13°C where work involves strenuous physical effort) to be maintained in all indoor workplaces.

Thermometers must be placed in appropriate places to allow employees to ascertain the temperature. It should be noted that at present there is no legal maximum temperature (SI 1992/3004, Reg 7).

- To ensure that heaters or cooling systems supplied do not produce noxious fumes (SI 1992/3004, Reg 7(2)).
- To provide adequate lighting in the workplace. Where reasonably practicable, this must be natural light (SI 1992/3004, Reg 8).
- To provide emergency lighting where necessary for health and safety, eg where lighting failure could create a particular risk of danger such as on emergency exit stairways (SI 1992/3004, Reg 8(3)).
- To ensure that workplaces, and everything they contain, are kept clean. It must be possible to clean the floors, ceilings and other walls. Employers must ensure that rubbish does not accumulate (SI 1992/3004, Reg 9).
- To ensure that all work rooms have enough space to ensure health and safety – 11 cubic metres per person is considered suitable taking into account fixtures and fittings (SI 1992/3004, Reg 10).
- To ensure that all workstations are suitable for their purpose (SI 1992/3004, Reg 11).
- To ensure that all floors and other surfaces used as a traffic route are made of a suitable material and kept clear of slip and trip hazards (SI 1992/3004, Reg 12).
- To ensure that there is adequate drainage (SI 1992/3004, Reg 12(2)).
- To ensure that measures are taken to prevent people falling from heights or being hit by falling objects (SI 1992/3004, Reg 13).
- To ensure that all clear panels in doors and gates, etc are made of safety glass or other safety material, and are marked so that people can tell there is a barrier (SI 1992/3004, Reg 14).
- To ensure that all windows and skylights that can be opened must be able to be opened, closed, etc safely and that open windows do not create a risk to safety (SI 1992/3004, Reg 15).
- To ensure that it is possible to clean windows and skylights safely (SI 1992/3004, Reg 16).
- To ensure that all workplaces are arranged to ensure that vehicles and people move around safely (SI 1992/3004, reg 17). There are specific requirements for traffic routes (SI 1992/3004, Reg 17):
    - they must have suitable signs
    - there must be enough of them
    - they must be suitable for their purpose
    - they must be in a suitable location
    - they must be large enough to ensure safety
    - there must be separate ones for vehicles and people or, if they have to share a traffic route, they must be appropriately segregated
    - they must not present a hazard to people working nearby
    - they must allow enough space to separate any doors, gates, etc which open onto them

- To ensure that doors and gates are suitably made to prevent a risk to health and safety, and are fitted with any necessary safety devices (SI 1992/3004, Reg 18).

SIMPLY SAFETY

- To ensure that escalators and moving walkways are safe, and fitted with any necessary safety devices, including at least one emergency stop control which is easy to see, identify and operate (SI 1992/3004, Reg 19).
- To ensure that suitable sanitary conveniences and washing facilities are provided and are well ventilated and clean, and well maintained (SI 1992/3004, Reg 20).
- To ensure that there are separate facilities for men and women, except if they are in a lockable room.
- Showers must be provided if the type of work carried out makes this necessary: the washing facilities must have hot and cold (or warm) water, and soap and towels (or other methods of drying) (SI 1992/3004, Reg 21).
- To ensure that a supply of drinking water is provided at easy to access locations. The water must be wholesome and where necessary there must be a sign saying that it is drinking water (SI 1992/3004, Reg 22).
- To ensure that somewhere suitable is provided for employees to store their work clothes and personal clothes (SI 1992/3004, Reg 23).
- If people have to change into work clothes, the employer must provide suitable changing facilities, which allow for men and women to change separately (SI 1992/3004, Reg 24).
- To ensure that suitable rest facilities are provided in easily accessible locations. Pregnant women and nursing mothers must also be provided with suitable rest facilities, preferably containing somewhere to lie down (SI 1992/3004, Reg 25).
- If there is a risk that food might become contaminated in the workplace, the employer must provide employees with suitable eating facilities in the rest areas. There must be somewhere suitable for people to eat their food in all workplaces where food is normally consumed (SI 1992/3004, Reg 25).

Personal Protective Equipment at Work Regulations 1992

For more information on PPEWR in practice please see 2.144: Personal protective equipment.

These regulations set out the principles for selecting, providing, maintaining and using personal protective equipment (PPE). PPE should only be provided as a last resort when all other aspects of control measures identified within the risk assessment have been exhausted.

PPE is defined as all equipment, designed to be worn or held, to protect against a hazard. It includes most types of protective clothing and equipment, such as eye, foot and head protection, safety harnesses, life jackets and high visibility clothing. There are some exceptions:

- ordinary working clothes
- uniforms (including clothing provided for food hygiene)
- PPE for road transport (for example, crash helmets)
- sports equipment

Health and Safety (Display Screen Equipment) Regulations 1992

These regulations require the employer to carry out risk assessment of all Display Screen Equipment (DSE) workstations within their premises, and implement any control measures that are required to prevent or reduce the risks identified. These assessments must be reviewed when necessary (SI 1992/2792, Reg 2).

The employer is also required:

- To make sure their DSE workstations meet the requirements set out in the Schedule (SI 1992/2792, Reg 3).
- To set up a work routine for DSE users which will give them regular breaks from using DSE (SI 1992/2792, Reg 4).
- To provide DSE users with appropriate eye and eyesight tests, paid for by the employer, carried out by an ophthalmic optician. You as the Employer are required to pay for special spectacles if the optician prescribes that they are needed for use with DSE and normal ones cannot be used (SI 1992/2792, Reg 5).
- To provide DSE users with appropriate health and safety training and information on the use of their workstation and the risks involved (SI 1992/2792, Reg 6).

Other Legislation

This checklist contains a number of main statutes and regulations, the provisions of which are most likely to have an impact on most workplaces apart from those described already:

- Control of Substances Hazardous to Health Regulations 2002 (SI 2002/2677) (COSHH 2002).
- Electricity at Work Regulations 1989 (SI 1989/635) (EWR 1989).

SIMPLY SAFETY

- Lifting Operations and Lifting Equipment Regulations 1998 (SI 1998/2307) (LOLER 1998).
- Health and Safety (First Aid) Regulations 1981 (SI 1981/917) (HS(FA)R 1981).
- Health and Safety (Safety Signs and Signals) Regulations 1996 (SI 1996/341) (HA(SSS)R 1996).
- Reporting of Injuries Diseases and Dangerous Occurrences Regulations 1995 (SI 1995/3163) (RIDDOR 1995).
- Health and Safety (Consultation with Employees) Regulations 1996 (SI 1996/1513) (HS(CE)R 1996).
- Safety Representatives and Safety Committees Regulations 1977 (SI 1977/500) (SRSCR).
- Health and Safety (Young Persons) Regulations 1997 (SI 1997/135) (HS(YP)R 1997).
- Construction (Design and Management) Regulations 2007 (SI 2007/320) (C(DM)R 2007).
- Noise at Work Regulations 2005 (SI 2005/1643)
- Disability Discrimination Act 1995 (DDA 1995).
- Safety Representatives and Safety Committees Regulations 1977 (SI 1977/500).

CONTROL OF SUBSTANCES HAZARDOUS TO HEALTH REGULATIONS 2002

These regulations cover hazardous substance safety in the workplace. A hazardous substance is practically any substance, preparation or agent, which is capable of damaging human health, including biological agents and carcinogens (SI 2002/2677, Reg 2). However the Control of Substances Hazardous to Health Regulations 2002 (SI 2002/2677) (COSHH) does not cover lead, asbestos and radiation; these are covered by other regulations.

The regulations require employers to carry out a risk assessment of all activities which may lead to exposure to hazardous substances (SI 2002/2677, Reg 6). Their risk assessment must be recorded and reviewed when necessary.

Employers also need to prevent exposure to hazardous substances, wherever reasonably practicable. If prevention is not reasonably practicable, employers must reduce exposure by implementing control measures (SI 2002/2677, Reg 7), such as the following:

- enclosure
- safe systems of work
- engineering measures
- personal protective equipment (PPE) (this must only be used as a last resort where other control measures do not provide adequate protection)

Employers are required to make sure that all the control measures they provide for protection against hazardous substances are well maintained and in good working order (SI 2002/2677, Reg 9).

The regulations require employers to carry out appropriate monitoring of hazardous substances in the workplace. Monitoring records must be made and kept for at least five years (or at least 40 years if the monitoring identifies the exposure of an individual to hazardous substances) (SI 2002/2677, Reg 10).

Employers are required to carry out suitable health surveillance, where appropriate. Records of health surveillance must be made and kept for at least 40 years (SI 2002/2677, Reg 11).

The regulations require employers to provide all employees exposed to hazardous substances with suitable information, instruction and training (SI 2002/2677, Reg 12), including the following:

- results of the risk assessment
- control measures they must use and how to use them
- results of monitoring and health surveillance

The regulations also require employees to make proper use of control measures, and report any defects they find (SI 2002/2677, Reg 8(2)).

Manufacturers Safety Data Sheets (MSDS) are produced by the manufacturer or distributor to accompany the material and provide details of the emergency arrangements including first aid and environmental impacts and in practice for this reason should remain with the material at all times e.g. If a colleague had some in his eye how would you know how to treat him/her?

ELECTRICITY AT WORK REGULATIONS 1989

For more information on Electricity and for EWR in practice see Chapter 9.

The Electricity at Work Regulations 1989 (SI 1989/635) (EWR 1989) apply to all workplaces, and set out general requirements for employers to provide and maintain safe electrical systems.

In the regulations electrical equipment is defined as 'anything used or intended to be used and installed, to generate, provide, transmit, transform, rectify, convert, conduct, distribute, control, store, measure or use electrical energy'.

As an electrical system is classed as anything connected to electricity, which includes stored electricity in the form of batteries, the regulations apply to complex wiring systems on the premises right down to portable appliances such as desk lamps and radios.

LIFTING OPERATIONS AND LIFTING EQUIPMENT REGULATIONS 1998

For more information on LOLER in practice see Chapter 9.

The Lifting Operations and Lifting Equipment Regulations 1998 (SI 1998/2307) (LOLER 1998) came into force in December 1998. They apply in all work premises and work situations subject to the Health and Safety at Work etc. Act 1974 (HSWA 1974). The regulations replaced most of the previously existing laws relating to the use of lifting equipment.

For the employer the requirements imposed by these regulations relate to lifting equipment provided for use or used by an employee at work. The types of equipment covered by these

SIMPLY SAFETY

regulations are such as cranes, lifts and hoists, and their components including chains, ropes, slings, hooks, shackles and eyebolts. Examples of equipment covered include a passenger lift, a dumb waiter, a vehicle inspection hoist and a scissors lift.

The employer should be aware that there is also an important link between these regulations and the Provision and Use of Work Equipment Regulations 1998 (SI 1998/2306) (PUWER 1998), which apply to all work equipment, including lifting equipment.

For further information on the requirements of PUWER see Chapter 9.

HEALTH AND SAFETY (FIRST-AID) REGULATIONS 1981

For more information on the first aid regulations risks, First Aid and for the first aid regulations in practice, First aid – what the law requires see Chapter 5.

These regulations place duties upon all employers to provide adequate first aid for their employees (SI 1981/917, Reg 3). The general duties are as follows:

- provide adequate first aid equipment and facilities appropriate to the type of work or operations undertaken
- appoint a sufficient number of suitable and trained people to render first aid to employees injured or who become ill at work
- to make provision to cover annual leave, planned, unplanned and exceptional absences of first aiders or appointed persons
- inform employees of the first aid arrangements, including the location of equipment and personnel

HEALTH AND SAFETY (SAFETY SIGNS AND SIGNALS) REGULATIONS 1996

These regulations cover the provision of safety signs in almost all premises, and set up a standard for safety signs so that they are easily recognisable. The principal duties for the employer under these regulations are as follows:

- Employers are required to use appropriate safety signs where the risks cannot be adequately controlled by using other measures. They must also consider hand or verbal signals, where appropriate. All safety signs must be maintained.
- The employer needs to provide employees with suitable information, training and instruction on safety signs, and how to react to them (SI 1996/341, reg 5).
- The Schedule within the regulations sets out the requirements that safety signs and signboards must meet, and cover the following:
    - types of safety signs
    - interchangeable and combination signs
    - safety colours
    - effectiveness
    - prohibition signs
    - warning signs
    - mandatory signs

- emergency escape and first aid signs
- fire fighting signs

It also covers the requirements for the following:

- pipes
- containers
- fire-fighting equipment
- traffic routes
- dangerous locations and obstacles
- illuminated signs
- acoustic signals
- verbal communication
- hand signals

REPORTING OF INJURIES, DISEASES AND DANGEROUS OCCURRENCES REGULATIONS (RIDDOR) 1995

The Reporting of Injuries, Diseases and Dangerous Occurrences Regulations 1995 (SI 1995/3163) (RIDDOR 1995) deals with the reporting of accidents, diseases and dangerous occurrences. It provides details of what type of injury or occurrence should be reported, when it should be reported, by whom and how it should be reported.

It is not just injuries to employees which are reportable to the authorities but also injuries to the self-employed, trainees, visitors or passers-by – in fact anyone who is injured as a result of work activities.

For more information on RIDDOR 1995 in practice and Accident reporting – what the law requires see chapter 5.

REPORTING OF INJURIES, DISEASES AND DANGEROUS OCCURRENCES REGULATIONS 1995 (RIDDOR) - CHANGED – 6 APRIL 2012

As from **6 April 2012**, RIDDOR's over three day injury reporting requirement changed.

As from this time the trigger point will increase from over three days' to **over seven days'** incapacitation (not counting the day on which the accident happened).

Incapacitation means that the worker is absent or is unable to do work that they would reasonably be expected to do as part of their normal work.

Employers and others with responsibilities under RIDDOR must still keep a record of all over three day injuries – if the employer has to keep an accident book, then this record will be enough.

The deadline by which the over seven day injury must be reported will increase to 15 days from the day of the accident.

SIMPLY SAFETY

New guidance that explains the change is available to download from the HSE website at www.hse.gov.uk.

HEALTH AND SAFETY (CONSULTATION WITH EMPLOYEES) REGULATIONS 1996 AND SAFETY REPRESENTATIVES AND SAFETY COMMITTEES REGULATIONS 1977

The Safety Representatives and Safety Committees Regulations 1977 (SI 1977/500) (SRSCR) stipulate that the employer needs to consult with safety representatives in regard to both 'making and maintaining arrangements that will enable him/her and his/her employees to co-operate effectively in promoting and developing measures to ensure the health and safety at work of the employees, and in checking the effectiveness of such measures' (SI 1977/500, reg 4).

Trade unions have the right to appoint an individual to represent the workforce in consultation on all matters of health and safety at work and to carry out periodic inspections of the workplace for hazards (SI 1977/500, reg 3).

The employer has a duty to consult such union-appointed representatives on health and safety arrangements.

The employer must set up a safety committee within three months if two or more appointed representatives make a written request (SI 1977/500, reg 9).

In addition to representing employees in consultations with the employer, a safety representative can have the following functions (SI 1977/500, Reg 4):

- To investigate potential hazards and dangerous occurrences at the workplace and to examine the cause of accidents at the workplace.
- To investigate complaints by any employee they represent relating to that employee's health, safety or welfare.
- To make representations to employers on general matters affecting the health, safety and welfare of employees they represent.
- To carry out inspections of the workplace following notifiable accidents and, if relevant to the inspection, see certain documents.
- To represent the employees in consultation with enforcing authorities.
- To receive information from enforcing authorities.
- To attend safety committee meetings.
- To receive information relating to risk assessments affecting employees they represent.

To extend these principles to organisations with employees where there are no trade unions, the Health and Safety (Consultation with Employees) Regulations 1996 (SI 1996/1513) (HS(CE)R 1996) were introduced. These regulations require that the employer consults with all employees about any matter that affects their health and safety at work as well as other duties which tie in with the duties set out in SRSCR 1977.

The employer is required to consult employees in good time on matters which could affect their health and safety (SI 1996/341, Reg 3) and especially on the following:

- Measures introduced which may affect their health and safety, including the introduction of new technology.
- Arrangements for appointing competent persons to assist with health and safety.
- Information which should be passed to employees under other regulations (such as on hazardous substances).
- Training required under other regulations (such as on the use of PPE) but the regulations do not apply if the employees are already represented by appointed safety representatives.

HEALTH AND SAFETY (YOUNG PERSONS) REGULATIONS 1997

These regulations set out the rules for the employment of a child and a young person. To clarify the difference between the two the regulations define them:

- a child is defined as someone who is not over compulsory school age (currently 16 years) (SI 1997/135, Reg 2(b))
- a young person is defined as someone who has not attained the age of 18 years (SI 1997/135, Reg 2(e))

SIMPLY SAFETY

An employer may not employ a young person unless they have made or reviewed a full risk assessment in accordance with the Management of Health and Safety at Work Regulations 1999. and taking into account a number of characteristics associated with young persons, as follows:

- lack of experience
- lack of awareness of risks, eg perception
- physical and psychological immaturity

Again, before the child or young person is employed, the employer must provide, in addition to the general information requirements, a parent or guardian of the child with comprehensible and relevant information on (SI 1997/135, Reg 8):

- the risks to health and safety identified by the assessment
- the preventative and protective measures
- the risks notified to him in accordance with these regulations

The employer must ensure that young persons are given protection at work from the risks to their health or safety which are due to their inexperience or lack of knowledge of existing or potential risks (SI 1997/135, reg 13D).

The employer must ensure that young persons are not employed for work, subject to training which involves: (SI 1997/135, reg 13D):

- tasks beyond their physical or psychological capacity
- harmful exposure to agents which are toxic, carcinogenic, cause heritable genetic damage or harm to the unborn child or in any other way chronically affect human health
- harmful exposure to radiation
- risk of accidents which it may be reasonably assumed cannot be recognised or avoided by young person's owing to their insufficient attention to safety or lack of experience or training
- risk to health from exposure to extreme heat or cold, noise or vibration

The employer may employ young persons (not children) in work which involves the above risks provided they have received suitable and sufficient training; however, they must be supervised by a competent person and the risks must be reduced to the lowest level that is reasonably practicable.

CONSTRUCTION (DESIGN AND MANAGEMENT) REGULATIONS 2007

For more information on construction projects see Chapter 9.

The Construction (Design and Management) Regulations 2007 (SI 2007/320) (C(DM)R 2007) place duties upon the employer when he/she is undertaking construction work.

'Construction work' is defined as meaning the carrying out of any building, civil engineering or engineering construction work and includes:

- The construction, alteration, conversion, fitting out, commissioning, renovation, repair, upkeep, redecoration or other maintenance (including cleaning which involves the use of water or an abrasive at high pressure or the use of corrosive or toxic substances), de-commissioning, demolition or dismantling of a structure.

- The preparation for an intended structure, including site clearance, exploration, investigation (but not site survey) and excavation, and the clearance or preparation of the site or structure for use or occupation at its

- The assembly on site of prefabricated elements to form a structure or the disassembly on site of prefabricated elements which, immediately before such disassembly, formed a structure.

- The removal of a structure or of any product or waste resulting from demolition or dismantling of a structure or from disassembly of prefabricated elements which immediately before such disassembly formed such a structure.

- The installation, commissioning, maintenance, repair or removal of mechanical, electrical, gas, compressed air, hydraulic, telecommunications, computer or similar services which are normally fixed within or to a structure.

It does not include the exploration for or extraction of mineral resources or activities preparatory thereto carried out at a place where such exploration or extraction is carried out.

It is important that the employer realises that under the new C(DM)R 2007 he/she is unable to appoint a clients agent or representative to undertake the responsibilities and duties allocated to the employer. The employer is therefore unable to shift his/her duties to the agent/representative.

The provisions of the regulations apply to any construction project where work:

- last longer than 30 days; or
- involve more than 500 persons days of construction work

Any day on which construction work is carried out (including holidays and weekends) should be counted, even if the work on that day is of short duration. A 'person day' is one individual, including supervisors or specialist trades, carrying out construction work for one normal working shift.

Construction work for a domestic client is not notifiable and although a domestic client does not have duties under CDM, those who work for them on construction projects will. A domestic client is someone who lives, or will live, in the premises where the work is carried out. The premises must not relate to any trade, business or undertaking.

Where projects are notifiable under C(DM)R 2007, the employer must also:

- appoint a CDM co-ordinator
- appoint a principal contractor

SIMPLY SAFETY

- make sure that construction work does not start unless a construction phase plan is in place and there are adequate welfare facilities on site
- provide information relating to the health and safety file to the CDM co-ordinator
- retain and provide access to the health and safety file

CONTROL OF NOISE AT WORK REGULATIONS 2005

For more information on the Control of Noise at Work in practice, see Chapter 4.

The Control of Noise at Work Regulations 2005 (SI 2005/1643) (CNWR 2005) also imposes exposure limit values and action values (Reg 4).

Under CNWR 2005, the employer has a duty to:

- Identify noise hazards in the workplace.
- Undertake a noise assessment for employees who are liable to be exposed to noise levels above the lower Exposure Action Value (EAV) (Reg 6).
- Identify measures required to eliminate or reduce risks, control exposures and protect employees.
- Maintenance of records of what measures have been taken.
- Provide employees with hearing protection, making its use mandatory in areas where noise levels are above the Upper Exposure Action Value (EAV). (Reg 7).
- Provide information, instruction and training of employees on the risks from noise, the control measures, hearing protection and safe working practices.
- Ensure correct maintenance of any noise control equipment and hearing protection in order to control exposure (Reg 8).
- Provide health surveillance for those at risk (Reg 9).

CONTROL OF VIBRATION AT WORK REGULATIONS 2005

The Control of Vibration at Work Regulations 2005 (SI 2005/1093) (CVWR 2005) came into force on 6 July 2005 and introduced Daily Exposure Limit Values and Daily Exposure Action Values for both Hand Arm and Whole Body Vibration. However, the limit value may only be exceeded if all other aspects of these regulations are being complied with.

The employer has duties to assess the risks from vibration in the workplace, eliminate vibration at source, provide health surveillance where appropriate and provide information, instruction and training.

Exposure Limit and Action Limit Values (Reg 4)

These exposure limit values are daily exposure levels over an eight-hour period, which must not be exceeded except in circumstances applicable to the transitional period. The exposure action levels are daily exposures which, if exceeded, mean that the facility manager has additional duties to reduce the risk.

Table 11.02

Vibration Type	Daily Exposure Limit Value	Daily Exposure Action Value
Hand Arm	5 m/s2A(8)	2.5 m/s2A(8)
Whole Body	1.15 m/s2A(8)	0.5 m/s2A(8)

Vibration Risk Assessment (Reg 5)

This requires the employer to assess the risks of vibration in the workplace and to identify measures required to control the risk to ensure that employees are not exposed to vibration at or above an exposure action value or above an exposure limit value. A typical vibration risk assessment should consider:

- The magnitude and duration of exposure.
- The environment in which work being undertaken, eg cold damp conditions may increase the effects of exposure.
- The possible effects of vibration upon the employee, eg pregnant women or some one with a retinal problem.
- Vibration effect upon the workplace, eg stability of structures and reading of controls.
- Manufacturers information.
- Health surveillance information.
- Whether it is possible to replace equipment with vibration-damped equipment.
- Whether it is possible to substitute the process.

Elimination or Control of Exposure (Reg 6)

The employer is required to eliminate the vibration at source or, if that is not possible, then to implement control measures that are reasonable practicable. A typical strategy would be the hierarchy provided in the Management of Health and Safety at Work Regulations 1999 (SI 1999/3242) (MHSWR 1999) and should typically consider the following:

- The choice of work equipment.
- Alternative work methods.
- Additional work equipment to reduce the risk of injuries from vibration.
- Maintenance programmes to ensure work equipment in best possible condition.
- Appropriate information, instruction and supervision for employees.
- Suitable work schedules to ensure rest periods and to limit duration of exposure.

SIMPLY SAFETY

- Adequate protection of employees from the weather and any environmental conditions.

Health Surveillance (Reg 7)

A tiered approach to health surveillance is recommended in cases where the vibration risk assessment identifies that there is a risk of employees developing vibration related medical conditions or where employees may be exposed at or above the action levels. It is imperative that the facility manager maintains adequate records of health surveillance and if a vibration related disease such as Hand Arm Vibration Syndrome (HAVS) is discovered then the employer should take the following action:

- The employee is to be provided with information and advice from a qualified person.
- Make arrangements for further health surveillance.
- Undertake a review of the vibration risk assessment.
- Review the control measures.
- Review the health of other employees who may have been engaged in any similar activities.
- Consider offering the employee alternative work that does not involve vibration.

Information, Instruction and Training (Reg 8)

The employer must supply appropriate information and training to employees where there is a risk or where they may be exposed to vibration at or above the exposure action value. Such training should include details of exposure action values and exposure limits, findings of the vibration risk assessment, control measures and what to look for to detect early signs of injury and health surveillance.

The Health and Safety Executive have also produced a very useful vibration calculator which can be downloaded from *www.hse.gov.uk/vibration/hav/vibrationcalc.htm*.

See Chapter 4 for further information on Hand Arm Vibration (HAVS).

DISABILITY DISCRIMINATION ACT 1995

From 1 October 2010, the Equality Act replaced most of the Disability Discrimination Act (DDA). However, the Disability Equality Duty in the DDA continues to apply.

EQUALITY ACT 2010

The Equality Act 2010 aims to protect disabled people and prevent disability discrimination. It provides legal rights for disabled people in the areas of:

- Education
- Employment

- Access to goods services and facilities including larger private clubs and land based transport services
- Buying and renting land or property
- Functions of public bodies e.g. issue of licenses

The Equality Act also provides rights for people not to be directly discriminated against or harassed because they have an association with a disabled person. This can apply to a carer or parent of a disabled person. In addition, people must not be directly discriminated against or harassed because they are wrongly perceived to be disabled.

As an employer, your obligations remain largely the same. The Act harmonises and replaces previous legislation (such as the Race Relations Act 1976 and the Disability Discrimination Act 1995) and ensures consistency in what you need to do to make your workplace a fair environment and to comply with the law.

The Equality Act covers the same groups that were protected by existing equality legislation – age, disability, gender reassignment, race, religion or belief, sex, sexual orientation, marriage and civil partnership and pregnancy and maternity. These are now called 'protected characteristics'

The Disability Discrimination Act 1995 (DDA 1995) was passed with the intention of ending discrimination against disabled people and improving their access to employment, goods, facilities and services and the management, purchase or renting of property or land. The law itself is only a framework and there are additional regulations, amendments and codes of practice that also need to be observed.

All businesses or facilities open to the public, whether or not they are free of charge, have obligations and responsibilities under DDA 1995 as both service providers and employers. DDA 1995 defines a person as disabled if the following apply:

- the person must have either a physical or mental impairment
- the impairment must have adverse effects that are substantial
- substantial effects must be long term
- long-term substantial effects must adversely affect the carrying out of normal day-to-day activities

Discrimination occurs if a disabled person is treated less favourably for a reason that relates to their disability and the treatment cannot be justified on reasonable grounds.

The provisions contained in DDA 1995, Parts II and III are most relevant to employers.

DDA 1995, Part II makes it unlawful for employers to discriminate against disabled applicants for jobs, existing disabled employees and employees who become disabled. It imposes a duty on employers to make reasonable adjustments to assist disabled employees or applicants. This might include changes to the following:

- The physical environment: structural aspects of the premises (such as doorways, stairways), fixtures and fittings (such as lighting, door and window furniture, floor coverings), furniture and its layout and equipment (such as telephones, computer equipment).

SIMPLY SAFETY

- Employment arrangements: working hours, selection and interview procedures, terms and conditions of employment relating to training, promotion and so on and the methods of giving instructions.

In addition, steps such as those listed here, or a combination of steps, will sometimes have to be taken:

- Making adjustments to premises.
- Allocation of some of the disabled person's duties to another person.
- Transferring the person to fill an existing vacancy.
- Alteration of the person's working hours.
- Assigning the person to a different place of work.
- Permitted absence during working hours for rehabilitation, assessment or treatment.
- Acquisition of special equipment or modifying existing equipment.
- Modification of instructions or reference manuals.
- Provision of a reader or interpreter.
- Provision of supervision.

DDA 1995, Part III makes it unlawful for a service provider to discriminate against disabled people in the provision of goods, facilities and services. This part of the DDA also makes it unlawful to discriminate against disabled people in the management, sale or rental of property.

A service provider is anyone who provides goods, facilities and services to the general public, whether paid for or free.

Under Pt III of the DDA, service providers have a legal duty to take reasonable steps to make these services available to disabled people. They should not discriminate by:

- Refusing to provide a service.
- Providing a service of a lower standard or in a worse manner.
- Providing a service on less favourable terms than they would to service users without a disability.
- Failing to comply with the duty to make reasonable adjustments to a physical feature of their premises that makes it impossible or unreasonably difficult for a disabled person to make use of the service.

Service providers will also be required to make reasonable adjustments such as the following:

- Changing practices, policies and procedures that make it impossible or unreasonably difficult for a disabled person to use a service (for example, a video rental shop normally offers membership only to people who can provide a driving licence as proof of their identity – this automatically excludes some disabled people from joining, so the shop would be required to accept an alternative form of identification).
- Providing auxiliary aids and services (such as the provision of information on audio tape, a sign language interpreter, extra assistance, or a temporary ramp).
- Removing a physical feature that makes a service impossible or unreasonably difficult for a disabled person to access.

- Altering the physical feature so that it no longer has a discriminatory effect.
- Providing a reasonable means of avoiding the physical feature (eg in a building whose services are accessed by stairs – allowing a wheelchair user to use an entrance normally used by staff which is fully accessible).
- Providing the service by a reasonable alternative method (eg offering a telephone or Internet service).

The duties to make reasonable adjustments are continuing, which means that service providers will have to constantly review the adjustments they make and may have to make further adjustments in the light of changing circumstances, customer expectations, new technology and experience. They will also be expected to plan ahead and anticipate changes.

For detailed guidance on Part III, its implications on facilities, access design specifications, access audit strategies and case studies, see Ian Waterman and Janet Bell, Disabled Access to Facilities, Butterworths Tolley, 2002.

WORK AT HEIGHT REGULATIONS 2005 AND WORK AT HEIGHT (AMENDMENT) REGULATIONS 2007

The Work at Height Regulations 2005 (SI 2005/735) (WAHR 2005) came into force on 6 April 2005 and apply to all working at height where there is a risk of falling which is liable to cause personal injury.

These regulations also apply to those who work at height providing instruction or leadership to one or more people engaged in caving or climbing by way of sport, recreation, team building or similar activities in Great Britain.

The regulations place duties on employers, the self-employed, and any person who controls the work of others, where working at a height is involved.

As part of the regulations the employer must ensure that:

- all work at height is properly planned and organised
- those involved in work at height are competent
- the risks from work at height are assessed and appropriate work equipment is selected and used
- the risks from fragile surfaces are properly controlled and
- equipment for work at height is properly inspected and maintained

The HSE have drafted a simple hierarchy for managing and selecting equipment for work at height. These state that the employer must:

- avoid work at height where they can
- use work equipment or other measures to prevent falls where they cannot avoid working at height and
- where they cannot eliminate the risk of a fall, use work equipment or other measures to minimise the distance and consequences of a fall should one occur

SIMPLY SAFETY

The regulations include schedules giving requirements for:

- existing places of work and means of access for work at height
- collective fall prevention (eg guardrails and working platforms)
- collective fall arrest (eg nets, airbags etc)
- personal fall protection (eg work restraints, fall arrest and rope access) and
- ladders

'Don't let a Fall Shatter your Life'

The Work at height, Access equipment Information Toolkit (WAIT) is a free on line HSE toolkit of advice and guidance aimed at people who occasionally need to work at height. It helps you select the right access equipment for the planned work. When inspecting your workplace or indeed when investigating an accident the HSE or local Environmental Health Officer will use the WAIT tool to assess whether you have used the correct means of access e.g. Ladder or other work equipment.

Ladder Exchange

This annual initiative provides UK businesses with an easy and simple way to replace broken, damaged or bent ladders and trade them in for safe new ones. Since its launch, Ladder Exchange has resulted in nearly 7 000 dodgy ladders being removed from use.

For further information regarding the WAIT toolkit or Ladder Exchange please visit the HSE website *www.hse.gov.uk*

CORPORATE MANSLAUGHTER AND CORPORATE HOMICIDE ACT 2007

This Corporate Manslaughter and Corporate Homicide Act 2007 (CMCHA 2007) is a landmark in law as for the first time companies and organisations can be found guilty of corporate manslaughter as a result of serious management failures resulting in a gross breach of a basic duty of care which leads to death. Although the new offence is not part of health and safety law it introduces a new important element into the corporate management of health and safety. The employer is advised to be aware of the new Act in case they are called upon to advise the board of their organisations.

The new Act came into force on 6 April 2008 and clarifies the criminal liabilities of companies where serious failures in the management of health and safety result in a fatality. The wording of the offence is that an organisation will be guilty of an offence if the way in which its activities are managed or organised:

- causes a person's death; and
- amounts to a gross breach of a relevant duty of care owed by the organisation to the deceased.

An organisation is only guilty if the way in which its activities are managed or organised by its senior management is a substantial element in the breach.

The employer needs to look at the practical steps that their organisation can take.

For example:

- Consider and obtain all relevant legislation and health and safety guidance applicable to their business.
- Consider their industry standards and best practice – to what benchmarks are the company working?
- Take action to improve record-keeping generally.
- Ensure all risk assessments are up to date and reviewed on a regular basis especially where there are any changes.
- Ensure that all staff involved in the risk assessments are aware of the contents of the assessments and the control measures that have been put in place.
- Implement a consistent and documented enforcement regime for health and safety issues across the business:
    - Does the policy state that breach of health and safety rules is considered to be gross misconduct which will result in disciplinary action?
    - What actually happens to employees when they fail to comply with health and safety rules?
- Consider what element of the company's budget is spent on health and safety and is it sufficient.
- Regularly review the company's accident and near-miss reports, procedures and investigations and ensure that
    - Any findings are acted upon.
    - The results are passed on to the health and safety committee and health and safety representatives.
    - All relevant information is brought to the board's attention.
- Regularly review the company's policies and assessments in relation to vehicles and work-related driving.
- Consider and keep under review the company's hierarchy and determine who would be considered 'senior management' for the purposes of the Act.
- Regularly review the training of senior management and the competence of individuals within the business responsible for managing health and safety.
- Regularly review the company's 'safety culture' – regardless of documents, policies and procedures – what happens 'on the ground'?
- Regularly review the company's policies on the appointing of, and control of, contractors.
- Ensure that employees are able to report health and safety concerns confidentially and ensure that it is working.
- Check the extent of the company's main insurance cover for criminal costs (both prosecution and defence). Most policies cover defence costs to the magistrates' court only, which will be inadequate for any corporate manslaughter prosecution.
- Check the extent of any insurance policies in place covering criminal costs for directors or officers of the company.

SIMPLY SAFETY

Further advice may be obtained from:

- The Sentencing Council has produced a set of guidance documents on sentencing which are available for download on its website: http://sentencingcouncil.judiciary.gov.uk/guidelines-to-download.htm
- The SAP has recommended fines of up to 10% of turnover in corporate manslaughter cases and 7.5% for charges involving a fatality under the HSWA 1974.
- The Ministry of Justice has detailed information available on its website: www.justice.gov.uk/guidance/manslaughteractguidance.htm.
- The Institute of Directors and the HSE have published guidance for directors detailing their responsibilities for health and safety, entitled Leading Health and Safety at Work INDG417.

THE HEALTH AND SAFETY OFFENCES ACT 2008

The Health and Safety Offences Act 2008 (HSOA 2008), which came into force on 16 January 2009, amends s 33 of the Health and Safety at Work etc. Act 1984 to raise the maximum penalties available for offences in the lower courts from £5,000 to £20,000. It also makes most offences imprisonable. For example, magistrates and judges can now imprison individuals convicted under HSWA 1974, ss 7, 8 or 37, which cover breaches by individual directors and employees. The Minister for Work and Pensions (Lord McKenzie) has stressed that prison should be reserved for the most serious offences.

There are strict guidelines which are observed by the regulators in their approach to the prosecution of health and safety offences. The HSE Enforcement Policy Statement. makes it clear that prosecutions should be in the public interest and where one or more of a list of circumstances apply. These include where:

- death was a result of a breach of the legislation
- there has been reckless disregard of health and safety requirements
- there have been repeated breaches which give rise to significant risk, or persistent and significant poor compliance, or
- false information has been supplied wilfully, or there has been intent to deceive in relation to a matter which gives rise to significant risk

Prosecutions of individuals by health and safety regulators are not undertaken lightly. Any prosecutions of individuals for example employers will be subject to the same strict considerations set out above and are only taken if warranted, and not in lieu of a case against their employer.

HEALTH AND SAFETY INFORMATION FOR EMPLOYEES (AMENDMENT) REGULATIONS 2009

The Health and Safety Information for Employees Regulations 1989 (SI 1989/682) had always required the employer to provide health and safety information, including the contact details for the local health and safety enforcing authority office and Employment Medical Advisory Service

(EMAS) office, to employees by displaying in the workplace the approved poster or giving each employee the approved leaflet. The Health and Safety Information for Employees (Amendment) Regulations 2009 (HSIE(A)R 2009) have allowed the Health and Safety Executive (HSE) to approve and publish new posters and leaflets which do not require the addition or updating of enforcing authority and EMAS contact information

From 6 April 2009, the HSE has published new versions of its approved health and safety poster and a new leaflet.

The new versions are modern, eye-catching and easy to read. They set out in simple terms, using numbered lists of basic points, employer and their staff must do, and tell you what to do if there is a problem. The new poster and pocket card also reduce the administrative cost for employers, who no longer have to add further information and keep this up to date.

Employers can, if they wish, continue to use their existing versions of poster and leaflet until 5 April 2014, as long as they are readable and the addresses of the enforcing authority and the Employment Medical Advisory Service are up to date. This information can be obtained from HSE's website at www.hse.gov.uk

There is also a leaflet that employers can give to workers, instead of displaying the poster, which is in the form of a pocket card that is better suited to the workplace..

Equivalent easy read and large print leaflets will be produced, along with an MP3 version on the HSE 'Talking leaflets' website: www.hse.gov.uk/pubns/tlindex.htm. The poster and pocket card will also be available in Welsh.

The new law poster, pocket cards and other formats can be ordered from HSE Books (tel: 01787 881165) and is also distributed by HSE Books and booksellers.

Employers will be able to check that they have a genuine HSE law poster by checking the unique, serially numbered hologram on each poster.

CHEMICAL (HAZARD INFORMATION AND PACKAGING FOR SUPPLY) REGULATIONS 2009 – TO BE KNOWN AS CHIP 4

The current CHIP Regulations have been amended as a consequence of the adoption and entry into force of the European Regulation on the Classification, Labelling and Packaging of Substances and Mixtures, known as the CLP Regulation. The CLP Regulation adopts in the European Union, the internationally agreed Global Harmonised System (GHS) on the classification and labelling of chemicals, known as the 'GHS'. Although the CLP Regulation will be directly acting on member states, without the need for transposition, the proposed amendments will allow CHIP to be aligned with the transitional period of the CLP Regulation and to ensure that the provisions of the CLP Regulation can be enforced in Great Britain, both throughout the transitional period and beyond.

The new regulations (CHIP 4) came into force on 6 April 2009 and employers who are required to manage the use of chemicals as part of the operational activities within their workplace will need to be fully conversant with the requirements of the regulations.

SIMPLY SAFETY

These regulations concern the identification of harmful properties of chemicals (hazards) and the communication of this information to users by means of labels. To be known as CHIP 4, they cover hazards to health, safety and the environment, and use of chemicals both in the home and at work. They consolidate, revoke and re-enact with amendments the Chemicals (Hazard Information and Packaging for Supply) Regulations 2002 (CHIP 3).

The CHIP 4 regulations:

- consolidate all amendments to the Chemicals (Hazard Information and Packaging for Supply) Regulations since 2002
- set out the procedures for classifying dangerous substances and preparations (reg 4)
- dovetail the requirements of CHIP with EU Regulation 1272/2008 on classification, labelling and packaging of substances and mixtures (the CLP Regulation), which adopts in Europe the Globally Harmonised System for the classification and labelling of chemicals (GHS)
- require safety data sheets as specified in Art 31 of EU Regulation 1907/2006 concerning the Registration, Evaluation, Authorisation and Restriction of Chemicals (REACH)
- impose requirements relating to the packaging of dangerous substances and dangerous preparations
- impose requirements in respect of the particulars that shall be shown on the labels for dangerous chemicals
- specify labelling requirements and the methods of marking and labelling of packages that contain dangerous chemicals
- require that the packaging of certain chemicals be provided with child-resistant fastenings or tactile warning devices or both, and sets out the standards to which they must conform
- require a person who classifies a dangerous preparation to retain the data used for the classification for at least three years after the preparation was last supplied
- provide for enforcement of the CLP Regulation in Great Britain
- make consequential revocations and amendments to a number of other regulations

The CHIP 4 Regulations also provide for transitional periods for compliance with the CLP Regulation.

Suppliers must:

- continue to classify both substances and mixtures to CHIP 4, reg 4 until 1 June 2015
- classify, label and package substances according to the CLP Regulation from 1 December 2010 for substances and 1 June 2015 for mixtures.

NOTE: The new regulations do not extend to Northern Ireland.

FACTORIES ACT 1961 AND OFFICES, SHOPS AND RAILWAY PREMISES ACT 1963 (REPEALS AND MODIFICATIONS) REGULATIONS 2009

The Factories Act 1961 and Offices, Shops and Railway Premises Act 1963 (Repeals and

Modifications) Regulations 2009 (SI 2009/605) came into force on 6 April 2009 and for the employer will go some way towards simplification and reduce the administrative burden of form filling.

These regulations amend the Factories Act 1961 and the Offices, Shops and Railway Premises Act 1963 with their main purpose being to remove the requirement for the employer to register factories, offices and shops with the relevant health and safety authority has been abolished, forms such as F9 (for factories) and OSR1 (for offices and shops). It also removes the requirement to keep a general register under the Factories Act.

NOTE: The registration or form filling requirements in relation to other regulations (eg food standards registration or registration in relation to the transportation or storage of hazardous material) still apply.

HEALTH AND SAFETY AT WORK ETC. ACT 1974 (APPLICATION TO ENVIRONMENTALLY HAZARDOUS SUBSTANCES) (AMENDMENT) REGULATIONS 2009

The Health and Safety at Work etc. Act 1974 (Application to Environmentally Hazardous Substances) (Amendment) Regulations 2009 (SI 2009/318) came into force 23 March 2009.

The Health and Safety at Work etc, Act 1974 (Application to Environmentally Hazardous Substances) Regulations 2002 extended the reference to dangerous substances in s 1(1)(c) of the Health and Safety at Work etc, Act 1974 (HSWA) to include environmentally hazardous substances. This is for the purpose of enabling regulations to be made under HSWA s 15 to implement the directives referred to in Health and Safety at Work etc, Act 1974 (Application to Environmentally Hazardous Substances) Regulations 2002, reg 2.

The new regulations amend the Health and Safety at Work etc, Act 1974 (Application to Environmentally Hazardous Substances) Regulations 2002, reg 2 to add a reference to Directive 2008/68/EC on the inland transport of dangerous goods, so that regulations can be made under HSWA to implement that directive. This will be to the extent that it relates to substances which are dangerous to the environment but not to people.

The regulations apply to Great Britain.

NOTE: The provisions of Directive 2008/68 are transposed by the Carriage of Dangerous Goods and Use of Transportable Pressure Equipment Regulations 2009 (SI 2009/1348), made under HSWA, s 15

SIMPLY SAFETY

APPENDIX 2 - ASSOCIATIONS AND ORGANISATIONS - ALPHABETICAL

BRITISH INSTITUTE OF FACILITIES MANAGEMENT (BIFM)

Number One Building
The Causeway
Bishop's Stortford
Hertfordshire
CM23 2ER

Tel. 0845 058 1356

Email admin@bifm.org.uk

www.bifm.org.uk

BRITISH SAFETY COUNCIL

70 Chancellors Road
London
W6 9RS

Tel. 020 8741 1231

Web - www.britsafe.org

BRITISH STANDARDS INSTITUTION (BSI)

389 Chiswick High Road
London
W4 4AL

Tel. 020 8996 9000

Fax 020 8996 7400

Email - cservices@bsi-global.com

Web - www.bsi-global.com

CHARTERED INSTITUTE OF BUILDING SERVICES ENGINEERS (CIBSE)

222 Balham High Road
London
SW12 9BS

Tel. 020 8675 5211

Fax 020 8675 5449

Email enquiries@cibse.org

Web - www.cibse.org

Site contains link to:
Society of Public Health Engineers

CHARTERED INSTITUTE OF ENVIRONMENTAL HEALTH

Head office
Chadwick Court
15 Hatfields
London
SE1 8DJ

Telephone: +44 (0)20 7928 6006
Fax: +44 (0)20 7827 5862

CONSTRUCTION BEST PRACTICE PROGRAMME

PO Box 147, Bucknalls Lane
Garston
Watford
Hertfordshire
WD25 9UZ

Tel. 0845 6055556

Fax 01923 664690

Web - www.cbpp.org.uk

ERGONOMICS SOCIETY

Devonshire House, Devonshire Square
Loughborough
LE11 3DW
Tel. 01509 234904
Fax 01509 235666
Email - ergsoc@ergonomics.org.uk

Web - www.ergonomics.org.uk

HEALTH AND SAFETY BULLETIN

LexisNexis irs
Web – www.irsonline.co.uk

HEALTH AND SAFETY EXECUTIVE

HSE HEAD OFFICE

Health and Safety Executive
Redgrave Court
Merton Road

SIMPLY SAFETY

Bootle
Merseyside
L20 7HS

Web – www.hse.gov.uk

Please refer to http://www.hse.gov.uk/contact/index.htm or your local telephone directory for your local office

HSE Books

PO Box 1999
Sudbury
Suffolk
CO10 2WA

Tel. 01787 881165

Fax 01787 313995

Email - hsebbooks@prolog.uk.com

Web - www.hsebooks.co.uk

International Institute of Risk and Safety Management (IIRSM)

Suite 7a
77 Fulham Palace Road
London
W6 8JA
United Kingdom

Enquiries: +44 (0)20 8741 9100

Fax: +44 (0)20 8741 1349

Email: - info@iirsm.org

Institute of Engineering and Technology (IET)

The Institution of Engineering and Technology
Michael Faraday House
Six Hills Way, Stevenage
Hertfordshire,
SG1 2AY

www.theiet.org

Tel: +44 (0)1438 313 311
Fax: +44 (0)1438 765 526
Email: - postmaster@theiet.org

INSTITUTE OF OCCUPATIONAL SAFETY AND HEALTH (IOSH)

The Grange,
Highfield Drive
Wigston
Leics
LE18 1NN
Tel. 0116 257 3100
Fax 0116 257 3101
Web - www.iosh.co.uk

LIGHTING INDUSTRY FEDERATION

207 Balham High Road
London
SW17 7BQ
Tel. 020 8675 5432
Web - www.lif.co.uk

NHS STOP SMOKING HELPLINE

Tel. 0800 022 4 332 – 7 days a week, 7am to 11pm
Web - http://smokefree.nhs.uk

ROYAL INSTITUTION OF CHARTERED SURVEYORS

Parliament Square
London
SW1P 3AD
Tel. 0870 333 1600
Web – www.rics.org/uk

ROYAL SOCIETY FOR THE PREVENTION OF ACCIDENTS

Edgbaston Park, 353 Bristol Road
Edgbaston, Birmingham
B5 7ST
Tel. 0121 248 2000
Fax 0121 248 2222
Email - help@rospa.co.uk
Web - www.rospa.co.uk

SIMPLY SAFETY

SANITARY MEDICAL DISPOSAL SERVICES ASSOCIATION

111 Wollaston Road
Irchester
Northants
NN29 7DD
Tel./fax 01933 311223
Email **infor@smdsa.com**
www.smdsa.com

SMOKEFREE ENGLAND

Web - www.smokefreeengland.co.uk

Unions

Free health and safety sheets are available from the following unions:

Unison: - www.unison.org.uk

GMB: - www.gmb.org.uk

Acknowledgements

A number of people have supported us in the writing and collation of this book not least our respective families with a very Special thanks to Jill Davies and Karin Morgan for their patience and encouragement at times when it seemed an uphill struggle to complete.

A special mention must go to Clara Hartle who stepped in at the very last moment to act as our editor and dealt with our numerous spelling and grammatical errors.

A special thanks has to go to the Health and safety executive (HSE) whose website has been invaluable for its rich sources of information, reports and legal updates.

Finally a big thank you to all of our employers and clients which over the years have provided us as authors with such a rich tapestry of scenarios and problems to solve which has provided us with a lifetime of experience in order write this book.

Thanks to all.

Printed in Great Britain
by Amazon.co.uk, Ltd.,
Marston Gate.